BEFORE ENDEAVOURS FADE

A GUIDE TO THE BATTLEFIELDS OF THE FIRST WORLD WAR

BY ROSE E. B. COOMBS, MBE

AN
AFTER THE BATTLE
PUBLICATION

Credits

BEFORE ENDEAVOURS FADE

© Rose E. B. Coombs, MBE, 1983

Hardback: ISBN 0 900913 26 6
Paperback: ISBN 0 900913 27 4

Printed in Great Britain

First Published August 1976
Second Edition November 1977
Third Edition November 1979
Fourth Edition March 1983

Designed and edited by
Winston G. Ramsey
Editor *After the Battle* magazine

PUBLISHERS
Battle of Britain Prints International Limited,
3 New Plaistow Road,
London, E15 3JA
England
Telephone 01-534 8833

PRINTERS
Plaistow Press Limited
3 New Plaistow Road,
London, E15 3JA
England

PHOTOGRAPHS
All photographs are the copyright of the author, except those from the Imperial War Museum archives (designated IWM) and the aerial photographs which were taken by *After the Battle* magazine.

MAPS
All maps are the copyright of the Michelin Company and are reproduced with their permission.

FRONT COVER
The 41st Division Memorial at Flers.

BACK COVER
Newfoundland Memorial at Gueudecourt.

ENDPAPERS
Extract from Sheet 28 SW Edition 8A, Belgium and part of France, showing the front line as at August 29, 1918.

PAGE 3
Dawn over Ypres.

PAGE 4
Desplanque Farm Cemetery located at La Chapelle d'Armèntieres.

ABOUT THE AUTHOR
'You haven't talked to THE expert on the Great War until you have talked to Miss Coombs.' So ran one letter received at the Imperial War Museum, London, where, from 1946 until 1982, Rose Coombs worked, in latter years as Special Collections Officer.

Her interest in battlefields began at an early age but it was not until after the Second World War (in which she served as a Radar Operator with Nos. 10 and 11 Groups, RAF), that she was able to realise her ambition, through her rôle at the Imperial War Museum, to visit the battlefields of Europe.

During the years which followed she had the opportunity to make hundreds of visits to the Western Front of 1914-1918, on many occasions acting as guide to ex-servicemen's groups returning to the battlefields. She has accompanied authors writing on the period and lectured groups of all ages, giving freely of her detailed knowledge of the terrain, its history, the units and personalities involved, and what remains today. Miss Coombs has now combined years of study, travel and research in this profusely illustrated publication.

Contents

There will be voices whispering down these ways,
The while one wanderer is left to hear,
And the young life and laughter of old days,
Shall make undying echoes.

From *Looking Forward* by
Geoffrey Winthrop Young, 1909

The Anxious Dead

O Guns, fall silent till the dead men hear
   Above their heads the legions passing on;
(Those fought their fight in time of bitter fear,
   And died not knowing how the day had gone.)

O flashing muzzles, pause, and let them see
   The coming dawn that streaks the sky afar;
Then let your mighty chorus witness be
   To them, and Caesar, that we still make war.

Tell them, O guns, that we have heard their call,
   That we have sworn, and will not turn aside,
That we will onward till we win or fall,
   That we will keep the faith for which they died.

Bid them be patient, and some day, anon,
   They shall feel earth enwrapt in silence deep,
Shall greet, in wonderment, the quiet dawn,
   And in content may turn them to their sleep.

JOHN McCRAE

Introduction by the Author...

A visit to the battlefields should begin at one of the traditional entry ports for the BEF—Boulogne, Calais, Dieppe or Le Havre. However, today the modern traveller can also take advantage of the routes through Dunkerque, Ostend or Zeebrugge, by ferry or hovercraft. As it is the nearest port to the English coast, I have chosen Calais as the starting point for this itinerary and Boulogne for the departure.

I have travelled all the routes described in an ordinary saloon car. On the whole the main roads now have excellent surfaces but here and there the camber of the roads is not ideal and care should be taken to maintain a suitable speed to counter this.

The motorways which now criss-cross the old front line have access points to many of the areas covered in this book and views of parts of the battle-front can be obtained from them, but to really see the country it is necessary to keep to the old roads — the Routes Nationales (N); the Chemin Departmentals (D) or (CD), and the Vicinaux Ordinaires (VO).

Frequently I have found these latter two categories are better surfaced than those nationally maintained roads, although narrower. Distances throughout are quoted in kilometres.

Maps are a necessity for any tour. Whilst I have indicated the route to be taken on black and white extracts, I recommend the visitor to purchase the following Michelin 1:200,000 maps: Belgium Sheet 2; France Sheets 51, 52, 53, 56 and 57. The scale is 1cm to 2km (very approximately half-an-inch to one mile) and all the features are indicated in colour.

The text is correct to June 1982 but visitors are warned to expect varying road numbers from both my text and the current Michelin maps.

Another problem for the visitor today has been caused by the changes in place names due to the recent adoption of modern Flemish as opposed to the traditional spellings used for Belgian towns and villages as they were known to the BEF. For ease of navigation, I have indicated the version which is now to be found on signposts.

MISS ROSE E. B. COOMBS, MBE

About this book...

It is now over sixty years since war raged here. Thousands of soldiers died daily. Their relatives have visited their graves, their comrades also. Pilgrims have come from all parts of the world to say a prayer or bring flowers. An old soldier has tried vainly to find the trench he knew so well. But the old warriors — the majority of them — have disappeared; as have their loved ones. History is made but who will remember it? From far off, the descendants of those who fought here come to visit the villages whose names, for some four years, made people hold their breath. School children come with their teachers, cars of tourists with guides and the casual visitor. To all this guide is indispensible.

The author spares no pains to attract your attention but she does not go in for melodrama. You will find all the details you need with the historic background to the events. As for the itinerary you will find little is missed. All battle sites and monuments are included, even to the smallest or the most modest. Graves of the known and unknown are pointed out and this is done with the utmost respect for all.

When the author asked me to write an introduction to her work, she recalled our many trips over the battlefields of France and Flanders. I would like to thank her for this expression of friendship and wish this guidebook every success.

Dr. Alfred A. Caenepeel

Vice-Chairman, Last Post Committee
Founder and Curator, Ypres Salient Museum

THE LATE DR ALFRED A. CAENEPEEL

Demarcation Stones

In the decade following the Armistice, 119 small monuments were erected in Belgium and France, at intervals along the 960 kilometres of the Western Front, to mark the limit of the German advance in 1918. The Touring Club de France and the Touring Club de Belgique were the prime movers of this scheme which caught the imagination of the public.

Of pink granite, the monuments were no more than a metre in height. They were designed by the sculptor Paul Moreau Vauthier who produced three basic types, differing mainly in the helmet of the capstone. These were either of the British tin helmet or the French and Belgian 'Poilu's' helmet design. On the side of the stones were decorations consisting of a soldier's equipment — gas mask case, water bottle, etc., and each bore the inscription. 'Here the Invader was brought to a standstill' in either French, Flemish or English. On the front face, the

name of the place they were to stand in or near was inscribed.

The stones which became know as Demarcation Bornes or Stones were placed in positions where the battle line crossed a road or street, in town or country, at points decided by Maréchal Pétain and the General Staffs of France, Belgium, and Britain.

Funds to help in the erection of the monuments came from many sources beside the two Touring Clubs, which bore the main charge, and local authorities, ex-Servicemen's organisations and private people all contributed to their cost.

The number of stones remaining in-situ today is much depleted as many were destroyed or lost during the Second World War or have become the victims of the motor vehicle. For instance, of the seven donated by the Ypres League and erected in the Salient, only two or three have survived. Others have been broken up by the explosion of old ammunition which had been placed against them by farmers.

Where our itinerary passes a stone, I have usually drawn attention to it.

The Poppy Legend

The poppy legend originated in China. A white flower from which a potent drug was distilled was called the Flower of Forgetfulness. Ghengis Khan brought some of the seed westward but after a battle the flower became red. In the centre of each was a cross.

It was found that on many battlefields, when everything else had been laid waste, the

landscape was soon ablaze with the blood-red blooms. On the Somme battlefield in 1917, (and again after the war was over), the land burst forth in a blaze of scarlet with patches of yellow charlock and white chamomile. Many graves of those buried near the front line were soon marked by the charlock due to the seeds being released when the grave was dug.

Lord Macauley drew attention to the strange link of the poppy with battle and put forward the suggestion it should be regarded as the flower of sacrifice and memorial.

Battlefield Debris

The colossal expenditure in shell and ammunition during the First World War has left a dangerous legacy for the careless visitor today. Often, as the battle areas are traversed, small piles of rusting shells will be seen on the verge. These neat piles of ammunition are usually the result of a field being ploughed — the 'Iron Harvest' I call it — and still to this day, regular collections are made by the military authorities to take these very dangerous objects away for safe demolition.

The sight of such things seems to turn many visitors into collectors and, with little thought of the danger of these seemingly inoffensive objects, they are bundled into the car. Please leave them where you see them — or if it is within any of the memorial parks draw the attention of the Superintendent to them. Explosives do not improve with age and many French children are still maimed and blinded by handling such objects.

Even the apparently innocent rusty bayonet or length of barbed wire carries with it the danger of tetanus if carelessly handled. Recently scientists have been working on one aspect of the spread of the deadly disease rabies, as it has been realised that the old battle-torn woods and shrublands are

breeding grounds of the most frequent carrier — the fox. The French medical authorities have been investigating some of the untouched regions and have found evidence that careless wandering through dirty infectious ground can be dangerous.

Remember also that the removal of anything from private land is stealing. It is often possible to acquire material quite safely and legally for a small sum. However, always bear in mind the strict Customs Regulations on the import of weapons and ammunition.

Accommodation

The traveller should be warned that, for the most part, the regions through which these routes pass are off the normal tourist track and, therefore, hotels are often few and far between. Beyond the coastal resorts or the cities of Amiens, Reims, or Arras, there is not a great deal of choice. The French and Belgian National Tourist Offices can supply lists of approved hotels in the area but it will

be found that few are of three or four star classification.

Ypres has a fairly good selection of moderately priced hotels and out in the country, within easy access, there are some more expensive (but not outrageously so), country house type hostelleries. Usually in the small towns there are cafés which have a few rooms.

Nowhere in France is one far from a good restaurant. In my travels I have never failed to find the Buffets de la Gare of the larger or main line stations of very good value. Amiens, Lille, Arras and Reims—all are good. Some

stations have more than one restaurant on the premises catering for differing tastes or pockets. Often if there is no such café on the station, one will be found in the vicinity, for example, in Albert and Armentières.

For those doing their own catering there is no village in France where bread cannot be bought daily (except between the hours of 12.00 and 2.00 p.m.). For reasonable prices I can highly recommend the ever increasing number of hypermarkets which have sprung up close to every large town. It is sometimes a little more difficult in Belgium but the conditions are improving.

Calais–Ypres

ROUTE I VIA BERGUES

Calais. Hôtel de Ville Belfry

Now a modern sprawling industrial area and busy port, **Calais** was a most important British base particularly for the ordnance services and the auxiliary units for the BEF. Hospitals, training camps and depots all grew up behind the town and, in February 1918, the train ferry link with the then new Richborough military harbour was established.

Little of the Calais the first BEF knew remains, and the new residential and industrial zones now spread over the flat land behind the sand dunes where the troops encamped. Here and there, however, little bungalows (originally temporary wooden huts) remain as residences.

During the Second World War, Calais was almost entirely destroyed in 1940; thereafter to be encircled by concrete bunkers of the German defences. Many of these were added to the old forts which had previously been its main defence. Gradually many of these have

been removed to make way for new building. The huge modern complex of the ferry terminal, geared to the requirements of motor vehicles—cars, coaches and huge trucks—is surrounded by open areas for parking.

The recommended route to leave the terminal for destinations other than Calais centre now takes the coast road between the Bassin des Chasses and the old fort with the ruins of concrete bunkers scattered drunkenly as the demolition continues. The road hugs the old moat up to the roundabout where it is joined by the road from the hoverport. In the sand dunes around the hoverport a few bunkers remain.

To visit the town, follow the signs for 'Centre Ville' which lead across the Pont Mobile, through the Place de Suède, the rue Cdt Bonninque, the Place d'Armes and the rue Royale and Place Maréchal Foch, past the Parc Richelieu and the bridges — Pont George V and Pont Jacquard—and the Central Station to the Parc St Pierre and the famous Hôtel de Ville. Another route is from the Place de Suède, which leads down the rue de Moscou and the open railway.

In the **Parc St Pierre** is the **Musée de Guerre**. The exhibits are mainly related to the 1939-45 conflict. In front of the nearby **Hôtel de Ville**, a magnificent building in the Flemish Renaissance style with its famous Belfry, in the Place du Soldat Inconnu is the equally famous sculpture by Rodin of the Six Burghers of Calais.

From the roundabout the currently rather narrow road and poor surfaced rue de Nord connects with the access road for the wide bypass which now encircles Calais. The N1 on the left leads towards Gravelines and Dunkerque through modern residential areas amid which the occasional large concrete bunker can be glimpsed, but most of these have now gone. The little single storey dwellings in the rue de Phaisbourg are replacements for the wooden bungalows already mentioned.

The N1 is straight and very uninteresting. The rather drab ribbon development gives way to the flat agricultural region of beet and corn fields, market gardens and the occasional old sugar factory standing idle now the crops are taken direct to the modern refineries outside Dunkerque.

A more interesting route to Dunkerque and Belgium is now signposted from the first turning to the left after the railway crosses the rue du Nord. This passes through part of the new industrial zone for about 1 km then a sharp right turn followed ½ km later by a left onto the D119. This road winds its way through the immediate hinterland of the sand dunes, through **Fort Vert** with a number of desolate

bunkers, defences for the **airfield** at **Marck** which is on the right (8 kms), and for coastal artillery protecting both Calais and Fort Philippe, all of Second War vintage. Waldam is a small modern village passed through before the hamlets of Le Tap Cul and L'Etoile, part of Oye Plage where the road rejoins the N1 on the modern outskirts of Gravelines. The nuclear power station and oil refinery at Petit Fort Philippe have caused considerable extension of the residential areas of both Grand Fort Philippe on the west bank of the River Aa and Gravelines. The N1 now curves round to the south of the ancient town.

During the Great War **Gravelines** was a Belgian headquarters. It is possible to visualize the encampments located where light industry amid the workers' estates is now in view below the new road. There are still vestiges of the old fishing port with military connections dating back many centuries. Within the crumbling walls and ramparts, largely designed by Vauban, the narrow and busy streets follow a spider's-web pattern. It is a quaint place and can be approached by a continuation of the D119 instead of turning right and then left onto the N1. The old road through the town centre with its attractive church tower rejoins the N1 at a new crossroad on the eastern side. The main road makes a sharp right hand turn here. About 1 km further east is one of the **best preserved windmills** in Flanders, away to the right among the beet fields.

After 5 km, Loon Plage, a suburb of the ever spreading complex of Dunkerque, is bypassed to the north. New roads have been constructed to carry the heavy traffic the new docks have caused and several further access routes are proposed to form a complete ring-road for the old port.

In 5 kms, at a major crossroad, the N1 swings to the left to enter Dunkerque. Keep ahead on the D940 to the next major crossing where the N225, a fast dual carriageway, is the access road for the A25 autoroute. A short way along the N225 there is a lake for small craft and nearby there is a road sign which announces 'Zero altitude'.

The quickest route to Ypres is via the A25 to the Steenvoorde turn-off (28 kms) but if a visit to Dunkerque has been made, leave by the D916 which follows the Canal de Berques for 9 kms, passing the old **Fort Vallières** about midway, to the quaint old town of Bergues. It can also be reached from the N225 by taking the left turn to Bierne and Bergues on the D352.

Bergues is a sleepy country town surrounded by fortifications designed in 1667 by one of France's illustrious sons, Sebastien Le Prestre

Above: **The Porte de Cassel at Bergues.** *Left:* **Until recently, a Bailey Bridge, dating from the Second World War, straddled the moat at this spot.**

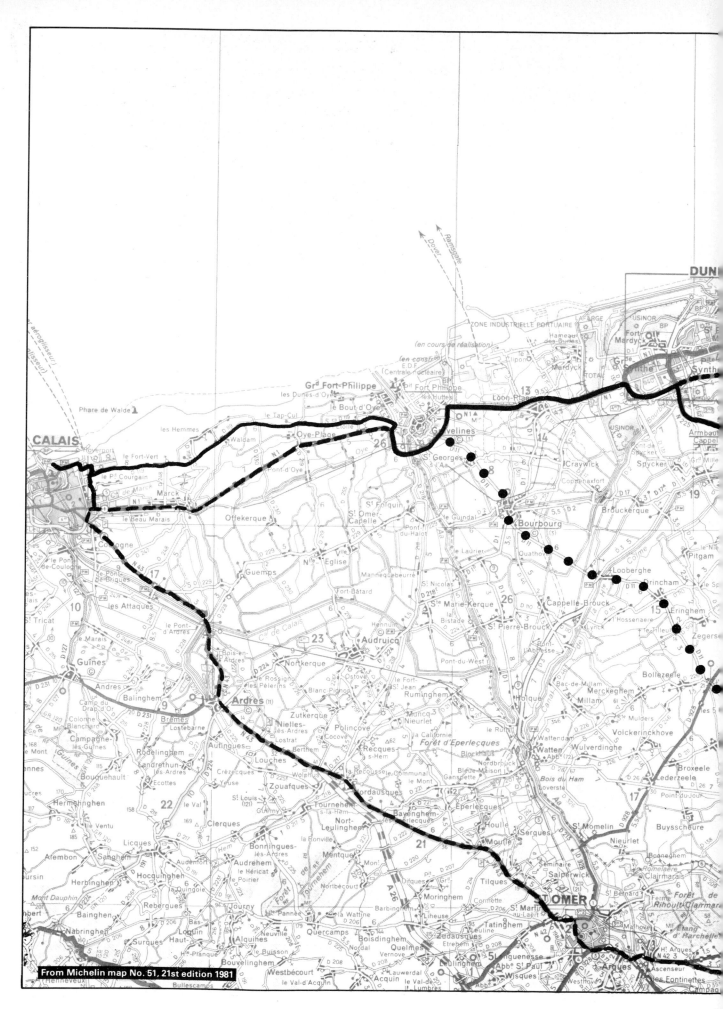

From Michelin map No. 51, 21st edition 1981

8

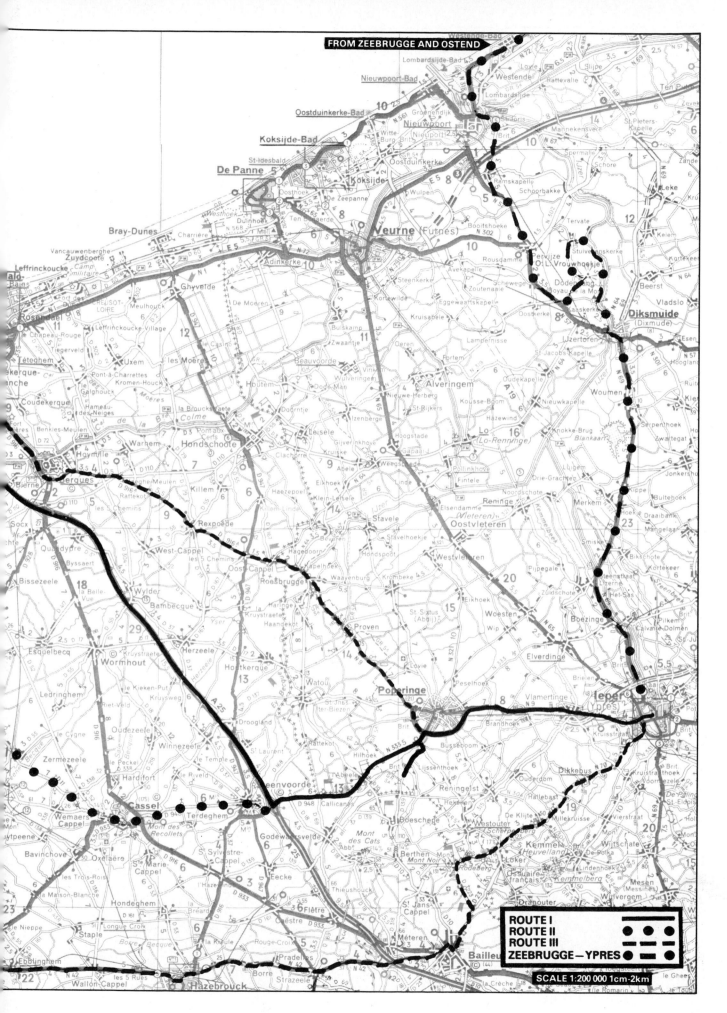

ROUTE I
ROUTE II
ROUTE III
ZEEBRUGGE — YPRES

SCALE 1:200 000 1cm-2km

Proven. La Lovie Château, headquarters for many BEF units and a base for King George V for his visit to the Western Front in July 1917.

de Vauban, Marshal of France (1633-1707). He is remembered on the **Porte de Cassel** by a plain memorial plaque. This gate is one of the narrow gateways which gave entry to the town across the moat fed by the three canals whose junction is in the town. These canals were a vital asset to the BEF. The Inland Waterways Transportation units operated barges to carry stores and casualties over many miles through Flanders. Bergues was a staging post to and from the coast.

Belgian troops used the town as a rest centre during the Yser battles and being only 25 kms behind the front line, it was bombarded in 1915. In 1940 it was badly damaged and many of the old houses were destroyed. Vauban's walls survived, as did the Port de Cassel with the emblem of the Sun King (Louis XIV) on the outer side, although the bridge over the moat did not and was replaced by a Bailey Bridge in 1944; now this has gone too after many years' service.

The D916a, the road to the frontier at Oostcappel via Rexpoede, crosses the fertile agricultural plain with its tiny farmhouses set amid neat fields, and church spires of the villages dominate the landscape which was the southern boundary of the Belgian front.

After 13 kms we reach Oostcappel frontier post—a small uninteresting hamlet. Driving straight on, the road has become the N9. Then, 7 kms further on is **Proven** well known to the BEF as a rail centre which, by 1916,

was vast. Training areas and hospitals were set up all over the commune. **Mendinghem British Cemetery** on the right of the road just before the village is one of a trio of cemeteries in the locality which served the hospitals and casualty clearing stations. The other two are

Dozinghem and **Bandaghem**, all three names being coined by the British troops to sound like the local Flemish ones.

In the woods to the east of the village the divisions grouped prior to the Third Battle of Ypres and, at **La Lovie Château** 2½ kms down the road to Poperinge, was the Fifth Army Headquarters from June to November 1917. From May 1915, the house was commandeered as an Army headquarters. At that date the VI Corps took the house over and the base set up by them remained until February 1916 when XIV Corps took over. In July the VIII Corps took their place, being in residence until the advent of the Fifth Army, who were followed by II Corps, and from April 1918 34th, 41st and 49th Divisions each used the house until August when II Corps returned. In July 1917 King George V stayed here during his visit to the Front. Today La Lovie is a spastic children's school and hospital.

Halfway between Proven and Westvleteren is the **Abdij St Sixtus**, a Trappist monastery where the monks brew a strong beer with mead from their bees to improve the taste and aroma. A casualty clearing station and other military establishments were housed in the Abbey grounds. In the Second War, General Montgomery paused here briefly with his 3rd Division Headquarters on their way to Dunkerque.

Above: **The Germans captured Poperinge on October 4, 1914 but were driven out eleven days later. The photo of Scottish troops in the Grand Place was taken in 1917.**
Below: **Transport of another age in the square renamed Groot Markt with the graceful Stadhuis in the background.**

Proven. The Abdij St Sixtus. This is the wall against which a deserter is said to have been shot in 1915.

Toc H, Everyman's Club in Poperinge. Over 25,000 used the attic chapel 1915-18.

7 kms **Poperinge**. 'Pop' to every British soldier was the forward base for the Ypres Salient from the autumn of 1914 onwards. The town, briefly occupied by the Germans in October 1914, was recaptured on the 15th and soon became the venue for the military. Training camps, depots and hospitals sprang up amid the hop fields. Refugees from Ypres crowded in and the station became one of the most important behind the lines, as almost all troops going up to the front or returning on leave entered the war area from its platforms.

The main square bustled with transport, horses, mules and men with lorries of all shapes converged here, as all the roads leading from it led to one facility or another. Restaurants and estaminets did a roaring trade despite frequent bombardments among the thousands who sought relief and relaxation from the rigours of trench life.

Follow the signs for the centre and you will arrive in the pleasant **Grote Markt** with the elegant Gothic **Stadhuis** at the eastern end and nearby St Bertin's church. Gasthuistraat curves away on the western side of the square with the old chapel which gives it the name on the right, a doorway beside it leads to the hospital. Further along a tall white house, perhaps the most famous in 'Pop', comes in view. The beautiful iron doors are the entrance to **Talbot House**.

The Reverend Neville Talbot, senior chaplain of 6th Division, had been searching for a house which he could open as a church club for the division in 1915 when by chance the owner of No. 16 rue de l'Hôpital (as the street was then called) left to find less dangerous quarters — the house had been hit several times by artillery shells — and the Padre persuaded the Army to rent the house for the duration. In charge of the project he placed an old friend, the Reverend Philip Byard Clayton. A rotund little man in 'specs' with a contagious sense of devotion and fun, he had been padre at No. 16 General Hospital in Le Tréport earlier in 1915 and in November arrived at GHQ Montreuil expecting to be sent to the Guards Brigade but his tall friend (Talbot stood 6 foot 7 inches) asked for him. And so 'Tubby' arrived in Pop and the house was opened on December 11, 1915 as a club for Everyman with rooms where men could relax and enjoy comparative comfort and a delightful garden, but the most important place in the house was the Upper Room—the chapel in the old hop and fruit attic. It was named **Talbot House** after Neville Talbot's brother Lieutenant Gilbert Talbot who had

been killed at Hooge on July 30, 1915 and who lies in Sanctuary Wood Cemetery.

The house remained open with few interruptions until, in May 1918, enemy bombardment forced its closure for a few months before re-opening on September 27, 1918. In January 1919 the owner reclaimed his house and the Club had to close but the spirit which had been born there did not die. In 1919, the Christian Movement Toc H was founded to help men and women who in the harsh days of peace searched vainly for employment and the 'brotherhood of the trenches'. Thus the name was perpetuated and the organisation grew worldwide. Branches sprang up in almost every country, all working to aid people through their life 'to think fairly, to love widely, to witness humbly and to build bravely'. This their founder did throughout his long life, travelling extensively from his base near the Tower of London until his death in December 1972. Each branch on formation was presented with a lamp, similar to those used in the time of Christ, to recall that which burned in the Upper Room at Pop.

In the years after the war, Tubby and other Toc H members made pilgrimages to the Salient but it was not until 1926 that they could persuade the owner of the Old House to allow visits. However, Lord Wakefield, who in 1928 had purchased the mine crater at Spanbroekmolen, the Pool of Peace, bought the house in 1929 and soon once more its doors were open wide. During the German Occupation from 1940 to 1944 the people of Poperinge hid the treasures from the house which they had stripped as the Germans came; all were back in their familiar places when Tubby made his first post-war visit. It is still a venue for pilgrims, not necessarily Toc H members, and is presided over by a Warden and a small band of volunteers to help him and his wife. There is always a cheerful welcome.

Further along the street, following the curve, you will see another famous building. Now a private house, it was known the world over as **Skindles** — the sign is still proudly worn above the front door. Originally the **Café de la Commerce des Houblons,** it was opened under the direction of Madame Beutin and her two daughters. Their friendly welcome made it an extremely popular venue for the young army officers who crowded into Poperinge right throughout the war. When the Beutin's opened at the then **No. 43 rue de l'Hôpital,** one young blade from Oxfordshire was reminded forcibly of a similar establishment at Maidenhead, Berkshire — Skindles Hotel — and in time this name was adopted by Madame Beutin. It has been recorded that General Plumer was there the night before the Battle of Messines began and legend has it that ten seconds before the great arc of mines was detonated, he ordered a Vermouth!

Immediately after passing Skindles, take the next turn to the left and turn back into the

Hotel Skindles—Haig's HQ, which later became the famous Officers' Club. Now a private house.

Grote Markt skirting St Bertin's church. To the right in St Bertinstraat is the **College Stanislas**, an episcopal establishment used as a hospital by the Friends Ambulance Unit for civilian casualties from Ypres in 1915. Although the 1915 and 1918 bombardments caused much damage, there are many old houses in the town and, in spite of modern building going on everywhere, there is much of the town recognisable to those who knew it over sixty years ago.

Leave Poperinge by the N9 Ieperstraat and pass the real target for the enemy artillery — **the station**. It has been written that whenever a leave train was due to depart, the enemy artillery interfered, but this did not prevent the place being the most popular and the most loathed spot in the vicinity; always thronged with travellers waiting for the trains. Returning men, however, did not loiter with the same indifference. A rumour which took a great deal of scotching was that the stationmaster of Pop had been shot as a spy due to the suspicious regularity of the shelling.

The twelve kilometres along the straight road to Ypres were travelled by all not using the railway running parallel to it. The road was lined by encampments, hutted and tented, hospitals, dumps and offices. Today, all sign of these has gone with the passage of time. Across the railway now runs a great new highway which eventually will encircle the town as a bypass. Only the cemeteries remain to remind us of the thousands who passed this way. Even the tall trees which survived the bombardments have been felled to make way for the four-lane road and replenished with saplings.

The forecourt of 'Pop' station was rarely devoid of soldiers during the war.

Red Farm Military Cemetery, Brandhoek, with a headstone to a civilian on the left.

On the outskirts of the town the N9 crosses the new ring-road which will shortly be connected with a new highway to Ieper (Ypres) (that bypasses Brandhoek and Vlamertinge running to the south of the N9, Poperingsweg) and narrows at the approaches to **Brandhoek** 3½ kms. On the left is one of the smallest cemeteries in the Salient — **Red Farm Cemetery** where in April-May, 1918, 46 British soldiers and three civilians were buried. A right turn in the centre of Brandhoek leads to the new highway and across it some of the cemeteries made when the hamlet was the centre of hospitals and casualty clearing stations. Cross the railway and the new road and immediately go right and bear left and, in a few metres, two cemeteries are reached. In that on the right — **Brandhoek New British Cemetery** lies Captain N. G. Chavasse, VC and Bar, MC, RAMC, who died from wounds on August 4, 1917 (Plot III Grave B15). Medical Officer to the 1st Bn. Liverpool Scottish, he went to France with the battalion in November 1914. He was awarded the Military Cross in 1915 in recognition of his gallantry at Hooge, and for his devotion to duty and his self-sacrifice and extraordinary energy and inspiration at Guillemont in August 1916, the Victoria Cross. For similar services in July and August 1917 he was awarded posthumously the Bar to the VC. He died two days after his action in Brandhoek Military Hospital. His headstone is unique for it bears two small representations of the VC in place of the usual large one.

Returning to the crosstroads, the third

The hop store near Vlamertinge—once a casualty clearing station.

cemetery of Brandhoek is seen on the right. Turn right on to the N9 again. About 2 kms further along on the north side of the road stands a tall red brick building, the **Hop Store**. Just beyond the trees behind it is the **Hopstore Cemetery** recalling the casualty clearing station there. Until they were rebuilt recently, against the wall of the abutting cottage was a water pump from which men and horses going to and from Ypres were refreshed.

Another kilometre and **Vlamertinge** is reached. Almost totally destroyed in artillery barrages, the village was held by the Germans between October 7-10, 1914. All around, the BEF built camps and stores and the inevitable hospitals and casualty clearing stations. By 1918 only the battered tower of the church remained. Behind the church is **Vlamertinge Military Cemetery** which is entered by a pair of unusual gates. These are of special design in memory of Lieutenant Mitford who lies

within this cemetery, also it is the last resting place of Captain Francis Grenfell, VC (Plot II, Grave B14).

In the second Vlamertinge cemetery, the **New British Cemetery** on the Ouderdom road to the south of the village, there lies another VC—CSM John Skinner, VC, DCM, King's Own Scottish Borderers. He won his award in 1917 for bravery in the Third Battle of Ypres when he put three blockhouses out of action in one continuous battle in August. He returned to England for the investiture by King George V and the customary fourteen days leave. At the end of this time, when he reached Folkestone, he was sent to hospital and posted to the Reserve Battalion in Edinburgh. However, a few days later he was seen with his company back in the Salient. He had refused to go to Edinburgh and, having his return

In Memoriam—to Lieutenant Mitford.

The grave of a VC. John Skinner in Vlamertinge New British Cemetery.

Totally destroyed, the Asylum on Poperingseweg was rebuilt in identical style and flourishes today as a psychiatric centre.

leave warrant in his pocket, after two days in hospital he had risked a court-martial to return to his men. He also had a bet with a pal, QSM Ross. Both had been wounded eight times and the wager was: who would get the ninth first. Skinner won the bet on March 17, 1918 when he was shot between the eyes when trying to rescue a wounded man.

His funeral was remarkable. The South Wales Borderers' Padre, the Rev. Kenelm Swallow, officiated at the ceremony in the pouring rain when his body was brought to the cemetery in Vlamertinge on a gun carriage drawn by a magnificent team of horses and then his body was carried to the grave (Plot XIII, Grave H15) by six brother VCs of the 29th Division. The ceremony took place on March 19, 1918 and is unique in military history.

Another 2 kms along the N9 and the spires of **Ypres** are in full view ahead as the straight road bends and is crossed by the railway. In the trees, before the crossing, once stood a solitary house. Set in a pleasant garden with ponds before the front door, this was

Rossières Château, or better known as 'Goldfish Château'. It was hardly damaged during the war, despite its occupaton by many formations' headquarters including V Corps, the Canadians and other divisions, and the proximity of the railway and enormous stores dumps nearby. Then, in 1920, it was entirely destroyed when an ammunition dump blew up. It was said that the German General von Bissing, who occupied it briefly in October 1914, was enchanted by it and stated then that he wanted it as his 'prix de guerre' and therefore the German artillery carefully avoided it!

Another kilometre and Ypres is entered. On the left a red brick wall encloses the famous **Asylum**. This Victorian-style building has been rebuilt in almost identical form as it was completely destroyed during the bombardments. In 1915, the Friends' Ambulance Unit, which had established itself there in December 1914, was driven to the cellars before it and the nuns who assisted, evacuated it in May 1915. At a ceremony in 1965, three of these gallant ladies were present although

all have now passed away, the last in 1979. Sister Marguerite became famous for her work with the wounded and wrote a book about her experiences. Now, new quarters for the patients have been erected in the gardens.

A few hundred metres further on, the road crosses the old canal and the level crossing known as **Bridge No. 10** or 'Devil's Bridge'. Turning right on to a new road towards the station, because of the one-way traffic system it is not possible to go ahead into Elverdingestraat where the **headquarters of the Commonwealth War Graves Commission** is to be found at No. 82. This is the office of the Superintendent of the north-west Europe area.

Also along this street is the **prison** in whose cellars many British soldiers found refuge, including the Guards and, I believe, on occasion the Town Major. Taking the first main turning on the left which is Botterstraat, the main shopping street, the Grand Place is reached and the Cloth Hall comes into view.

The rebuilt Cloth Hall, Ypres.

ROUTE II VIA CASSEL

Leave Calais by the N1. In 22 kms the outskirts of Gravelines are reached. Turn right onto the D11 from the ring-road signposted Bourbourg-Cassel. The road crosses the flat meadows and small fields with their attendant farms to the country town of Bourbourg astride a canal. Follow the signs for Cassel (8 kms) through the town, having crossed the canal and railway, and continue onwards over the Canal de la Haute Colme at Loobergue and thence through the Erkelsbrugge road junction to Arneke.

After 21 kms we reach **Arneke**, a sleepy village belying the fact that it was a busy railway centre surrounded by training depots and reinforcement camps. Ahead the solitary hill of Cassel rises above the gently undulating landscape. The road climbs up and around the wooded slopes of the steep hill and joins the N42 from St Omer after 7 kms at the entry to the town.

Cassel. As the narrow street rises, a square, until recently Place General Plumer now Place Général Vandamme, opens on the left. Immediately thereafter, the main road, even narrower, proceeds downhill to the Grand Place. The town clings to the crest and slopes of the 156-metre-high **Mont Cassel** which, since Roman times, has been an important road junction as major highways converge from each cardinal point.

The scene of many sieges through the centuries, it had been burnt and devastated no less than nine times when, in 1914, once more it became an important military centre. Once more the medieval streets, houses and cellars rang with the voices of soldiers and, not for the first time either, English accents were heard. An earlier occupation placed it forever in the nursery literature of British children, for here it was that the Grand Old Duke of York marched his 10,000 men up the hill only to march them down again. This was during the 1793-1794 campaign in Flanders mounted by the Duke of Coburg when the Duke of York led the English contingent against the French revolutionary army and was soundly beaten in a nearby battle.

In October 1914, Sir John French set up a base in Cassel for the period of October 11-24, but it is as the headquarters of Maréchal Foch (from October 1914 to April 1915 and again in April 1918) and as that of General Plumer's Second Army (from 1916 to 1918) that Cassel will be remembered.

Although the town suffered considerable damage in the Second World War, in many aspects it still appears much the same as those who served there 60 years ago will recall, as the rebuilding has been in character and style.

On the summit of the Mont de Cassel are the **Jardin du Publique,** once the **Place de Castel Moulin** now the **Terrasse du Château,** which can easily be reached from the square below, up the narrow winding street passing the tall red brick house, **Castel Yvonne,** where Lord Plumer lived. His rooms overlooked the great plateau with Ypres and the grey mass of the Messines Ridge in the distance.

The Jardin du Publique is dominated by a wooden windmill of the type which, until the early years of this century, were found throughout this part of Flanders. This mill, which is open to the public, is a reconstruction based on a mill salvaged from Arneke.

Nearby is the equestrian statue by Georges Malissard of Maréchal Foch, a copy of which

The Castel Yvonne in Cassel was once occupied by General Plumer.

is in Grosvenor Gardens, close to Victoria Station, London. The statue, on a pedestal of Soignies and Breton granite, was unveiled by Raymond Poincaré in the presence of the Maréchal on July 7, 1928 and looks out over the battlefields of the Yser, Ypres and Messines. The square face of the pedestal represents the stubborn resistance of the Allied armies. An arc of trees frames the statue which is set on the spot from where Foch was given to watching the smoke of battle rise from the trenches in the distance.

Above: **Cassel. A surviving bunker on the summit in the Jardin du Publique. Beneath were underground offices.** *Below:* **The vista seen today over Flanders from Cassel.**

Maréchal Foch surveys the battlefields from Mont Cassel.

The Hôtel de Schoeberque was used by King George V and other notable visitors to the Ypres Salient.

Beneath the gardens are the cellars of the old castle which stood here and were used by the military in both wars. Second Army Headquarters also used the large building (now a café), as well as other houses in the town. In front of the café, in the centre of the car park, is a memorial to the three major battles of Cassel, 1071, 1328 and 1677. An archway leads from the garden direct to the main square by an extremely steep path and road. Near the path leading to the gateway is a concrete bunker and an entrance to the cellars.

At various strategic points around the park orientation tables are set into the tops of the balustrades. Distance and directions for towns all over the globe are etched in slate. From these viewpoints the magnificent panorama unfolds. In bygone times it was said that from the summit of the Mont de Cassel could be viewed five kingdoms: those of France, England, Belgium, Holland, and of God. Certainly on a clear day the view encompasses the hills of Kemmel and the Mont de Cats, Vimy Ridge and the lighthouse of Dunkerque. With the aid of binoculars the spires of Ypres, or the pillars of the Vimy Ridge memorial, can be discerned. Closer at hand, the old Roman roads and those built by Napoleon's engineers like spokes from a wheel can be determined. The roofs of the Renaissance-style buildings straggle immediately below the park, among them the Hôtel de Ville with its many dormer windows, each said to represent one of the cantons in the province of Flandres Maritime of which Cassel was the capital.

In the **Hôtel de Ville**, the erstwhile Hôtel de la Noble Cour set on the Grand Place, Maréchal Foch had his office. It is preserved as a **museum** with photographs and documents displayed together with the Maréchal's furniture and other treasures. More exhibits relating to the war effort of Cassel are on show in the **Town Museum** with relics of past glories in the same building. The museum is open on Sundays from mid-June to mid-September, 2.00 p.m. to 6.00 p.m.

The rue d'Ypres, now renamed **rue du Maréchal Foch**, leads from the Grand Place eastwards. At **No. 32-34**, the **Hôtel de Schoeberque** was the residence of the Maréchal during his tour of duty and it was here he received notabilities and where King George V, the Prince of Wales, the King of the Belgians and Sir Douglas Haig stayed on different occasions. A plaque on the wall of the modern hotel commemorates these dates and visits.

The road bends past the white buildings at the end of the street as it begins its tortuous descent to the valley. At the corner is an old archway, the ancient Porte d'Ypres. The town cemetery is on the precipitous slopes in between two very dangerous hairpin bends.

At the foot of the hill, the road to Poperinge and Ypres crosses the D916 for Bailleul. Just off this road, some 2 kms away, is the hilltop village of **St Marie Cappel** below which are the fields where the **Royal Flying Corps aerodrome** was established. Today, little or no sign of the aerodrome can be traced.

After crossing the D916 the road (D945) enters the wooded slopes of the Mont des Recollets and some further dangerous corners have to be negotiated before the long straight road to Steenvoorde (6 kms).

Steenvoorde is a dusty market town with an unusual church spire. It can be bypassed on the eastern side by one of the link roads to the Dunkerque-Paris motorway, but it is just as simple to carry on through the town and out on to the same road before crossing the motorway.

Among the copses on the right of our road is the hunting lodge so vividly described by R. H. Mottram in his *Spanish Farm* trilogy. Between the French customs post and the Belgian one at **Abeele** is the site of another **RFC aerodrome**, reverted of course to agricultural uses. Just to the left of the road

can be seen the Cross of Sacrifice of **Abeele Military Cemetery**. This stretch of the road is international as France lies on the right and Belgium on the left. Abeele (6 kms) is a small village almost buried under the weight of the juggernaut lorries waiting for customs clearance along the length of its curving main street.

After 6 kms we reach **Poperinge** *(see Route 1)*. By taking the road 3½ kms from Abeele, and almost immediately another right and traversing the hopfields, it is possible to visit the beautiful **Cemetery of Lijssenhoek**, the second largest in Flanders. Here men of many nationalities lie amid beautiful gardens and trees. Begun in 1914 by the French (who had established a casualty clearing station at **Remi Farm**, on the boundary of the cemetery, to which a railway spur was laid from the Poperinge line) the cemetery bears the unusual dates 1914-1920. In these peaceful surroundings Frenchmen are the earliest burials but close by lies the last officer to die in the Salient—Lieutenant-Colonel Beatty Pownall—together with his comrades who lost their lives in September and October 1918. Men from the Commonwealth and the Chinese Labour Corps, Algerians and the only Americans to be buried in the Salient lie close to a large German plot.

Remi Farm has changed little over the years. In the great barn, where men were sheltered during the war of 1914-1918, the beams bear signs of earlier military occupations. Etched on them and on the walls are initials and dates of soldiers' visits of a previous century. Graffiti of Poilu and Tommy are intermingled.

On the southern side of the cemetery is the **Commonwealth War Graves Commission nursery garden** for the region. Here shrubs, trees and perennial plants are propagated.

A casualty clearing station was established by the French army at Remi Farm *(above)* beside which a burial ground was laid out. Here combatants of both sides were buried in what was to become the second largest cemetery in the Ypres Salient—Lijssenhoek British Military Cemetery.

ROUTE III VIA ST. OMER

Leave Calais by the N43. This road for most of its length to St Omer and beyond has a good even surface and is a most pleasant drive. Near Pont d'Ardres the road runs close to two of the major canals of the region, both of which played an important role in the Great War carrying supply barges up to the back areas and depots.

Pont d'Ardres (12 kms) was a bustling base bristling with soldiers working on the barges and in the dockside establishments. Today it is little more than a village near the new bridges which span the canals on whose banks new industries are springing up.

Ardres (5 kms). A quaint little town through which the road climbs as it leaves the flat plain for the more undulating country before St Omer. In these fields the training camps and ranges were built. The occasional rough mound and bramble-strewn ditch may be the remnants of practice trenches and the full-size replica of sectors of the front line which were made in 1916 and 1917.

St Omer (23 kms). A quiet and attractive town set on hills between the canals. From October 12, 1914 to April 31, 1916 the British General Headquarters was based here. In 1917 it became the Royal Flying Corps and Royal Air Force Headquarters until the end of the war. In 1917 it also began to become a regular target for enemy air raids and, with the opening of the German Spring Offensive in 1918, it came within easy artillery range.

Evidence of the destruction can be noted now only in a few isolated buildings, as much of the town has been repaired or rebuilt. In the Second World War, the town was a German Luftwaffe base and was raided by the Allied air forces more than twenty times inflicting further damage, now made good.

The arrival of the BEF in 1914 was far from being the first time that contact with England had been felt. This started in Saxon times, when Hereward the Wake stayed here and later during the sieges of the Middle Ages and the 18th Century wars of Marlborough. In the **Jardin Publique** remnants of the Vauban ramparts are preserved below the eminence on which stands the Basilica of Notre Dame. This large 13th Century church is crowded with reminders of the town's historic past and still bears witness to the attacks of both wars.

Among the few remaining signs of the British presence in 1914-18 is a small, faded, bluish-green circular plaque, similar to those seen around London, on the crumbling walls of **No. 50 Avenue Carnot.** It records the death in this house of Field-Marshal Lord Roberts

St Omer. Place du Maréchal Foch, scene of Lord Roberts' funeral in November 1914.

on November 14, 1914. The grand old man had been visiting the Indian Corps when he returned to Sir John French's Headquarters with a chill which turned to pneumonia. On November 17 his body was moved in military state to the Hôtel de Ville, the streets being lined by troops from every unit in France. A large number attended the short service held in the **Place Gambetta** (as the Place du Maréchal Foch was then known) before the cortege moved to the station through troop-lined streets.

Also in the Avenue Carnot is the **Hôtel Sandelin**, a beautiful 18th Century house which is an excellent provincial museum and art gallery. **No. 37 rue St Bertin** bears no marks to recall it being the residence of Sir John French and later Sir Douglas Haig. Further down this street, which leads to the ruins of the **Abbey of St Bertin**, are the old buildings of the **Hôpital Militaire**, previously a school solely for the education of Roman Catholic boys from Britain. Opened in 1592 it was moved firstly to Bruges and later, in the 18th Century, Liege, before going to Stoneyhurst in Lancashire in 1794 where it still flourishes.

St Omer was a very popular leave town as it provided many amenities for leisure not readily available closer to the front. In the unique marshes to the north and eastern outskirts called the **Watergangs** (from the curious labyrinths of canals and drains of this reclaim-ed region), many estaminets were opened for the officers and men who enjoyed the fishing or boating. In the forest of Clairmarais were huge camps and supply depots and special facilities for the men on leave. Within the walls of the ancient farms whole battalions could be accommodated and several of these are situated at the forest edge. Near one farm rises the ruined tower of the **Abbey of St Omer** — a refuge where Thomas à Becket sought shelter after his contretemps with Henry II.

Taking the N42 eastward through the new suburbs and industrial complex growing up on the dried marshes, **Arques** is reached in 4 kms. The road crosses the major Canal de la Haute Colme, and at **Les Fontinettes** it was connected by a remarkable hydraulic barge lift to the Canal de Neuf Fosse. The lift transported the barges up and down the 50ft difference in levels. It was built in 1887 and was in use without a break until recently replaced by a slope, as in both wars there was an unwritten agreement between belligerents not to bomb it. Beside the new facilities the old Assenseur des Fontinettes can still be seen with a barge in the lift.

Just beyond the crest of the rise outside Arques, a wide flat plateau is reached and the **site of the aerodrome** comes into view. The roads were lined with concrete shelters but these are now crumbling and gradually disappearing amid the beet fields.

To the south of St Omer is the residential

No. 50, Avenue Carnot, where Field-Marshal Roberts died.

No. 37, rue St Bertin — used by both French and Haig.

suburb of **Blendeques** in whose pleasant valleys and woods are a number of elegant homes, many being classifed as châteaux. Here HM King George and Queen Mary resided during their visits to the troops. Some of the châteaux still bear military placards on their walls proclaiming the offices which they once housed. The **Château de l'Eminence** proudly displays a fire point notice by its crumbling front door; another, the **Château Bellevue**, was the main office of an officer school.

To the west of St Omer on the Boulogne road (N42) at the **Wisques** crossroad is the **Abbey of St Paul**, and, a short distance up the road to Wisques village, its sister convent. To these were brought the typhoid victims from Ypres in 1915 and here were established schools for the evacuated children. Between here and **Wizernes** to the south was a complex for the V-2 missiles of 1944.

After 2 kms the road forks; take the N42 for Hazebrouck, passing through **Renescure**, a railway station well known to the BEF, and **Ebblinghem**, a village with associations with the training camps.

Hazebrouck (18 kms). A name known to every British soldier. Thousands passed through the station en route for Ypres or the Somme. From the outbreak of war, the name of this quiet market town and vital junction for road and rail communications was rarely out of the news, having become an Army headquarters in October 1914.

In the first German drive westwards, the town was surrendered peacefully by the Abbé Deputy, Lemire, to avoid destruction, but the British Cavalry Corps cleared the town and nearby Forest of Nieppe and the I British Corps set up its headquarters here. Once again a British Army, the First Army, was based in the town, for in 1815 Wellington used it as one of his major bases. In 1915 the Second Army took over. General French resided in one of the graceful houses in the then Grand Place but now, as the traveller enters from the rue Warein, it will be noticed the name has changed to **Place Général de Gaulle**.

This huge rectangular market place, with its unusual Classical Hôtel de Ville, was always bustling with troops and is still the hub of a thriving town. Here and there uneven cobblestones survive from earlier times to shake the unwary driver. In another square — **Place de la Victoires**—is the town war memorial and one of the few ancient buildings remaining—the church of St Eloi dating from the 16th Century.

Hazebrouck was a major advance base, there being ordnance, signals, engineer, medical and transport depots crowded around this important railway junction. Army workshops, where all manner of equipment was produced from odds and ends, opened in the town. Administrative offices occupied the large halls and other requisitioned buildings. Training areas and reinforcement camps opened in the surrounding countryside; to the south-west were sited the hospitals and casualty clearing stations.

Towards the end of 1917, the town, which had previously suffered occasional bombardments, was seriously damaged by shellfire. One gun operating from near Lille was said to be a British high velocity piece captured during the Battle of Cambrai. The Forest of Nieppe, the scene of the British cavalry action in October 1914 which cleared the advancing German troops, was threatened again in the Spring Offensive from the south-east and heavy fighting ensued in April 1918. Hazebrouck was menaced and the civilian population was evacuated but the stands of the 29th, 31st and Guards Divisions and the 1st Australian Division which stemmed the onslaught saved the town. Casualty clearing stations which had operated from 1916 to 1917 returned in the summer of 1918 as did No. 9 Field Hospital.

Château de l'Eminence where the King and Queen resided during tours of the front.

Hazebrouck's magnificent town hall overlooks the Grand Place.

In the Second World War the town was again very badly damaged but, in many aspects, it is still very recognisable as the soldiers' centre of rest and leisure and of the base works and junction for the front which it was for so long. Many of the billets and buildings the military used have been repaired in the old style.

Leave Hazebrouck by the rue de Bailleul (N42) out into the area of the 1918 battles for Hazebrouck, now once more a peaceful agricultural region which becomes slightly more undulating as the road approaches **Strazeele**, 7 kms away.

This village was the German's first objective in their attack on Hazebrouck from the east in April 1918, but the 33rd Division and the Australians stood in their way and held on. The nearby villages of **Méteren** (to the north-east) and Merris (to the south) were overrun but were recaptured by the 9th Scottish Division and 1st Australian Division respectively on July 9 and 19. In 1914, the German advance on Méteren was the scene of a bayonet charge by 2nd Bn. Seaforth Highlanders in III British Corps (General Poultney) checking and clearing action.

Four kilometres south of Méteren, the N42 crosses the Dunkerque-Lille motorway before entering **Bailleul** in 3 kms as the D944. A picturesque market town, famed since ancient times for its lacemaking which, with linen, is still one of the major industries, Bailleul was a

military base for much of the war—a real front line town. It fell briefly to the Germans but was recaptured by the British on October 14, 1914 and thereafter, for three-and-a-half years, it was to act as a forward base for the British and French before being almost totally destroyed in the savage fighting of the Battle of the Lys in the spring of 1918. Bailleul

Many buildings were used by the military. This chapel was signals HQ.

Bailleul. The reconstructed Hôtel de Ville beside the Belfry.

The memorial to the 25th Division which recaptured the ruins on August 30, 1918.

The ruins of St Armand church form the backcloth for the town's war memorial.

provided a welcome respite to the fighting forces and a haven for the wounded in the hospital facilities of its well known asylum and clinic. Troops thronged its pleasant market square above which the **Belfry of the Hôtel de Ville** rose defiantly. Cafés and estaminets flourished and one in particular, 'Tina's', in the rue de Dunkerque, became a famous and popular officers' haunt.

The town had hardly suffered from artillery bombardment but in July 1917 the relative peace was shattered by heavy shells which caused much damage. Then the almost complete destruction of the town came when the Germans advanced to capture the ruins on April 15, 1918 after the heroic defence of the British 34th and 59th Divisions which were forced to retire exhausted. For four months the town was in German hands and then on August 30 the British 25th Division regained possession of the ruins.

Today, the old market square once more is the centre of a charming busy little town; the Hôtel de Ville and the Belfry have been rebuilt in warm red brick and the cafés and shops welcome both resident and visitor.

The road enters the centre of the town at a roundabout, in the centre of which is the obelisk memorial to the 25th Division, and, turning left, the square is reached. In the street behind the Hôtel de Ville can be seen the ruins of the **Church of St Amand** now forming an integral part of the town's **War Memorial**.

The road to Belgium, the D23, leaves the square at the opposite end and almost immediately a green CWGC sign can be seen indicating the way, down a small street on the right, to the **Bailleul Communal Cemetery and Extension**. The entrance to these cemeteries is just beyond the main gates to the town cemetery, after which the road deteriorates into a muddy track. Whilst the Communal Cemetery is relatively small, the Communal Cemetery Extension provides the last resting place of over 4,000 men of many nationalities. Alongside their British and Commonwealth comrades lie French, Russian, Chinese, and many Germans. From the cemetery walls a panoramic view of the Monts de Flandres provides a background to the **site of the old Royal Flying Corps base and aerodrome**. Among those buried here is Sergeant Mottershead, VC.

Returning to the D23, turn right on to the Loker (Locre) road for about a kilometre, passing round the walls of the **old asylum** and the hospital which was so vital to the troops. I understand the present day aspect resembles very closely that of 60 years ago.

'A good reputation endures for ever' . . . 'faithful unto death'. So are the Chinese Labour casualties remembered in Bailleul British Cemetery Extension.

Ahead now rise the hills of Flanders—Mont Noir, Mont Rouge and Mont Kemmel with the Mont des Cats far over to the left. At the first road junction keep to the Loker road but, a short distance beyond, take the left fork, the D223 for **Mont Noir.** As the road approaches the village one of the 1939-45 concrete bunkers which surround the hill comes into view on the right, and almost immediately on the left is the entrance to a **small cemetery** where British and French soldiers who died in the attacks of 1918 lie together. Between April and September 1918 there was heavy and prolonged fighting in this area when, having secured Kemmel, the Germans advanced to be thrown back by the 34th British Division.

The Bailleul Asylum and hospital cared for great numbers of casualties.

The wooded slopes of Scherpenberg today hide the dugouts built into its sides.

The 34th Division Memorial, Mont Noir. Note the divisional chequerboard sign.

Further up the hill, actually on the crest, is the **34th Division Memorial**. For many years this was known locally as Nurse Cavell for who else could be the Angel of Victory!

The customs post is at the main crossroads just below the summit. Around it now are cafés, hotels and souvenir shops. Between Mont Noir and Mont Rouge, across the valley and the lower Mont Vidaigne, is a téléphérique. On the slopes of both hills are sports facilities of many kinds with camp sites and caravan parks nestling amid the trees.

Three kilometres further on is **Loker (Locre)**. This village was almost entirely destroyed in the battles for Mont Kemmel. On the wall of the **Hôtel de Ville**, opposite the church, there are three memorial plaques commemorating French units who participated in the 1918 operations.

The direct route to Ypres, the N70, passes beneath the **Scherpenberg** rising on the right of the road. As it is approached, the entrance to a series of dugouts can be seen above the tree-line. Scherpenberg was heavily defended by the French and the British 21st, 25th and 49th Divisions when it was attacked on April 29, 1918 but it was not captured. A kilometre further along is the hamlet of La Clytte (De Klijte) where the Poperinge-Kemmel road crosses.

After 4 kms, **Dickebush** (Dikkebus) is reached, a familiar name to all who served in the Salient. The artificial lake was lined with trenches and hutments. Access to the lake is gained from the first crossroad after the village when, taking the right-hand road, the white brewery (which was a delousing station and bath centre) is passed. It is difficult today, as one sits on the terrace of the hotel overlooking the peaceful waters, to envisage the devastation and mud and the appalling conditions which prevailed in 1917 and 1918 along the banks, but, with the right light, traces of the revetments can be clearly discerned. After a further 5 kms, Ypres is reached by way of the modern station, now flanked by the bypass.

Sunset over the peaceful waters of Dickebush Lake.

19

Zeebrugge—Ypres

The old armoured cruiser HMS Vindictive alongside the outer wall of the mole. Special gangplanks were provided for the raiding party to reach the raised parapet and ladders enabled the troops to descend the other side (Charles de Lacey).

An interesting route to Ypres is via **Zeebrugge**—the port where the 3rd Cavalry Division disembarked in October, 1914. They had been sent there to cover the Belgian retreat from Antwerp, but five days later the Germans occupied the town. They set about converting the port into a front line naval and seaplane base and, by December, it was operational.

The modern ferry terminal is part of a huge new dock complex being built to cater for the container ships, tankers and freighters now plying into this port. To the west of the ferry terminal the **old mole** is disappearing to make way for new installations. Already to the landward the famous raised esplanade above the jetty, outside which HMS *Vindictive* tied up, has been demolished and a new approach road has replaced the old cobbled road along the wharves.

The old mole, built in 1895-1907, was 2½ kms in length and protected the entrance to the harbour and the Bruges canal. For much of its length it was some 150 feet wide with the esplanade being on the seaward side right up

Almost 60 years later, a British ferry rounds the end of the rebuilt mole.

Left: The damaged wall, where Vindictive went alongside on April 23, 1918, photographed after the war (IWM). *Above:* The plaque marking the spot.

to the narrower extremity and the lighthouse. Near the place where HMS *Vindictive* with the tiny *Daffodil* and *Iris* came alongside on St George's Day, 1918, there is still a battered, weatherbeaten bronze plaque, but gone are the quay over which the Marines and sailors swarmed and fought and the bridge which connected the mole to the shore, penetrated by the old submarine *C3* under Lieutenant Sandford. The site of the Lübeck Battery has disappeared in the new complex as has the place where in 1925 an elegant monument, some 46 feet high, was erected. It was surmounted by a bronze sculpture of St George and the Dragon and was the scene of an annual ceremony during the pilgrimage of the men of the Zeebrugge Association. In 1942 the Germans destroyed the memorial and melted down the bronze. Until the work on the new access road to the docks began, a more modest stone memorial stood on the identical spot. When the construction work is completed the memorial is to be returned to a suitable place in the vicinity.

Another casualty of the enlargement of the harbour is the **Palace Hôtel**, the basement of which until September 1978 was the home of the **Zeebrugge Museum**. The building had been German Headquarters and the museum contained reproductions of the murals they had used to decorate the walls of the various rooms. The exhibits were relics of the men and ships (including Captain Fryatt and the SS *Brussels*), the uniforms, medals, badges and items of equipment, photographs and documents, together with other artefacts relative to the Second World War and the two occupations of the port. Actual portions of the ships, models and dioramas depicting the raid and coastal defence, a typical small Belgian parlour where examples of booby-traps were demonstrated, made this an interesting and unusual museum. All the collection has been removed temporarily to Bruges, where some of the objects are on view in the city's main museums but, on the completion of the port works, a new museum will be inaugurated and once more Zeebrugge will boast a fine reminder of its historic past.

Leaving the terminal, turn left at the traffic

The second memorial with the old Palace Hotel in the background.

Above: 'In memory of St George's Day, 1918 when every moment had its deed and every deed its hero.' So read the inscription on the original memorial at Zeebrugge unveiled in 1925. *Below:* In 1942, German forces destroyed the monument—all that was salved were a few of the stones which were set in the pavement after the war.

Above: German and British casualties from the raid were buried together in Zeebrugge churchyard near the Salvage Corps Memorial. *Right:* The smallest Memorial to the Missing—to four men who lost their lives during the attack.

lights onto N72; in about 1½ kms **Zeebrugge church** will be seen off to the right between the new highway bounded on the left by the sprawling new container port complex and the old main road, the Heiststraat, to the left of St Donaasplein. Here in the **small cemetery** are buried together British seamen and Royal Marines killed on April 23, 1918 and a number of Germans. Here also is the smallest of the **Memorials to the Missing**, a small stone panel set in the wall commemorating three officers and one mechanic who had lost their lives on that memorable day and have no known grave. Among them is Lieutenant Commander A. L. Harrison, VC, killed whilst leading one of the storming parties from HMS *Vindictive*. There is also a simple memorial erected in 1920 to the British Salvage Corps.

Return to the N72 5 kms to **Blankenberge**. In the **Communal Cemetery** Lieutenant-

Above: HMS Vindictive alongside Ostend mole, October 1918 (IWM), and *right* the bow of the ship preserved today.

The Nieuwpoort Memorial to the Missing, remembering those who lost their lives at Antwerp in 1914 and along the coast between 1914-18 and have no known grave.

The Memorial to King Albert beside the lock gates at Nieuwpoort. These were the sluices opened by the lock-keeper in 1914 to flood the surrounding countryside.

Commander G. N. Bradford, VC, of the *Iris* lies buried.

Another 21 kms and Ostende is reached. At various places along the road will be seen bunkers of the Atlantic Wall but none of the old 1914-18 fortifications or gun sites remain.

Ostend (Oostende) is one of the main holiday resorts on this long sandy coastline as well as being a major port for ferries to the UK. A railway terminus for the long distance continental trains and an airport add to its importance. The N72 enters Ostend over a series of bridges crossing the locks into the inner harbour and the canal to Bruges (Brugge). As the road rises and turns to the left over the outer end of the lock leading into the dry dock, a small park will be noticed laid out beside the basin. It can be reached by turning left (one-way traffic). There, amid the flower beds, rests the **bow section of the Vindictive and the masts of the Intrepid and Thetis**. The upper sections of the mast of HMS *Thetis* (nearest the road) is fairly new as the original fell to pieces with wood-rot. (I know for I gave a section of it to the Imperial War Museum, London!)

On August 27, 1914, a small force of Royal Marines landed in Ostend to protect the evacuation of thousands of refugees to England. On October 4, the Royal Naval Division disembarked for the ill-fated expedition to Antwerp and two days later the 7th Division landed to proceed to the front.

When the Belgian Government and King Albert had to evacuate Antwerp, they made their HQ in Ostend. However on October 13, the Government left for Le Havre and the King went to lead his army on the Yser. Ostend was occupied by the Germans on the 15th.

Here, as at Zeebrugge, the Germans constructed a naval base for their submarines but, because it was constantly under attack from both the air and sea, the repair shops and stores were moved to Brugge and Zeebrugge. Ostend then became a secondary port for small craft only and Zeebrugge took precedence both as a destroyer and submarine base.

On April 23, 1918, at the same time as the major attack on Zeebrugge, an attempt was made to block the canal and harbour entrances using two old cruisers, the *Brilliant* and *Sirius*. This was unsuccessful and on May 9-10 another attempt was made, this time with HMS *Vindictive* which had been filled with concrete and was sunk between the piers in the harbour entrance sealing the large craft in the basins. After doing a great deal of demolition, the Germans left Ostend on October 17, 1918.

There is a choice of roads from Ostend to Nieuwpoort: the N318 runs close on the coast along the dunes and large modern blocks of flats through the busy streets of the resorts, whilst the N72 runs behind the built-up area

passing the airfield and gives views over to the left of the Yser battlefields.

In 16 kms, the roads converge close by the huge circular **Memorial to King Albert** erected above the multiple sluices for the canals at the inland end of **Nieuwpoort.** The striking, brick archways surround a mounted statue of the King; on one wall is a small bronze plaque to his wife, Queen Elizabeth, who died in 1968. A lift takes visitors to the balcony at the top of the arch, giving magnificent views of the Yser, the canals, Nieuwpoort and Lombardsijde. This was the western end of the front line which ran 600 miles to the Swiss border; the whole region was utterly devastated.

This end of the line was usually in the hands of the French and Belgians but in June 1917, the British XV Corps took over the line with men of the 1st and 32nd Divisions and, later, the 66th Division. They held the line from St Georges, Ramskapelle to the sea at Nieuwpoort and withstood the onslaught of the major German attack of July 10, 1917. Although the battalions were cut off, they held on until the battle eased on July 17, when they were relieved by the 49th and 33rd Divisions after having suffered very heavy casualties. The 41st and 42nd Divisions came in September but the other divisions left the area which was now a stagnating front and, in November, these last two divisions were relieved by the French.

In a triangular plot beside the road, beneath the gaze of King Albert, three lions guard the cenotaph of the **British Memorial to the Missing**, Nieuwpoort. This memorial is to the 566 officers and men who died in the operations at Antwerp in 1914 and later actions on the Belgian coast, particularly those in 1917.

The six sluices over which runs the road to Ramskapelle, control the canals to Veurne and Dunkerque, the Canal de Paschendaele (to Brugge) and two regulate the Yser. These were opened by the lock-keeper during the Battle of the Yser in 1914 thereby flooding the lower reaches of the Yser and stemming the German advance. The garrison in Nieuwpoort was aided by British naval machine gunners.

Take the N67 for a short distance and then the Ramskapelle road to the right, beside **Ramskapelle St George's Road Cemetery**. Here are buried men from scattered graves in the region, a group of Russians who died in 1919 and Belgian graves of October 1944.

British, Czech and Russian headstones in Ramskapelle St George's Road.

Above: **The Franco-Belgian memorial in the centre of Ramskapelle village.**

Ramskapelle village (3 kms) was a vital position on the railway to Dixmude in the Yser Battles of 1914 and was on the edge of the flooded areas. Go straight through the village and out on the N57, noticing the **Franco-Belgian memorial** on the churchyard wall in the centre of the village. On the edge of the village, just before joining the main road, will be seen a model windmill, actually a

transformer station, set in a small triangular patch. On one side a **Demarcation Stone** stands in a break in the hedge. This was damaged in the fighting here in 1944. Every year on October 31, a ceremony is held here in memory of the battle of 1914.

Take the N57 to the left and travel 5 kms

A tower in Pervijze used as an OP.

Oud-Stuivekenskerke. This is the Memorial Chapel of the Belgian Army built close to the ruins of the old one defended by the Belgians in 1914.

through the rich pasture of this fen and marshland to **Pervijze**. An observation post used during the 1914 actions was situated in **a tower** in the village.

Keep with the N57 for 2 kms then turn left onto a small road and almost immediately another left. After 1 km take a right turn by a café to reach, by a very narrow road, the **Belgian Army Memorial Chapel**. This is set in a remote point on the Belgian front line at **Oud-Stuivekenskerke** (it is shown on the map as O.L. Vrouwhoekje). The modern chapel is built close to the ruins of the old one which was fortified and defended by the Belgian Army during the Yser battles of 1914 and October 1918.

Around the chapel are tablets bearing the badges of many Belgian regiments and several memorials including **a Demarcation Stone** bearing the name Dixmuide. In the porch of the chapel are maps of the actions. The chapel is worth visiting purely for the beautiful stained glass windows—portraits of the King and Queen of the Belgians and Belgian soldiers. Part of the old fortified chapel nearby remains with a memorial to a militant priest.

Return to the road and continue to Stuivekenskerke, keeping to the right in the village, and then right, along the banks of the canalised Yser. Dotted about the area will be seen concrete shelters, mostly of French origin but some German and a few Belgian.

In 5 kms we reach the **Boyau du Mort**—the Trench of Death. This is a section of trench along the river bank which is preserved, somewhat artificially but based on genuine Belgian trenches. They were repaired by Belgian Army Engineers in 1974. The trenches are entered through a small museum, and nearby are the ruins of a blockhouse and the old mill which was here when the trenches were built. Within the trench area is another **Demarcation Stone**.

Dixmude (Diksmuide), 2 kms further on, is once again the sleepy market town it was when the war came in October 1914. It was defended to the death by the French troops of Général Jacques, the French Marines of Admiral Ronar'ch and the Belgian Army. Fighting against a much stronger opponent, who bombarded the town incessantly, it fell on November 10. Many artillery batteries were then emplaced in and around the town. It was not recaptured until the end of September 1918 when it fell to the Belgians.

Our road actually arrives in Dixmude close to the **Ysertoren**, the huge memorial tower of the **Free Flemish** — **VVK-AVV**. This

memorial has been an object of political strife and the original was blown up in 1946. The present tower stands a little behind the site of its predecessor which is in ruins near the entrance to the park. In the crypt are various memorials to the Flemish patriots. In the new tower is a museum which has some quite interesting and varied exhibits, including a comprehensive collection of the work of the Belgian artist, Joe English. There is a good explanation of the battles involving Dixmude and collections of papers and other relics. There is a lift to the top where the windows look out upon the town and surrounding countryside.

In the **main square** of Dixmude is a **statue of Général Jacques** and in the local park, a **Memorial to the French Marines and Admiral Ronar'ch**. The **town hall** is in the old Flemish style (as are the other houses in the square) and was rebuilt in the late 1920s. It possesses a small but very interesting collection of relics relative to the war and includes objects retrieved from the ruins.

Leave Dixmude by the N69 and travel 23 kms to Ypres. This road crosses much of the region of the floods and the 1914 battlefield. Now it is once more a rich agricultural plain with a large nature reserve at Blankaert.

The huge Free Flemish VVK-AVV tower in Dixmude—an earlier memorial was blown up in 1946.

This is the Boyau du Mort—the Trench of Death. Situated near Stuivekenskerke, it is a section of Belgian trench which has been preserved, rather artificially, with concrete. There is a blockhouse and old mill nearby, all dating from the First War.

This is the skeleton of Ypres as seen from the air in 1918. The ruins of St Peter's church are visible. The ramparts in the foreground lie either side of the Lille Gate (IWM).

YPRES

Ypres—Ieper—Ypern—there are said to be at least 27 different ways in which the name has been spelled over the centuries — dates from about 962. Centuries earlier there had been a settlement on the site, vestiges of which can still be seen beneath the Lille Gate.

By the Middle Ages the town had become one of the strongest and wealthiest in all Flanders and was the centre of a flourishing textile trade. Only Bruges and Ghent rivalled it and the inter-city squabbles were frequent and warlike. In the 13th Century, the centre of a population of around 200,000, Ypres reached its zenith. At this time its most famous building—the Cloth Hall—the largest of its type, was built. Work commenced about 1260 when the Belfry and the east wing were built; by 1286 the west and side wings were completed and the whole magnificent hall was finished in 1304. The purpose of the building was as a covered market and storage space to which ships could sail to load and unload their cargoes onto the covered quay on the banks of the Yperlee. Forty-eight doors led from the street direct to the vaulted sale area, with store rooms on the upper floor. No great additions were made until 1619 when the Nieuwerck was constructed along the eastern walls.

In 1383 the town was besieged by the English under the Bishop of Norwich assisted by 20,000 troops from Ghent. Ypres withstood the siege but the flourishing trade was severely affected as the weavers in the neighbourhood left rather than starve, taking the livelihood of the town with them. The importance and influence of Ypres then continually diminished until two centuries later the population had been reduced to 5,000.

Commercially, the position of Ypres may have waned, but never so its strategic importance. Since the 14th Century it has undergone many sieges and been vassal to

several princes. The centre of resistance to Spanish domination, it was sacked by the Duke of Parma in 1584 and throughout the next ninety years was constantly fought over by the French and Spaniards. Each left their mark on the fortifications and outlying defences. By the Peace of Nijmegen in 1678, Ypres became French and Vauban was entrusted with the defence works. Previously there had been six gates, a wall and moat beyond which the Spanish had formed defences of demi-lunes. On the eastern front, where the Antwerp gate had stood, they built a pentagonal-shaped citadel. This Vauban removed and replaced with a strong work — the Corne d'Anvers. Between it and the Corne de Thourot to the north a passage led to the Menin Road. Crenellated stone walls were replaced by stone and brick finished ramparts and bastions. Casemates in the ramparts behind St Jacques church were constructed in 1690. Vauban also reduced the number of gates to the town to four, three of which had ornate facades. The Antwerp gate was the most beautiful and bore on its inner face a long Latin inscription to the glory of Ludovicus Magnus dated 1688. These defences withstood the wars of 1689-1712 when Ypres was not taken. However, in 1713 the Dutch took the city and held it until 1744 when King Louis XV forced the surrender.

In 1792, Ypres was taken and retaken several times during the war between France and Austria. In 1793, the Austrians entered the town again and rebuilt some of the earlier defences which had been dismantled by Emperor Joseph II. These were in their turn levelled in 1794 after the French regained the city.

In 1804 Napoleon visited Ypres and the main gate was named after him, having an imperial eagle carved into the stonework. Thus, in name at least, the Antwerp gate disappeared.

In 1815, prior to Waterloo, all the exterior works were hastily rebuilt under Colonel

Carmichael Smyth of the Royal Engineers and were manned by British troops from Ostend and Nieuwpoort.

After Waterloo, when Belgium was united with Holland, Ypres was again strongly fortified against any possible French invasion and, at this time, the Napoleon Gate was renamed the Menin Gate. With the grant of independence to Belgium in 1838, Ypres became Belgian. The Belgian government in 1852 decided that Ypres no longer required to be a fortified town and levelled all the outer works and pulled down the Vauban walls on the north front. A year later the western ramparts were removed to make room for the railway and the old gates demolished to give wider passage for the roads. Only the Lille Gate was retained.

In 1914 Ypres once again lay in the path of the warring nations and, during the advance of the German IV Cavalry Corps, was entered by their 3rd Cavalry Division on October 13. They requisitioned 75,000 BFr and held the Burgomaster to ransom. The BEF reached the town on the next day and occupied it entirely.

Then began the first agony of Ypres; the great artillery barrage started on November 22 wreaking great damage to the ancient buildings and setting the Cloth Hall on fire. The civilian population suffered considerable casualties and the names of the Abbé Delaere and Sister Marquerite are remembered to this day for the gallant work they did among the homeless and wounded. Not until May 9, 1915, during the month-long barrages of the Second Battle of Ypres, when the Cloth Hall together with the Collegiate Church of St Martin and many other important houses and buildings were destroyed, were the civilians finally and compulsorily evacuated and Ypres left to the military. This was the second agony of Ypres and lasted until after the Third Battle of Ypres in 1917. However, during the comparative quiet of 1916, many people briefly returned to the ruins of their homes.

In the spring of 1918 Ypres came perilously

near to falling to the Germans but, although they reached the outskirts on the eastern and south-eastern flanks, the British lines held and, in the final Allied advance Ypres was relieved when, on September 28, the last German troops were ousted from the Salient.

The principal sites of interest of Ypres

The **Grote Markt** — the Grand Place, one of the most impressive in Flanders, is dominated by the reconstructed **Cloth Hall**. Under the guidance of architects J. Coomans and P. A. Pauwels, this great building was rebuilt in its original form externally between 1920 and 1962. Internally the great halls on the first floor were constructed much as they had been but, for the most part, the other rooms—offices, council chambers, etc.—are of modern aspect. In 1967 King Baudouin unveiled a stone in the main foyer to commemorate the actual completion and re-occupation of the Nieuwerck as the offices of the Burgomaster and his staff. The entrance is to be found beneath the eastern arcade from where one also enters the **Salient 1914-1918 War Museum** (entrance fee 30 BFr).

This excellent collection consists of displays of equipment, weapons, badges and insignia, medals and documents, photographs and maps of Belgian, British, French, American and German origin. All aspects of the conflagration and the battles of the Salient are represented and every item has either been found in the area or is similar to that used or worn there. Relics of some of the personalities connected with the war are included: Sir John French, later the Earl of Ypres, is represented by his banner and a pair of shining boots; Lord Plumer's hat rests nearby; the travelling tea service presented by Lady Haig in memory of her husband, and the sword of Prince Maurice of Battenburg presented by his sorrowing mother. Fragments of the old buildings, commemorative medals and specimens of trench art lie in cases beside the many types of ammunition from which they were made. In addition to the many

photographs taken during the war are those of some of the famous cemeteries and memorials supervised by the Commonwealth War Graves Commission and their German equivalent. Dioramas of a typical airfield of 1917-18, the old Menin and Lille Gates and battlefield scenes, models and a fine collection of trench signs with a map showing the original locations. Guidebooks to the region are on sale at the entrance to this museum including those which support the various routes signposted by the West Flanders tourist authorities. Among these is the Route '14-'18 which is incorporated in the itineraries which follow.

The Belfry is also open to the public and from the upper chamber gallery above the bell chamber a fine view of the town and surrounding countryside is gained. On a clear day the coast can be seen across the flat plain. The bell chamber houses the famous carillon which plays each day at set hours and the chiming bells which toll the hours half-an-hour before their due time. It is not advised to visit this chamber when the hour of midday is tolled as the reverberations and vibrations can be injurious.

On the first floor of the Cloth Hall, a collection of modern Flemish art is displayed. In due course it is hoped that a more local collection of ethnographical material will be shown. Concerts and large meetings are also held on this floor including banquets where some hundreds can be seated.

The most important Council Chamber is on the first floor of the Nieuwerck. It is lit by a huge window of stained glass, the design being a modern conception of the history of Ypres and its traditions and legends carried out in vivid reds and blues.

Of the original Cloth Hall of 1260, only the lower portion of the Belfry around the 'Donkerpoort', and a few of the pillars in the museum and the western hall remain. On the walls above the Donkerpoort are the municipal coat-of-arms and flanking the passage are the statues of Earl Baldwin IX and his Queen, Margaret of Champagne, King Albert and Queen Elizabeth. Above is

Almost an exact match . . . taken 60 years later.

the statue to Our Lady of Thuyne, the patroness of Ypres since the siege of 1383. A plaque commemorating the dedication of the town to the Sacred Heart (on the Jubilee feast of Our Lady of Thuyne in 1933) is to the left of the gateway, and on the right is the **Memorial to the French killed during 1914-1918 in the Salient**.

The present-day aspect of the Grote Markt closely resembles that which it held in the 18th Century as most of the houses are, externally at least, copies of those destroyed. Among them is the old house of the canteen of the Cloth Hall, now the **Klein Stadhuis restaurant** which dated from 1624. A near neighbour, now another café **'Den Anker'** was a copy of its 1611 counterpart. Further along beyond the Dixmudestraat is the old **Kasseirij** building which until 1967 officially housed the Burgomaster and served as Hôtel de Ville during the years of the reconstruction of the Cloth Hall. Opposite between Menestraat and K. Torhoutstraat is the **Court of Justice** which was formerly the Hospital of Our Lady. On the southern side the hotels are close copies of earlier houses but, as the years go by, the modern shop fronts are detracting somewhat from the grace of the Renaissance facades.

Through the Donkerpoort — beneath which is a large shell and the entrance to an inner courtyard of the Cloth Hall (where remnants of the old buildings are stored) — access to the **St Martin's Cathedral** is reached, across some of the few remaining old cobblestones of Ypres. High above the south door is the magnificent **Rose Window** which is the **British Army and RAF Memorial to King Albert**. During the design process for the window, it was discovered that there was no official crest for the British Army and one had to be created and approved by King George V. This is to be found in the upper segment of the window opposite those of the RAF and the Fifth Dragoon Guards.

The Ypres Salient 1914-1918 War Museum. *Left:* **A general view of the museum with relics from a German recently uncovered from the battlefield near Zandvoorde.** *Above:* **Original trench signs removed from the Salient.**

The church was completely destroyed during the war and, when it was rebuilt, the design included the present spire, which, although included in the pre-1914 plans, had never been built. The original cathedral was built in the 13th Century on the site of an earlier church founded in 1073 and was the seat of a bishop until it became the collegiate church under the administration of a dean in the 19th Century. The church is in Gothic style and is lofty and full of light from the many windows.

On the wall of the north transept is a **Memorial Plaque to the British Commonwealth War Dead in the Ypres Salient**. It is one of several placed in cathedrals all along the 1914-1918 front line. In 1973, archaeological excavations in the north aisle resulted in the discovery of the grave of Robert of Béthune—the Lion of Flanders—one of the greatest of the Counts of Flanders who died at Ypres in 1322. Long and widespread research led to this discovery and one of the most vital documents used was a photograph taken in early 1915 by Professor Barbour, then attached to the Friends' Ambulance Unit, which he took the day after one of the bombardments. This photograph showed a mural on the wall of the north aisle and, from a copy of the photograph made by the Imperial War Museum in 1972, it was possible to read the inscription which identified the figure as being

Robert of Bethune and referred to his tomb being close by. After the bombardments nothing was left of the wall and no other photographs were known.

Behind the cathedral are the remains of the old cloisters, now a repository of fragments from the ruined church. In the garden to the south-east of the church is the **Munster Memorial**—a beautiful Celtic Cross commemorating the men of the Munster Regiments who died in the Great War.

Across the Vandenpereboomplein—once partly a waterway to the Cloth Hall—is the **St George's Memorial Church**. The main door is in Elverdingestraat which carries the traffic to the west. The church was designed by Sir

The spire of St Martin's Collegiate Church . . . a pre-war dream fulfilled.

A typical CWGC British Memorial plaque; this one in St Martin's, Ypres.

The memorial commemorating the men of the Munster Regiments.

Reginald Blomfield and was built in 1928-29 as part of the British settlement. The idea came from Earl Haig who suggested that a church should be founded for use as the place of worship for the British colony (which was quite large immediately after the Great War) and for pilgrims to the Salient. The site also included the Eton Memorial School for the children of the gardeners and other officials working in the region and the community centre for them.

Today, the church, a memorial to all who died in the Salient, and the British Legion clubhouse next door are all that remain of the settlement. The school closed after the Second World War and the community buildings were sold. The church foundation stone was laid by Field-Marshal Lord Plumer on July 24, 1927. Almost every item contained within the precincts is a memorial. The windows, the furnishings and the decorations all commemorate a unit or an individual. Recent additions include memorials to Sir Winston Churchill, Field-Marshal Montgomery and a number of officers and men. Services are held regularly each Sunday evening and the Chaplain is in attendance on certain other occasions. The vigorous Friends of St. George's Memorial Church, Ypres, who are always glad to welcome new members, keep it in repair; their meetings are held usually in London under the auspices of the Bishop of Gibraltar in Europe.

The offices of the **Commonwealth War Graves Commission** are to be found at the other end of **Elverdingestraat** at **No. 82** which lies on the right-hand side beyond the town prison. In a street behind the Grote Markt—Merghelynkstraat—is the **reconstructed town house of an 18th Century gentleman** and it is well worth a visit as it depicts the pure French style of the period. From the gracious exterior in the Louis XV and Louis XVI style to the beautifully proportioned interior and period furnishings, it is possible to gain a fair idea of the way people of the upper classes lived in this merchant town.

The west face of the Menin Gate which was dedicated in July 1927.

By far the most important edifice in Ypres to the British visitor is the **Menin Gate**. Built on the site of the original Hangoart Gate (later the Antwerp Gate) this magnificent archway was also designed by Sir Reginald Blomfield and was inaugurated by Field-Marshal Plumer on July 24, 1927 in the presence of King Albert. At the time of the Great War, there was no actual gate on the site. It was indicated by the presence of two lions, one on each side of the roadway which cut through the walls. These lions are now in Canberra,

Some of the 'Old Contemptables' return to Ypres . . . and the memorial, in August 1982. All around them are the inscribed names of fellow soldiers . . . over 54,000 of them . . . who fought and died in the Salient and yet have no known grave. The missing who fell subsequent to August 16, 1917 are commemorated at Tyne Cot.

Australia. Through this cutting, many thousands of men wended their way to the Salient. A tag line at the time was, 'Tell the last man through to bolt the Menin Gate'.

Now the archway forms the **British Memorial to the Missing** and bears the names of 54,896 of those who died between 1914 and August 15, 1917 and who have no known grave. Their names are engraved on panels which form the walls both inside the archway and on the walls on the terraces and stairways to them. Over the archway, a British lion broods above the inscription detailing the purpose of the memorial. On either side of the arch, the Commission maintains a quiet garden of green lawns and shrubs. Incorporated into the foundations of the memorial is one of the bastions of the old ramparts with one of the sallyports on the northern side.

Immediately after the conclusion of the inauguration ceremony in 1927, the buglers of the Shropshire Light Infantry sounded the Last Post, and pipers of the Scots Guards played a lament. The simple ceremony of sounding the Last Post each and every night at 8.00 p.m. was conceived by Mr P. Vandenbraambussche, the then-Superintendent of the Ypres Police, soon after the unveiling. The buglers of the Ypres Fire Brigade co-operated with the police chief and early in the summer of 1928 the nightly ceremony began. In October of that year it was discontinued until the following spring. The Last Post Committee was formed and soon afterwards the Brussels and Antwerp Branch of the British Legion announced their wish to present to Ypres four silver bugles. In 1935, the British Legion of the County of Surrey subscribed £400 to go towards a fund to fulfil the aims of the Committee:

'. . . to ensure the sounding of the Last Post each evening for all time at the British Memorial at the Menin Gate in honour of the soldiers of the British Empire who fell at Ypres or in the neighbourhood during the war of 1914-1918 and in addition to do everything . . . that could increase the significance of this tribute to the Armies of the British Empire.'

Thus was born a tradition. For ever since November 11, 1929, except for the break during the German occupation of Ypres (from May 20, 1940 to September 6, 1944) it has continued. The day the Germans left Ypres the Call sounded out in the evening.

Two more silver bugles were presented by the Old Contemptibles' Association of Blackpool and Fleetwood and, in 1959, Colonel J. Whitaker presented two silver

trumpets in memory of former Cavalry and Artillerymen and himself who served in the Salient. Each night, two of the firemen in civilian dress take up their positions in the centre of the road beneath the Salient face of the Memorial and the police halt the flow of traffic through the gateway. Then, in a simple ceremony, the pure tones of the silver bugles ring out and echo away, never to a completely deserted scene. On major anniversaries and ceremonies involving the British or Ypres

Municipal celebrations, up to five firemen in full dress blow the Call and often Reveille. The Chaplain of St George's and perhaps the Dean will say prayers before a congregation of hundreds and wreaths will be laid on the stairways.

The **ramparts**, which to this day encircle the eastern and southern sectors of the town, can provide a most pleasant promenade, from north of the Menin Gate to west of the Lille Gate. The stretch of walls adjoining this gate

Guarded by two lions, the Menin Gate in 1914 (IWM) was a busy thoroughfare . . .

Where 'Wipers Times' was printed.

have been retained in the condition they were left in 1918. Below them and within their massive body was the best shelter the troops could find in the devastated town. Just beyond the Menin Gate, a number of the **casemates** are in use by a cheese factory. Here was a signal headquarters, and evidence of the occupation by troops can still be seen, together with alterations made by the Germans during their occupation in 1940-44. Further along the inner side of the ramparts, where the individual casemates are utilised for a number of trades, one is a garage workshop. It was here that the famous *Wipers Times* was once published by the Sherwood Foresters.

The **Lille Gate (Rijselpoort)**, with its medieval round bastions was called the Messines Gate for centuries. In his defence works, Vauban retained the two main bastions of the old gate and these remain today as they were after the First World War. The balcony above the gate and the roadway over the Kasteel Gracht have been modified. The Lille Gate was perhaps even more familiar to the BEF than the Menin Gate as, due to the extremely exposed position of the latter, the more sheltered southern exit was used as the main route to the front by the troops leaving Ypres.

Within the gateway on the eastern bastion is a doorway from which entry is gained to the **vaulted chambers** within. For many years this was a museum and called 'Plumer's Headquarters'. The inner room was very probably

used as a signals office and was frequented by officers and men from Plumer's staff, but I have it on the authority of his secretary that never was it his headquarters. The outer bastion walls are pierced by loopholes from which machine guns were trained; one of these is still in position. The late Sergeant Back told me that on the night before the attack on the Messines Ridge there were staff officers here and that some of the orders for the attack were given from this site. Now it is used by the local authority as a store. Inside the western postern are traces of the old Roman-style walls and from here the Yperlee rises.

The old **'Wooden House'**, just inside the gate, is a replica of a similar building destroyed in 1917; at that time it was one of the oldest in the town.

Just across the Lille Gate is the **British Military Cemetery, Ramparts Cemetery**. This is the only one within the old walls of the town. From it is a very beautiful view over the moat.

The other cemetery in the town is the **Reservoir Cemetery** which lies on Plumerlaan, a road running parallel to Elverdingestraat, in the region of the Plaine d'Amour.

Beyond the Menin Gate alongside the town cemetery is the **Ypres Town BMC** and **Ypres Town Cemetery Extension**, the entrance to both being on Zonnebekeweg.

To return to the Ramparts and the moat; just beyond the cemetery, the walks meander over the corner bastion known as the **Lion Tower** which like the Lille Gate dates from 1383. From here a view of the two half-moon (demi-lune) defences erected by Vauban in 1678 can be seen across the moat. Incidentally, the moat is fed by three rivers — the Zillebeke, the Bollaertbeke and the Vyverbeke (Dickebush Lake), and this part of it is known as the Majoor Gracht. Around the next corner within the walls, is the local deer park and just a little way further along under the trees is the cupola of a machine gun post.

On the town side of the walls slopes the esplanade gardens where various sports can be played. Standing in this area is the **old powder magazine** built in 1818 on the foundations of an even older magazine built before Vauban's time. It is now the oldest building in Ypres. It was said to be bomb-proof and it seems this was true as it survived all the bombardments. The ramparts promenade ends in the square in front of the station — René Colaert Plein.

In addition to the churches already mentioned, there are in Ypres three others, **St Pieters, St Jacques** and **St Nicholas**. The oldest of these is St Pieters in Rijselstraat (Rue de Lille). All three were almost totally

destroyed but in St Pieters there are vestiges of the original 12th Century church and fragments of later embellishments.

In Rijselstraat there are several other interesting buildings. One of these is **No. 38—the Belle Alms House**. The present building incorporates some of the original 16th and 17th Century portions of the chapel to the Belle Institution founded in about 1276. On the wall in the side street is a plaque to the memory of Master Jan Yperman, the father of Flemish surgery, who was closely connected with this almshouse from 1304-1329. The building now houses the Public Assistance Organisations Museum.

Little Toc H stands in the rue de Lille alternatively named Rijselstraat.

At **No. 70 is the Post Office.** This building is a replica of one of the stone-built houses of 14th Century Ypres. It may have been owned by the Templars. A short distance further down the street on the opposite side is the building which once housed **Little Toc H**—the Ypres branch of the famous Poperinge club. In the Oude Vismarkt there are other replicas of the old architecture of Ypres.

. . . but the Lille Gate was the main route for leaving Ypres; it bears its wartime scars still today.

Battles of the Ypres Salient 1914-1918
A BRIEF OUTLINE SUMMARY

First Battle of Ypres, October-November, 1914

October: The front line extended from Langemark — Zonnebeke — Gheluvelt — Zandevoorde — Messines to Armentières. British Army held the line in the eastern and southern sectors with the French on their left and the Belgian Army to the north.

7: German Cavalry enter Ypres but remain only briefly.

13: Northumberland Hussars enter.

14: British and French troops enter and occupy Ypres entirely. The British force was IV Corps led by 7th Division. Their Divisional Headquarters was at the Château, later called Stirling Castle, on the Menin Road. IV Corps had their HQ in the convent in Poperinge, Advance HQ was set up in the Hôtel de Ville in Ypres with the overflow on the upper floor of the Cloth Hall. Below were the French Cuiraissiers who used the ground floor level as stables. General Rawlinson was billeted at No. 10 rue de Lille (Rijselstraat). In the 7th Division were the first members of the Territorial Army to see action, the Northumberland Hussars, a Yeomanry regiment. They were in Bruges on October 6 and in action on the 12th. The London Scottish and the Oxford Hussars, another Yeomanry regiment, were first in action on October 31.

22: German concentrated bombardment and attack on Ypres commences and they advance westward.

29/30: The front had contracted on to Ypres despite many gallant charges and stands by the British cavalry and infantry who were well outnumbered. The line now ran from Langemark—Broodseinde—Kleine Zille- beke—Hollebeke—Messines.

31: Germans pushed back to Gheluvelt.

November 1: Messines-Wytschaete Ridge cap- tured by Germans who reach Wulvergem and Neuve Eglise.

2: French XIV Corps recapture the Ridge and British I Corps held furious attack on Gheluvelt.

10: German second bombardment of Ypres commences.

22: Cloth Hall, St Martin's church and many other buildings destroyed or badly damaged.

1915
Front line stabilised from Bixschote— Langemark—St Julien—Broodseinde —Hooge—Zillebeke—St Eloi—Wytschaete —Ploegsteert. Line remained almost unchanged without much gain or loss although there was continuous activity.

March: Heavy fighting on the Lys front. St Eloi changed hands on two occasions. The civilian population who had fled Ypres during the bombardments trickled back to their ruined homes.

Second Battle of Ypres, April-June 1915

April 14: Battle opens. Germans commence bombardment of Ypres which continued for nearly a month, completely destroying the town.

17: British capture Hill 60.

22: First gas attack on French territorial and colonial troops holding the line near Bikschote. The Belgian Corps were on the French left and the Canadian 3rd Brigade on their right. The French were pushed back to Steenstraat but the Canadians held the line at St Julien.

25: Main thrust of the German attack on British line. By the end of the month the front line ran south from Steenstraat to Zuideschoote—Boesinge—Hill 60—Holle- beke—Wytschaete—Ploegsteert.

May: Heavy fighting with severe casualties to both sides continued.

5: Hill 60 attacked. British line pushed back on 3-4 from St Julien and Frezenberg and to Hooge later. Hooge Château fell but was recaptured on June 2.

July 22-26: British advance along Menin road near Hooge.

29-30: First use of liquid fire by Germans.

August 7: Gas attack on Hooge.

1915-1917
Front line remained almost static with artillery activity punctuated by infantry attacks on varying scales by both armies. Mining in certain areas constantly under- taken by both sides. St Eloi and Hill 60 were scenes of perpetual engagements.

1916: Hill 62 captured by the Canadian Corps who also stemmed the German advance in the direction of Zillebeke and Hooge, fighting over Sanctuary Wood and across the open country beyond to within 1,000 yards of Hill 60. The front line extended from Steenstraat and Lizerne to Zuidschoote and Pilkem to Weiltje and Frezenberg, Zillebeke and Hill 60 and Hill 62, St Eloi and Hollebeke, Kemmel and Wytschaete, Wulvergem and Messines, Ploegsteert Wood and St Yvon, gains and losses fluctuating on either side.

1917
June: Battle of Messines.
1-7: British offensive heralded by unusually heavy and prolonged artillery bombard- ment obliterating Messines and Wytschaete.

7: In the early hours of the morning, 19 mines extending along the whole curve of the front line from Hill 60 and St Eloi to Messines were exploded. The New Zealand Division captured the highest point on the Ridge and advanced to beyond Messines village.

11: The advance along two miles of the front had continued and consolidated east and north of Messines. German counter-attacks in the St Yvon-St Eloi regions were abandoned by June 14.

July: At the end of the month, the line ran from Dixmude along the Yser Canal to Lizerne, Het Sas and Boesinge, then down the Ypres-Bruges railway to Quatre Chemins crossroads on to the Pilkem road and continued west of Wieltje village to Verlorenhoek, then west of Hooge skirting Sanctuary Wood passing west of Hollebeke and to the east of Ploegsteert Wood.

Third Battle of Ypres, July-November 1917

July 31: The Allied offensive began in bad weather in the early morning. In the region of Bikschote the enemy trenches were over- come to a depth of nearly two miles.

August 1: St Julien, Frezenberg, Pilkem, Westhoek were captured and Sanctuary Wood and Hooge fell after very severe fighting.

16: After a lull the Allied offensive resumed all along the line. Despite desperate fighting, the advance continued until September 20.

September 20: Langemark and Zonnebeke attacked and many fortified farms and trenches captured. Polygon Wood was the scene of heavy fighting by the Australians and Tower Hamlets also under attack.

26: Polygon Wood fell to the Australians and Tower Hamlets to the British infantry divisions.

October 4: The offensive was maintained along the front from Langemark to Tower Hamlets against increasingly determined resistance, the Germans defending the Paschendaele Ridge with every means possible.

9: British front extended now some seven miles from Poelkappelle to Broodseinde with the right flank on the slope of the Ridge. Casualties continued to be extremely heavy on both sides.

30: Paschendaele Ridge finally cleared of the enemy after the bloodiest battle in history. Ypres relieved completely. November 6 Paschendaele taken.

1918
German Spring Offensive
April 9-20: The Spring Offensive broke through the lines south of Ypres and the British and Portuguese forces withdrew on an arc from Neuve Eglise, Bailleul, Meteren, Vieux-Berquin, Festubert and La Bassée.

22-24: Germans attack and capture Mont Kemmel. Locre changed hands several times.

29: Severe German attacks between La Clytte and Zillebeke were repulsed and Mont Kemmel recaptured. Later the British division was forced to withdraw to Kemmel village.

Fourth Battle of Ypres, July-October, 1918

July 19: Battle of the Lys begins. The British attack.

September 1: The Allied advance begun in August had by this date reached La Bassée, Laventie, Neuve Eglise, Mont Kemmel, Wulvergem and Voormezele.

October: Ploegsteert, Messines, Warneton, Gheluvelt, Houthulst Forest, etc., had all been recaptured.

14: Last shell dropped on Ypres town, as the last German forces were chased out of the Ypres Salient.

16: Menin occupied by British Second Army.

At the end of the war, the honours of the British Military Cross and the French Croix de Guerre were conferred on the town of Ypres. These decorations can be seen together with the documents relating to them on permanent exhibition in the Salient Museum.

Zonnebeke, October 1917

YPRES SALIENT BATTLEFIELD TOUR

Zonnebeke, April 1976

ROUTE I

Leave by the Diksmuidestraat (N69) on the north side of the Grand Place shortly crossing the Wieltjegracht, a narrow weed-covered waterway at the site of the **Old Dixmude Gate**, and bear left at the fork almost immediately thereafter. Reaching the canal basin at the Kaaie, known to the BEF as **Tattenham Corner**, turn left with the road and after

Tattenham Corner, also called Dead End.

crossing the canal bear right at the next major turning. This is **Salvation Corner**, so called from the hut which the Salvation Army ran about here for troops going up the line.

Salvation Corner, named after a Salvation Army hut which once stood nearby.

The road runs parallel to the little Yperlee and the canal. Amid the modern residential area on the right is **Duhallow A.D.S. Cemetery** which was used in 1917 during the Pilkem Ridge battles. About ½ km further along, after leaving the built-up area and

Duhallow A.D.S. This is the special memorial with the graves of the Fusilier Wood casualties.

passing beneath the new road bridge, the canal bank rises to the right and the obelisk of the **49th Division Memorial** comes into view. Access is through **Essex Farm Cemetery** before it. Recent road improvements have included a new lay-by which now enables visitors to park off the busy road. To the north of the

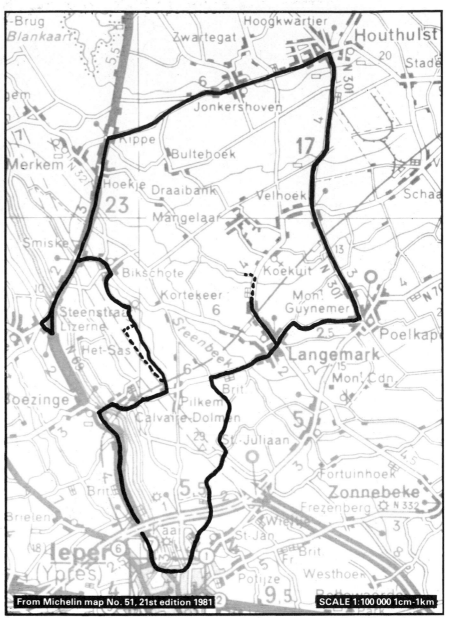

From Michelin map No. 51, 21st edition 1981   SCALE 1:100 000 1cm-1km

Essex Farm Cemetery with the 49th Division Memorial.

One of the youngest casualties to die in the Salient—Private Strudwick, aged 15.

cemetery is a track which leads down to the canal and the tow-path. It crosses a small bridge and on the further side are a group of **preserved British dugouts**. This bridge is at the west end of Bridge No. 4 or **Brielen Bridge**. The dugouts once stretched along both sides of it in the canal bank and were continuously used by the British divisions stationed in this area. Between the bridge and the memorial is the **site of the dressing station** above which Lieutenant-Colonel J. M. McCrae, Royal Canadian Medical Corps, wrote his famous poem *In Flanders Fields the Poppies Grow* in 1915.

In the cemetery are buried over 1,000 soldiers from the British and Commonwealth Forces and one German. Among the British graves are those of Private T. Barratt, VC, of the South Staffordshire Regiment, and Private Strudwick, who, at 15 years old, was one of the youngest casualties to be buried here.

Continuing on towards Boesinge remains of other canal bank dug-outs can be seen to the right whilst on the left, a little further up, is **Bard Cottage Cemetery**.

After 7 kms we reach **Boesinge**. Burned by the Germans during their brief stay here in October 1914, it was for the next three years the most northerly boundary of the British sector. This lay on the north side of the village and there is still a ditch between two fields beside a farm on the right which marks the boundary. Beyond this point the French held the line joining with the Belgian Army near Dixmude. Fierce battles were fought in the region in 1915 during the Second Battle of Ypres and again in the Third Battle in 1917, during which the French made a successful attack and crossed the canal to the eastern bank. On the left-hand side as the village is entered is a **Demarcation Stone** and in a garden is a **concrete blockhouse** surmounted by a German mortar—a Minenwerfer known as Kleine Berta.

To gain the eastern flank of the canal and to cross the Pilkem Ridge we now turn right, taking the Langemark road. In this part the canal has changed greatly as, previously, the only lock was at **Het Sas** a little further north. Since the First World War the southern lock has been added, the banks raised and now a new motorway cleaves its way through.

One km later, **Carrefour de la Rose** is reached. On the left is one of the most unusual and attractive memorials in the whole Salient. It is the **French 87th and 45th Divisions' Memorial** and is in the form of a Breton calvary and dolmen with a most useful and interesting orientation table and map. The map shows the stand made by the two divisions in the gas attack in April 1915. The calvary is a genuine one from Plouagat in Brittany and the dolmen was brought from Henanbiken. The small park is protected from the road by concrete posts in the form of the wooden posts which held up the barbed wire defences before the introduction of the iron pickets.

A short way down the road on the left lies **Artillery Wood Cemetery**, named after the small copse which was here, but continue straight on to reach **Pilkem** village. Turn left into Bikshootsestraat. Across the railway there is a road junction, the left turning, Slaaktestraat, takes you by the **largest German bunker** remaining (built as a signal station), whilst the right fork passes two bunkers on the right and one on the left. Both roads join the Bikschote road with two more bunkers. These are, like others in the area, part of the chain of defences built by the Germans in the winter of 1915-16. They form a huge arc across the northern and eastern sectors of the Salient. At the next fork go left past **Bikschote Mill** burnt down in 1977 now rebuilt.

The largest German bunker still to be seen in the Salient stands near the Pilkem Road.

British field dressing station bunkers at Bridge No. 4—Essex Farm.

Behind Boesinge Demarcation Stone, a 'Kleine Berta' rests on a German bunker.

The Breton Memorial to the French 87th and 45th Divisions at the Carrefour de la Rose. The map nearby shows their stand in the April 1915 gas attack.

The modern, gleaming Cross of Reconciliation near Steenstraat recalls the gas attack of April 1915. The original cross was destroyed by the Germans in 1942 who objected to the wording of the French inscription, shown in its present form *above.*

After 1 km turn left at the crossroads for Steenstraat. Two more bunkers can be seen along the road to the left. The road crosses over the path of the A19, the Veurne to Menen motorway, which now sweeps down to the south-east, cleaving its way across the Salient below St Julien and Zonnebeke, skirting Polygon Wood and Nonneboschen to Gheluvelt. In 1½ kms turn left to join the N69 and **Steenstraat**. This village, lying amid the rich fields, was at the western end of the French line on April 22, 1915. Their line ran eastwards to a point south of Poelcapelle where it joined the sector held by the Canadian Corps with the British 27th and 28th Divisions beyond them east of Zonnebeke and Polygon Wood.

April 22 had been a beautiful sunny day when, at about 5.00 p.m., a greenish-yellow cloud began to appear on either side of Langemark and slowly creep towards the French lines. Soon the whole four-mile length of the front held by the 87th and 45th (Algerian) Divisions was shrouded in the noxious cloud of chlorine gas. Within an hour the whole front had given way as the French and their colonial troops took the brunt of the unexpected horror which now hid their sector completely from view and they fell back to the canal. The Canadians on their right flank were, at the outset, beyond the field of the gas, but as they went to fill in the gap they were drawn into it, falling back to St Julien. The French recaptured Steenstraat on May 15 and some 2,000 Germans were found dead on the battlefield. On July 31, 1917, the French recrossed the canal by night with the aid of many pontoon bridges.

Having crossed the canal (1 km), the tall, graceful aluminium **Cross of Reconciliation** will be seen up the slightly rising ground on the right-hand side. This is a French memorial which replaced the original cross which had been erected to the memory of those who were gassed in April 1915. It was destroyed in 1942 by the occupation forces who objected to the reference in the inscription to the Germans as barbarians.

It was in this area that the French and Belgian lines joined during the 1915 battles and the short circuit from here through **Lizerne** (turning right at the crossroads) and then taking the first right will bring you back to the great Cross. There are several Belgian memorials in this district recalling the various attacks made here.

Turning left now onto the N69 again continue for 5 kms to the hamlet of **Kippe**. Bikschote, which was one of the centres of the gas attack of April 1915, lies over to the right. Kippe is the northern extremity of the Ypres Salient; to the left is the small town of Merckem, but we turn right for Houthulst, passing **Jokehoven** 3 kms further on.

After another 3 kms we reach **Houthulst**. Turn right at the crossroads. The road soon comes to the edge of **Houthulst Forest** whose western side it skirts for 3 kms. This forest was described by Napoleon as the key to the Low Countries. After a bitter defence by the Belgian Army, with support by French cavalry and territorial troops, it fell to the Germans on October 21, 1914. In the Allied advance during the Third Battle of Ypres the southern extremities were reached. The whole region was subjected to gas attacks and, although the defending Germans suffered very heavy casualties, all attempts to outflank the forest were defeated by their holding the Spriet Ridge. It was not until September 28, 1918 that the Belgians finally recaptured it. During their occupation the Germans had converted the entire forest into a fortress. From here their heavy artillery bombarded the Allied lines to the south. When the forest was captured, the Belgians took 150 guns and over 6,000 prisoners.

On the edge of the forest is the **Belgian Military Cemetery**. As the Belgian Army did not hold a sector in the Salient, this is their only cemetery in the immediate area. Besides the 1,704 Belgian dead, there are also some French and Italians buried here.

The Belgian army bomb disposal unit is based in the depths of the forest. For many years after the end of the Great War, the large numbers of shells, bombs, grenades and other types of ammunition found in the Salient (and elsewhere in this part of Belgium) were detonated and destroyed here. Even today shells and other relics of the past are still found by the farmers as they till the land, the spring and autumn ploughing bringing forth its deadly 'harvest of steel'.

After passing **Veldhoek** (4 kms), we reach **Poelkappelle** 3 kms further on. Although it had been reached by the British cavalry in October 1914, for most of the war it was well inside the German line. This small town was ravaged by bombardments and was the furthest point of the Allied advance in 1917. The 11th Division, supported by tanks, one of which was knocked out right in the centre of the town and still bedded down in the mud amid the ruins when, in July 1923, the **Memorial to Georges Guynemer** was unveiled.

The Guynemer Memorial, Poelkappelle.

The Belgian Cemetery in Houthulst Forest with its distinctive headstones.

The great French air ace was killed on September 11, 1917 during a combat with an Aviatik. His flight companion, Lieutenant Benjamin Bozon-Verduraz, did not see his Spad fall as at the vital moment he was busy attending to another group of enemy machines. It was later reported that the German infantry in Poelkappelle had found the wrecked machine and the dead pilot (who had been shot through the head), and had moved his body to a dugout, but that an artillery barrage had almost immediately destroyed the trench and the aircraft. I have been told that the flying stork—emblem of his squadron—flies in the direction of his crash.

At the crossroads, with the monument in its centre, turn right 2½ kms to **Langemark**. This town was attacked by the Germans on October 23, 1914 but the untried divisions were no match for either the 2nd British Division or the French, and the student troops suffered heavy casualties. In the wake of the gas attack of April 22, 1915, Langemark was occupied by the German 51st Reserve Division and it remained in German hands until August 16, 1917 when 20th Light Division recaptured the ruined town and 2,000 prisoners. In April 1918 the Allies withdrew in the face of the Spring Offensive and it was not until September 28 that the town was finally recaptured. By this time there was not a building left standing—all had been pulverized in the bombardments. At the main crossroads turn right, passing the square and the modern church on the left, and cross the railway. After a short distance the houses give way to beet fields (on the right) whilst, on the left of the road, is the sombre **German Military Cemetery, the Soldatenfriedhof**.

A long, low, dark red granite building houses the gateway and incorporates the student memorial. This is a small room containing the Registers of those who are known to be buried between the tall oak trees and in the newer section to the north of the entrance. A visitors' book is also provided. Both chapels are entered through magnificent cast-iron doors of intricate design. The chapel walls are covered with the names of the students who died and on the wall of the second is a map depicting the locations of the other German graveyards.

The cemetery is in two almost distinct sections. The **Alter Friedhof**—the old cemetery—is under the shade of the great oak trees, which stand like enormous Imperial Guardsmen above the greensward, and has grey, slatish stones with the names of the dead picked out in white-painted lettering. Here lie

Top: **Blockhouses of the Einbettungsfriedhof-Nord in Langemark German Cemetery.**
Above: **Graves in the Alter Friedhof of Langemark German Cemetery.**

10,143 of whom 3,836 are unknown. Here and there groups of small basalt crosses break the serried ranks of stones. Immediately behind the entrance building is the **Kameraden-grab**—the mass grave where 24,834 are interred beneath a relatively small shrub-covered area. Brooding over this solemn scene is a bronze group representing the mourning comrades. In front of the graves are

memorials to the regiments of various parts of Germany.

The northern end of the cemetery, beyond the protection of the oak trees and behind the three concrete bunkers and their linking memorial stones, part of the fortifications of the Langemark Line, is the **Einbettungs-friedhof-Nord** where 9,475 men lie buried. Divisional memorials are to be found on the

The 34th Division RA and RE Memorial stands sentinel in front of a German bunker.

slabs of stone between the bunkers. A quiet pool marks the boundary of the graveyard in which is reflected the Teutonic cross. This is a forbidding place with its subdued colours and gloomy atmosphere heightened by the very neatness and trimness of the lawns, hedges, walls and trees.

In the distance beyond the cemetery, a little

The 20th Light Division's Memorial.

Here lies Captain J. E. Knowles, Middlesex Regiment killed near Mons on August 23, 1914. His grave and those of his men were moved from Maisières.

way along the road behind the Broenbeek, is another large bunker of the same line as those in the cemetery. In front of it is the **Memorial to the Royal Artillery and Royal Engineers of the 34th Division**. After the bunker was captured in September 1918 it was used as an advanced dressing station under the command of Robert Lawrence, a brother of T. E. Lawrence. He described to me the frightful conditions in this region in 1917 and 1918. There were no trenches, just a sea of mud across which duck-boards led from shell-hole to shell-hole right back to Velhoek and Koekuit. The concrete pillboxes were the only stable buildings remaining. At certain times more men were lost by drowning than by the bullet.

Return to the centre of the town, the church being on the right and at the traffic lights go right on the Boesinge road. A short distance along the road, now flanked by modern villas, is the stark grey **Memorial to the 20th Light Division**. Over the Steenbeek and in the yard of a large farm is a square pillbox—**Cement House**. Next door to the farm is the large **British Cemetery** which bears this name. Until recently all bodies found in the Salient and identified as British were buried here. Some time ago, a tiny cemetery near Mons had to be closed due to roadworks at Maisières and the eighteen or so officers and men (who had died in August 1914) were transferred here. Among them is Captain Knowles, one of the first British officers to lose his life.

At the next crossroads, known as **Iron Cross**—a heavily bombarded spot as it was a main crossing of the transport routes to Langemark—turn left and in about ½ km turn right, thereby crossing the eastern side of the **Pilkem Ridge**. On the right, 2 kms further on, is a large and most interesting concrete bunker. It is a fortified Belgian farmhouse,

Cement House, a German bunker next door to the British Cemetery.

Goumier Farm. On some British maps it is called Gournier Farm. Although it has been in almost constant use by farmers as a cattle shelter or pigsty in the years since the war, it remains in fair condition. The Germans were the first to fortify it, enclosing the brick walls in concrete, and in places it is possible to discern the imprint of the shuttering. As a strong point with excellent visibility, it was under frequent attack and changed hands on many occasions until the end of July 1917 when the 38th Welsh Division captured Pilkem. The Royal Engineers added further strengthening and blast walls to Goumier and thus it is one place where the two differing styles of work can be studied closely. After again falling into enemy hands it was finally recaptured by the Black Watch. Some years ago a plaque, in memory of the 38th Welsh Division, was placed on the bunker and, with the farmer's permission, visitors can inspect it.

Keep to the right at the fork just beyond the farm and continue for about 2 kms along this road across the ridge, passing between small farms often with a blockhouse or concrete observation post now incorporated in their buildings, until a five-way cross is reached. Take the first left and, after a couple of bunkers have been passed, a panorama unfolds. After another km, another crossroad. Turn right and begin the descent to Ypres.

Over the crossroads—the **Boundary Road**—passing **New Irish Farm Cemetery** on the right. Here a number of Chinese Labour Corps are buried beneath the chestnut trees. A short distance beyond, cross the new highway which bypasses Ypres and enter the town via La Brigue and the **Dixmude Gate**.

38th Welsh Division Memorial Plaque.

Goumier Farm blockhouse with British and German concrete reinforcement.

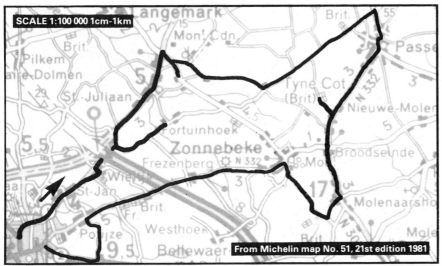

From Michelin map No. 51, 21st edition 1981

The 1st Bn. Monmouthshire Regiment.

ROUTE II

Leave Ypres by N70, passing the large **White House Cemetery** on the rising ground above the little **Bellewaerdbeek**. After ½ km we reach **St Jan** (Saint Jean), site of forward dressing stations all housed in cellars in 1915. The village was completely destroyed in 1917.

Travel ½ km and take the right fork for **Wieltje Farm Cemetery** along **Oxford Road**. The **cemetery** of this name will be seen on the right. Beyond the lane on the right is the **50th Northumbrian Divisional Memorial**. After the Second World War, an inscription relative to

The 50th Northumbrian Div. Memorial

the division's effort in 1939-1945 was added to the column. In the fields behind the memorial two lines of bunkers and emplacements, some of which are now only barely visible above the ground, mark the line of the **Cambrai redoubt** of 1917.

Returning to the main road, pass under the motorway and take the right-hand road, Roselaarstraat, for **Fortuinehoek**. It leads to Paschendaele and it was built shortly after the war. Soon after the turning on the right (note the bunkers in the fields), is the **grey limestone memorial** to the memory of Lieutenant H. A. Birrell Anthony and the officers and men of the **1st Monmouthshire Regiment** who fell in the Second Battle of Ypres on May 8, 1915. The memorial, set in a small stone-walled enclosure, is cared for by the Commonwealth War Graves Commission.

However, return to the N70, and turn right along the highway greatly widened here as it joins the Ypres ring-road. Off to the far side of this highway, from Wieltje village still runs the straight road to **Pilkem Ridge** known as **Admiral's Road**. The name derives from 1915 when an unnamed Captain of the 6th Division used to charge up and down it in an armoured car of the Royal Naval Division. Regrettably when the motorway is completed it may be diverted.

A little way along the N70 now is the site of the notorious **Mousetrap Farm**. Originally known as Shelltrap or Death Farm, the present house is nearer to the road. These names were considered too ominous and too famous name was acquired. It was the headquarters of the 3rd Canadian Brigade during the gas attack and, in the ensuing battle of St Julien, came into the line.

In the farm a little north of **Seaforth Cemetery** is **Cheddar Villa**. As the expenses of demolishing this typical German bunker would have been exorbitant, the farmer has designed his new extensions to incorporate it. It was captured in July 1917, and was utilised first as an aid post and then as a battalion headquarters by 1/4th Oxford and Buckinghamshire Light Infantry. The wide entrance of this bunker was the scene of a disastrous shelling on the night of August 7, 1917 when a platoon of the 1st Bn. Buckinghamshire Battalion was sheltering in it; direct hits killed many and all were wounded. It will be noted that the bunker, although set on the crest of a slope giving a wide field of vision, is also unsheltered.

In the distance to the north-east another bunker comes into view. This formed part of the German second line and is in front of the position **Kitcheners Wood**—now an open field—around which there was very heavy fighting in 1915.

One km further on we come to **St Julien** (St Juliaan). This village was captured by the Germans on April 24, 1915 after the gas attack and the gallant defence by the Canadians. By July 1917, the Germans had completed their lines of concrete blockhouses in the area. The heavy bombardments which preceded the Allied attack, and the thunderstorms of the last few days of the month, turned the area into a sea of stinking, yellowish, slimy mud. These strong points were the only firm places left and the battle was a series of actions from one strong point to another, and it was disastrous in the extremely heavy casualties which it cost. St Julien was finally captured on August 3 by the 39th Division, whose casualties were 145 officers and 3,716 other ranks killed, wounded or missing.

Kerselaar—**Vancouver Corner**—is 1 km further on. This crossroad is dominated by the **Canadian Memorial**, a pillar surmounted by the head and shoulders of a soldier resting on

his arms reversed, set amid a garden of roses, coniferous trees and juniper bushes. The tall trees, many recently replanted, are carefully clipped to represent a shell shape, whilst the juniper is so planted and cut to form small shell holes and craters. The inscription on the pillar, '2000 fell and here lie buried', is somewhat misleading as the dead lie in many cemeteries around and about and not in the confines of the memorial. The memorial faces the notorious **Triangle** of which the road junction formed part.

Centre: **The Canadian Memorial above Vancouver Corner and,** *above,* **the plaque with its misleading reference.**

A modern mill stands on the site of the Totenmühle, a German observation post.

Paschendaele — synonymous with the horror of war — from Crest Farm.

In the village church can be seen the 66th Division memorial window.

Turn right. Take either the first or second left turning. The first will, if the left fork is taken, lead past the mill built on the highest point in the sector. The Germans called it the **Totenmühle**—the mill of the dead—for it was one of their observation points constantly under attack. The present mill is a reproduction of the actual mill of 1915 and is often open to the public. From it can be gained a 360-degree view. After the mill, continue to the road junction and turn left. This road is a continuation of the second turning on the left from Vancouver Corner down to the Zonnebeke road. The name of the second corner is **Winnipeg**, a vital strong point in 1915 and 1917.

Travel 2 kms across the now peaceful meadows with small farms scattered beside clumps of trees and the inevitable pond. In 1917 this was completely torn up and many feet deep in Flanders mud. Only duck-board tracks were safe to use from one trench to another as few roads remained. The artillery was bogged down by the sticky, glutinous mud and many trenches were two or more feet deep in the slime. Crossing the region from east to west are the several small rivers or streams which, due to the continuous rain which followed the dry spell of July 1917, flooded the countryside. They were unable to be drained off due to the destruction of the ground by bombardments and entrenching.

The next crossroad, s'Graventafel, is marked by the **New Zealand Memorial** to their dead in the Paschendaele battles. Turn left

before the memorial and cross the area where the New Zealand Expeditionary Force made their stand.

After 3 kms, **Paschendaele New British Cemetery** is passed on the left. Then, reaching the main road (½ km), turn right and enter **Paschendaele** (Passendale). The village sprawls across the ridge at this point and, even though there has been much building beyond the old boundary of the village, it can be seen just what a valuable position it commands. For over three years the Germans held the ridge until, on November 6, 1917, in the culmination of the Third Ypres, the rubble which had been the village was captured by the Canadian Corps. Behind them were the gentle slopes of the western side of the ridge, a scene of terrible aspect of mud and blood, whilst ahead lay the green fields of an almost peaceful country hardly touched by war. In April 1918, following the German Spring Offensive, the Allied Command withdrew from the ridge and the Germans were once more in possession. On October 14, the Belgian Army drove the last of the enemy from the ridge.

In the centre of the village is the church, whose north windows form the **Memorial to the 66th Division**. From the porch it is possible to look down the slope to the clump of trees across a shallow valley where the **Canadian Memorial** is sited; this was **Crest Farm**. On the wall of the **Stadhuis** are several **memorials to the Belgian regiments** which took the village.

Continue along the N332 on the crest of the

ridge, now a modern highway, to **Broodseinde**. On the left, a short way out of the village, will be seen a small obelisk set in the beet fields. This is the **Memorial to the 85th Canadian Infantry Battalion**, the Nova Scotia Highlanders who participated in the capture of the ridge in 1917.

Above: **The 85th Canadian Infantry Battalion Memorial.** *Below:* **The text on the Crest Farm Memorial.**

s'Graventafel New Zealand Memorial.

Two kms along the ridge take the right-hand road, signposted to **Tyne Cot British Military Cemetery and Memorial to the Missing**, noting bunkers behind the houses. Here, within a kilometre of the farthest point in Belgium reached by the British forces, lie the greatest number to be buried in any Commonwealth war cemetery. There are 11,908 graves in this quiet place of beauty. The entrance is a flintstone lych-gate and the view up the gentle slope to the Great Cross and the arc of the Memorial to the Missing, which curves between the two domed pavilions in the background, is a never-to-be-forgotten experience.

Tyne Cot was so named by the men of the 50th Northumbrian Division, who were among the many who fought to capture the complex of bunkers and pillboxes which surrounded the old barn which stood about 50 metres west of the level-crossing on the Paschendaele to Broodseinde road. It was captured by the 2nd Australian Division on October 4, 1917. The five bunkers which formed the redoubt were part of the German Flanders I Line. The largest of the bunkers was then used as a dressing station by the 33rd

Tyne Cot British Cemetery and Memorial. Flanked by over 11,000 headstones, the original graves cluster below the Cross of Sacrifice.

Left: **The eastern bunker with the Memorial to the Missing.** *Above:* **The plaque on the Cross of Sacrifice.**

and 50th Divisions and two Canadian formations, burying their dead around it. The station and the cemetery were in use until the end of March 1918; when, after the Allied withdrawal, the area fell again into enemy hands.

After the war, over 11,500 dead were brought here from the surrounding battlefield; many of the missing listed on the panels of the memorial will be among them. The cemetery was designed by Sir Herbert Baker who wished to create the appearance of a huge English churchyard, and the flint walls and gateway were laid out with the walls of the precincts of Winchester College in mind. In May 1922 King George V included a visit to this cemetery in his pilgrimage. It was then in course of construction and, at the King's suggestion, the Great Cross was built above the largest of the remaining blockhouses, leaving a small section exposed to show the concrete. A plaque recalls its capture by the 2nd Australian Division. Thus, this Cross of Sacrifice differs from all others with its pyramid of gleaming white Nimy stone 'pierre romaine de Lens', lifting it above the serried ranks of headstones and the many varieties of flowers, shrubs and trees. From the base of the cross all the Salient stretching away to the south-west can be seen—a view right to Kemmel and beyond. On a bright, clear, sunny day the cross can be identified from the Dunkerque lighthouse. Tall trees guard the other two blockhouses retained within the cemetery.

Behind the Cross of Sacrifice are the original graves, well over 300 of them, which remain as they were found after the Armistice. Beyond them is the Stone of Remembrance and the terrace, raised up a few steps. At this

level the graves are in fan-like sections in front of the flint and Portland stone memorial panels. At intervals the wall is broken by groups of Tuscan pillars behind which open two circular cloisters on either side of a central apse which is the **New Zealand Memorial to their Missing**. From it iron gates open into quiet greenswards shaded by cedars.

There are 34,888 names on the panels of the memorial which covers the period from August 16, 1917 to the end of the war. Six recipients of the Victoria Cross are either buried or listed on the panels. Two of these lie buried close to the site of their heroic action—the spot where they lost their lives. They are Sergeant L. McGee, 40th Bn., AIF, and Captain Jeffries, 34th Bn. AIF.

Return to the main road and turn right. A new **memorial** has been erected to recall the French participation in the battles here on the **Broodseinde Ridge**. A short distance beyond the village on the Beselare road is the **Memorial to the 7th Division**. This is one of the earliest monuments to be erected in the Salient and it commemorates the actions of this division in the early days of 1914 and in 1917.

Continue for 1½ kms beyond Broodseinde and take the right-hand road for ½ km and then right again to bring **Zonnebeke** into view. This large village was completely destroyed as it was the focal point of many actions. In the First Battle of Ypres, it was successfully defended when Gheluvelt fell in October 1914, and then it was captured by the Germans in May 1915. It was recaptured by the 3rd British Division in September 1917. Once again, in April 1918, Zonnebeke was overwhelmed in the German advance westward

but in September, when the Second Army began their great push eastward, Zonnebeke was recaptured on the first day, September 28 (*see photographs on page 33*).

Turn left. In 3 kms we reach **Frezenberg**. The road runs down the northern edge of the ridge to which this village gives its name, and which was so vital in 1915 and 1917. The artillery, the 122nd Heavy and the 37th Howitzer Batteries being among those

Ex-Sergeant Nick Keating, 90 years old, whose battery was in action at this site in October 1914, beside the 7th Division Memorial.

The French National Cemetery at Potize. There are 3,748 graves and also the mass grave at St Charles de Potize.

This was once called the hottest spot on earth—Hellfire Corner. Here the Menin Road, the Potize-Zillebeke Road and railway all meet. Nearby is a British Demarcation stone recording the furthest advance of the Germans in 1918.

positioned here, stemmed the advance on April 24, 1915. On May 8 the 28th Division was holding the ridge but was forced to withdraw after very heavy bombardments. One battalion, the 1st Suffolk, was almost destroyed, there being only seven men left alive at the end of the day. By July 1917, Frezenberg was a virtual fortress. It was attacked by the 15th Division through the mud and, with the aid of tanks, in particular one called 'Challenger', the village was taken.

Another ½ km beyond, over the motorway, is **Verlorenhoek** also involved in the Frezenberg battles of 1915 and 1917.

St Charles is 1 km down the road. Set back amid the fields is a large British Cemetery, **Aeroplane Cemetery**, so named from the wreck of a machine close by. On the road edge on the same side (the left) is the **French National Cemetery** and the mass grave at **St Charles de Potize**. Here are buried 3,748 in individual graves, whilst 609 unknown lie in the mass graves. Amid the crosses near the road is the 1968 memorial of a grieving mother. It may be of interest to note that the road which goes off to the right here is **Oxford Road** leading to Wieltje.

In 1½ kms we reach **Potize** (Potijze). The village figured significantly in the British lines, being a divisional headquarters. **Potize Château**, also known as the White Château (one of the many), was used as an advanced dressing station but it was almost destroyed by shellfire.

Ypres is just over a kilometre straight ahead, but if one turns to the left a few yards further on at the crossroads, one of the best preserved British observation posts comes into view on the left. This is **Hussar Farm** which the Royal Monmouthshire Royal Engineers fortified, building the strong point inside the old farmhouse. Despite four years of enemy bombardment the OP survived and is today used by a farmer as a storehouse. As a result of the various hits, it is possible to see the manner in which the strengthening was carried out with lengths of railway line reinforcing the brickwork and concrete; even some of the original corrugated iron is still in situ.

A similar construction, **Red House**, lies a little to the west, being a tall, three-storey building emerging above the single-floor house built on the site of the former farm. Access is from Potize by a minor road on the east side of the N332.

Another 3 kms and Ypres is reached at the

Above: **Hussar Farm was a British observation post which was fortified by the Royal Monmouthshire Royal Engineers. Today it is used as a storehouse.**

most notorious place in the entire Salient—**Hellfire Corner**—the position on the Menin Road where the Potize-Zillebeke road crosses it and the railway. Almost hidden under the wall of a house on the left a **British Demarcation Stone** marks the limit of the German advance to the Channel ports in 1918. The Menin road sweeps away to the left and, after a downward slope, rises to Hooge. The exposed position can still be appreciated today, and it is no wonder that men did not loiter here. Right through the war this place was in the sights of either local or long-range enemy artillery and machine guns.

Turning right, Ypres is gained in a kilometre. The site of the **White Château**, General Haig's headquarters during the first battle of Ypres, is now occupied by a yellow brick house in a large garden on the right. Château Biebuyck was in constant use, even after it had been badly damaged, its cellars providing shelter. The large cemetery on the left is **Menin Road South Cemetery**. The wide highway now swings into Ypres and narrows to pass beneath the Menin Gate.

Below: **Château Biebuyck. The modern house marks the site of General Haig's White Château HQ which stood here in 1914.**

This is the lonely RE Grave, Railway Wood. Here lie one officer and eleven NCOs and men from the 177th Mining Company, all killed in the area.

Previously deep in the wood, the 14th Light Division Memorial is now at Hill 60.

ROUTE III

Proceed through the Menin Gate and bear right up the slope of the Menin road where after 1 km, we reach **Hellfire Corner**. The old railway embankment is discernible to the left. In ½ km is **Birr Crossroads** and its **cemetery** so named by the Leinster Regiment when in the line here in April 1915.

Take the next left turn, a narrow road. This is **Cambridge Road** which crosses the little Bellewaerdebeke fed by the lake. Pass the site of **Y Wood** to the right, the scene of the gallant actions of the 28th Division and 1st and 3rd Cavalry in 1915. Up on the ridge to the right the **Cross of Sacrifice of the RE Grave** is framed by trees. This unusual memorial marks the grave of one officer and eleven NCOs and men of the 177th Mining Company, RE, who were killed in the mining operations in this area 1915-1917. It can be reached via a track on the right ½ km further along or by a rough road from Hooge.

Continuing up the road we pass a little wood on the left. This is **Railway Wood**. Until September 1978, the **Memorial to the 14th Light Division** stood here. Subsidence and local needs to develop the area caused it to be removed to a new site at Hill 60. Remains of craters made by the many mines exploded around here can be discerned along the ridge behind the RE Grave. Attempts by the Germans in the Second World War to build a V1 site between the craters came to nothing.

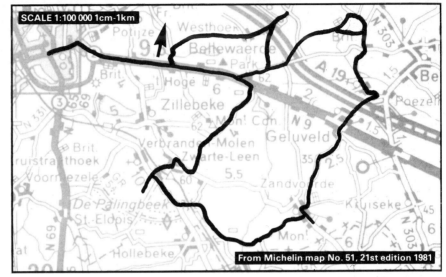

From Michelin map No. 51, 21st edition 1981

The Princess Patricia Canadian Light Infantry Memorial at Westhoek.

Turn right to cross **Bellewaerde Ridge**. Where the cattle now graze contentedly, trenches were obliterated by withering artillery fire and, in 1915 and in 1917, the shell-pocked slopes were again the location of severe fighting. Among the regiments which defended this position was the famous Canadian unit, the **Princess Patricia's Canadian Light Infantry** and in a short distance, just before entering the little village of **Westhoek**, the rather unusual **memorial** to the stand made by them is to be seen on the right. It is in the form of a circular stone seat built around a maple tree from Canada. It was planted and unveiled in 1958.

Cross over the motorway beyond **Westhoek** and note the lane to the right which skirts **Nonneboschen Wood** covering the rising ground and further, **Glencorse Wood**. Both were scenes of heavy fighting in 1914 and 1917. Here on November 12, 1914, Brigadier-General Charles FitzClarence, VC, was killed leading the survivors of the 1st Guards Brigade in a counter-attack on the Prussian Guard. This gallant soldier was known to the troops as 'GOC Menin Road'; his name is on the Menin Gate Memorial right at the top of Panel 3. Just south of Glencorse Wood was a farm which was named **FitzClarence Farm** in his honour. By 1917, it was a heavily fortified position with two well-sited bunkers and was valiantly fought over in the battles of August.

On the edge of Glencorse Wood is one of the private memorials to individuals which the CWGC cares for on behalf of the families by contract. This is the **pillar to Captain Ewen J. Brodie** of the 1st Bn. Cameron Highlanders who was killed on November 11, 1914.

In 1½ kms turn right and then left to skirt **Polygon Wood**. The motorway on our left cuts between Nonneboschen and Polygon Wood and a new bridge crosses it near the site of **Black Watch Corner** where the Royal Highlanders and the Cameron Highlanders fought the Prussian Guard in November 1914.

This expanse of fir and pine trees with its quiet glades is a state-owned forest. Before

Captain Brodie's private memorial in Glencorse Wood.

1914, the Ypres Military Riding School—the Polygon—was situated here and also the Belgian Army's old firing range which ceased to be used in 1870. The old butts, a large mound on the north-east side of the wood, still remain.

In October 1914, the wood, as it lay in the front line, was the scene of very heavy fighting and was attacked by the Prussian Guard. On October 24, 1914 the Northumberland Hussars were in action here, the first Territorial unit to be engaged. Despite terrible casualties the British held on and retained the area until May 3, 1915 when, in the wake of the gas attack, the Germans overran it. On September 27, 1917 the Australians retook the wood and the memorial obelisk of the 5th Australian Division now crowns the Butte.

In about ½ km along the edge of the wood, now a leisure park, will be seen the entrance to **Polygon Wood Cemetery** on the left and, on the right, the glade leading to the **Buttes New British Cemetery** and the **New Zealand Memorial to the Missing** and the **5th Australian Division Memorial**.

In the wood are the remains of several concrete shelters built by both sides during its occupation. The type of ground here made trenches difficult to dig and maintain and, by 1918, when the Australians evacuated it during the spring advance, only a few shattered tree trunks were left from the pulverising fire which had rained down on it. The bunkers were the only cover remaining.

Continue round the edge of the wood into open country, keeping to the right into **Reutel** (1 km), and take the left turn to **Beselare**, joining the N303, and turn right again for Gheluvelt (Geluveld). **Polderhoek Ridge** rises to the right off this road. The **château** was razed to the ground in 1917 having served both armies as headquarters. Now the whole region has been altered by the access roads for the motorway. At **Nieuwe Kruiseke** crossroads turn right on to N9 (Menin Road) for Gheluvelt. **Petit Kruiseke** in the vicinity was much fought over in the October 1914 German advance, and is depicted in the well known Matania painting of the 1st Bn. Grenadier Guards and the Green Howards barring the way. Private Henry Tandey of the Green Howards, later to win the VC, DCM and MM, is shown in the foreground carrying a wounded man. Adolf Hitler, a private in the 1st Bavarian Regiment, took part in this action.

As **Gheluvelt** is approached the **old windmill** comes into view on the right. A reproduction of the original, and much in need of repair, shelters the **Memorial of the South Wales Borderers**. In the centre of the village to the right of the church is the entrance to the **château**. The old Reutel road runs down

The South Wales Borderers' Memorial beside Gheluvelt Mill — still standing although in a sad state of repair.

Polygon Wood. The Australian Memorial and New Buttes Cemetery.

beside it, the route of 1st Division in October 1914. Here the 2nd Bn. Worcester Regiment counter-attacked after the 2nd Bn. Welsh Regiment in front of the village and the 1st Bn. South Wales Borderers were driven out of their trenches and forced to withdraw into the château grounds. In the counter-attack the 2nd Worcesters penetrated the captured village, driving the Bavarians before them and at the same time rescuing the South Wales Borderers in the park. The gallant actions of these men on October 31 stemmed the advance and barred the road to the west. Although the village was finally taken by the Germans, the stand of the division enabled the British line to be withdrawn without interference. The Worcesters' counter-attack from the château grounds was inspired by Brigadier-General FitzClarence. The château was hardly damaged during the war, even in the action recapturing the ruined village on September 28, 1918, and it is one of the few large mansions in the Salient which looks much as it did in 1914.

At the crossroad turn left and descend the ridge to **Zandvoorde** (2½ kms). The importance of Gheluvelt, as it strides the main road at the highest point of the ridge, can be appreciated well from here. Zandvoorde, on a hill, commanded a vital crossroads in 1914. The slope up from Zillebeke was the site of the charge by the Household Cavalry on October 26, 1914. During the next few days, other squadrons of the Household Brigade manned trenches in the village and the outskirts despite massive artillery fire which plastered the slopes. When the German XV Corps took the village they found two complete British cavalry squadrons with their machine guns, dead or dying in one meadow. On the eastern edge of the village (at the back of a garden on the right of the Ten Brielen road) is the tall column of the **Household Brigade Memorial**,

erected on the site of the place where Lord Worsley's body was found at the end of the war. This marks the centre of the position held on October 31. 1914.

Some little way down the slope, nestling into the hillside on the right before a small group of houses, is the only **German bunker** remaining in the Salient with its ground covering still in place. This large bunker was erected in 1916 and the date and name of the unit concerned is engraved on the wall.

Return to Zandvoorde and take the left-hand road for **Hollebeke**. After descending

The Household Brigade Memorial was erected on the spot where Lord Worsley's body had been found.

Gheluvelt Château. The 2nd Bn. Worcesters attacked in the grounds in October 1914.

the slope (2 kms) and crossing the Bassevillebeek, a small stream, there is a cluster of bunkers on the left and, on the right, the small mound in an orchard near a farm is the site of **Hollebeke Château**. Hollebeke, on the railway line and Ypres-Comines canal, was another of the hotly-contested positions in 1914 and 1917.

At the crossroad before the railway embankment turn right. The road runs parallel to the railway and in the embankment are several **bunkers and concrete shelters**. After crossing the stream again, turn left under the railway. The modern village of Hollebeke is on the left on the Comines road. It was entirely destroyed and, unlike the château, it was rebuilt.

Turn right. Almost immediately on the left is the ruin of **Lock 6 bis** of the old canal. This is also the eastern entrance to the leisure area, **Palingbeek Park**. The woodland beyond the lock stretches away to the west, along the canal and the hills on either side, right through to the site of **The Bluff**. It is possible to walk from Lock 6 bis the length of the canal to Spoilbank, along Kingsway and into Ypres near the station. Little remains to record the

Hollebeke. This is the site of the château which was entirely destroyed by the war and never rebuilt.

The old ruin of Lock 6 bis on the Ypres-Comines Canal, Hollebeke.

many operations which took place along this part of the canal but towards the western end at the Bluff there are several mine craters, now duck ponds, which recall the protracted mining operations of 1915 and 1916. To reach the main entrance and car park continue up the road, with **Battle Wood** on the right, and take the first road on the left. This comparatively new road, which follows an avenue of trees, terminates in a large car park in the middle of the park. A short distance from the car park is now a modern complex of an information and study centre for the nature reserve and café where once were bunkers and trenches. Nothing remains of the bunker on which the iron railings from the White Château gates were used for reinforcement. In the ravine and along the crests there are some reminders of the war—old brickworks from the canal, mine craters which are now ponds and broken hillsides. New paths take the visitor through this sanctuary today. Hidden beyond the woods on the southern flank is the **White Château**, for a long time a German base. Although the track remains, there is no public access to the château today and the Dammstrasse can no longer be reached from the canal and so make connection with the Warneton road. Among the many trenches which crossed and re-crossed the canal between the car park and the Bluff were the famous **International**, **Impudence** and **Imperial trenches**.

Return to the main road and turn left. Take

These German bunkers and concrete shelters can still be seen today in the railway bank at Hollebeke.

Remains of a 1915 mine crater on the Bluff. Until recent years, the remains of German bunkers, one reinforced with the old White Château gates, were still visible.

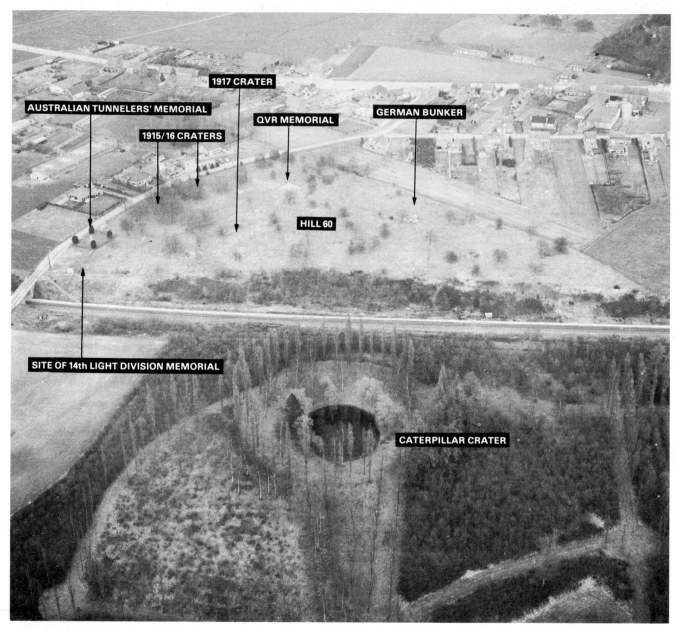

AUSTRALIAN TUNNELERS' MEMORIAL

1917 CRATER

1915/16 CRATERS

QVR MEMORIAL

GERMAN BUNKER

HILL 60

SITE OF 14th LIGHT DIVISION MEMORIAL

CATERPILLAR CRATER

the next turn to the right. Signpost for Hill 60. On the right, now outlined by tall poplar trees in private grounds is the **Caterpillar position**. Across the railway and on the right is **Hill 60**.

This hillock was created in the nineteenth century when the railway was built. The low mound formed from the spoil from the cutting, some 230 metres by 190 metres wide, was called 'Lovers' Knoll' or 'Côte des amants'. On top was rich, loamy clay; underneath came seven metres of firm, dry sand separated from the hard, underlying blue clay by a very wet two-metre layer of quicksand. This then was the problem which was to face the infantry, the artillery and, most important, the mining companies of the engineers of the French, British and German armies during four years of bitter fighting.

Early in November 1914, at the end of the battles of First Ypres, the cavalry under General Byng was dug in on the forward slopes, following the famous charge of the Household Cavalry at Zwarteleen on November 6. Then the French XVI Corps relieved the British and the French support troops on the hill until the German 39th Division captured it on December 10. It was then established as a strategic observation post, giving the Germans excellent views over the British lines to Ypres.

In the same month, preparations commenced to regain the summit and Lieutenant

Bruyeat was ordered to undermine and blow up the enemy fortifications on the crest. The Royal Monmouthshire Royal Engineers were brought in to assist in the mining which was completed in the spring of 1915.

In February 1915, 28th Division, II Corps, took over the line from the French. The officer in charge, Major D. Norton Griffiths, was one of the most colourful characters of the period, an eccentric but brilliant officer. One of his quirks was to use his own Rolls-Royce, adapted for military purposes, to travel around the battle area. Special mining companies were only then in the process of being formed and when, in April, the 5th Division relieved the 28th, the original mining parties were retained and reinforced by the new 171st Tunnelling Company, RE.

Five chambers were excavated and charged; the northern pair with 2,000lbs of powder each, the central pair with 2,700lbs each, and the southern one with 500lbs of gun cotton. As this last mine was very close to the German workings, it was not fully completed in order to avoid detection by the enemy. The 13th Brigade, who relieved the 15th Brigade on the night of April 16/17, 1915 in the line directly opposite Hill 60, were to carry out the initial attack following the explosion of the mines.

At 7.05 p.m. on April 17, after a very quiet day, the mines were blown in two pairs followed by the single one at ten-second intervals.

The famous Hill 60 and the Caterpillar mine crater at Zwarteleen have been preserved more or less as they were left in 1918. Now overgrown, our photograph shows how they appeared from the air in April 1976.

One hundred and fifty of the enemy and two REs were killed in the explosions. Immediately the first artillery barrage began by the 15th and 27th Field Artillery Brigades and the 9th Heavy Artillery Brigade, with two French and three Belgian batteries supporting them. At the same moment 'C' Company, 1st Bn. Royal West Kent Regiment, stormed the hill followed by the 1/2nd Home Counties Field Company, RE, and, with complete surprise, gained the crest of the slope and took the craters. Casualties to the storming party were light as the German garrison was overwhelmed. Another company of the West Kents and two from the 2nd Bn. King's Own Scottish Borderers came up and began to consolidate the position. At this time the 2nd Bn. Duke of Wellington's Regiment was in support near Zillebeke and the 2nd Bn. Yorkshire Light Infantry were in reserve. The machine gun section of the Queen Victoria's Rifles followed the first storming parties on to the crest.

A little after midnight, the KOSB began to relieve the West Kents, but before this task was completed, the Germans launched three

The remains of a Hill 60 bunker near the rim of a large crater.

counter-attacks. Previously there had been some wild artillery firing but, as these infantry attacks approached the craters in which the defenders were dug in, their fire became more accurate. Each counter-attack was repulsed by the extraordinary fine machine gun and rifle fire.

The Duke of Wellington's Regiment relieved the West Kents and KOSB at 8.30 a.m. to face heavy shelling and close fighting all day. The attacks by the Germans had won the right-hand sector by the railway cutting, but the tiny salient on the crest remained in British hands. At 6.00 p.m. the Duke of Wellington's, supported by the KOYLI, counter-attacked and won back the whole hill. That night (18/19) the 15th Brigade relieved the 13th Brigade. The 15th Brigade (1st Bn. Norfolk Regiment, 1st Bn. Cheshire Regiment, 1st Bn. Bedfordshire Regiment and 1st Bn. Dorsetshire Regiment). The 1st Bn. East Surrey Regiment (14th Brigade) was attacked and, with the Bedfordshires, were first in the front line.

On the evening of the 19th, the QVRs (13th Brigade) moved up in close support. It had been a fairly quiet day but on the 20th furious fighting broke out again and continued on the 21st. The 1st Bn. Devonshire Regiment (14th Brigade) relieved the two front line battalions that day. By now the hill was unrecognisable: the top gone in the mine explosion, the trenches had disappeared and the craters were a mass of debris and corpses.

On the 19th, the British accounts claim that the Germans used gas shells in the artillery bombardment although this is not confirmed in the German archives. The German Fourth Army records say it was on April 20 that sixty gas shells were fired at the hill. It is probable that the gas detected on the earlier date came from the cylinders dug into the hill ready for attack but, up to then, unused.

The hill remained in British hands until, on the evening of May 1, a gas attack was launched on the 1st Bn. Dorsetshire Regiment (15th Brigade) and the 1st Bn. Devonshires (14th Brigade) and the 1st Bn. Bedfordshires (15th Brigade). This was the first occasion that a gas attack failed to achieve its object for the British battalions, although suffering heavy casualties, held on.

On May 5, when the Duke of Wellington's (15th Brigade) were again holding the hill, another gas attack was launched. On this occasion the gas was released on a favourable wind along the British lines. This attack affected a great length of the line and the advancing Germans were able to get a foothold on the lower slope. Before

reinforcements could arrive a second gas attack was mounted, this time on the Bedfordshire and 6th Bn. King's Liverpool Regiments. In the evening, after a further gas attack, the 13th Brigade were ordered in to counter-attack and regain the hill but, although some KOSB did reach the top, they were pushed back by fire from the Caterpillar.

Another attempt to regain the hill was made by the KOYLI on May 7 but it was a failure, all the men taking part being either killed or taken prisoner. The Germans were in full possession of the hill; they fortified it and retained it until June 1917. In the two periods of fighting, and the comparative lull between them, the 5th Division suffered casualties of over 100 officers and 3,000 other ranks.

In the months following the great May battles, the main struggle went on underground. Deep mining began in August 1915 by 175th Tunnelling Company from an entrance in the bank of the railway cutting some 220 yards behind the British front line. It was to pass 90 feet below the surface. In April 1916 the 3rd Canadian Tunnelling Company took over and mines were commenced on the Caterpillar as well. After a long underground struggle between the miners of both sides, the Hill 60 gallery was finished in July 1916 and charged with 53,500lbs of high explosive. In October, the gallery under the Caterpillar was also completed and 70,000lbs of explosive was placed there. In order to achieve this, the German main gallery had to be destroyed by a camouflet.

In November 1916 the 1st Australian Tunnelling Company took over the maintenance of these mines. This entailed endless fighting

above and below ground to keep the enemy from discovering the galleries and charges.

The two mines were to be the most northerly in the long chain of twenty-four mines which were being prepared for the attack on the Messines Ridge. In the event only nineteen were blown. It was at 3.10 a.m. precisely on June 7, 1917 that these exploded with a tremendous shock, similar to that of an earthquake. It was felt even in London and other places in England.

Immediately after the mines had been fired and almost before the earth ceased to heave, the entire artillery force of the Second Army opened a three-pronged barrage on the German lines. Fifteen minutes later, at Hill 60, the men of the 69th and 70th Brigades, Yorkshire Bns. attacked the hill and gained the feature with few casualties and no trouble.

The craters which were left after the eruption can still be seen today all along the line of the Messines-Wytschaete Ridge—most of these are small ponds now used by farmers. In 1917, the Hill 60 crater was 60 feet deep and 260 feet wide at the rim, and the Caterpillar disappeared into a hole 90 feet deep and 334 feet wide at the brim. The 204th German Division, which held the two positions, lost 10 officers and 677 men killed by the explosions.

Hill 60 can be visited today as it is in the care of the Commonwealth War Graves Commission. The **Memorial to the Queen Victoria's Rifles**, although badly damaged in the Second World War, has been re-created on its old site despite the loss of the original stone mounting. One concrete bunker showing British as well as the basic German work remains on another high point whilst the remains of other dugouts can still be discerned. There are vestiges of five of the small craters and, although the walls have crumbled and the base filled in, the high crater, usually dry, still dominates the scene.

The following Victoria Crosses were among the many awards for gallantry in the Hill 60 operations:

Lieutenant G. R. P. Roupell, 1st Bn. East Surrey Regiment, for his magnificent example of courage and devotion on April 20.

Private E. Dwyer, 1st Bn. East Surrey Regiment, for gallantry in bombing and assistance under fire to wounded comrades.

Second Lieutenant G. H. Woolley, 9th Bn. London Regiment (Queen Victoria's Rifles). He was the first Territorial officer to receive the VC which was awarded for defence on the night of April 20/21 when, for a time, he was the only officer on the hill.

Second Lieutenant B. H. Geary, 4th Bn., attached 1st Bn. East Surrey Regiment, for conspicuous bravery and determination on April 20/21.

This bunker on Hill 60 built during the First War also saw service in the Second.

The Memorial to the Australian Tunnelling Company (with bullet marks from the Second World War) and that to the 14th Light Division on the right.

Hill 60 railway cutting with a modern 'Ypres Express' passing the Dump.

Queen Victoria's Rifles Memorial, Hill 60.

A small car park now overlooked by the **14th Light Division Memorial** is between the railway and the **1st Australian Tunnelling Company Memorial**. The entrance to the hill, which now bears no resemblance to its original shape, is beside the enclosure of the shrapnel-pocked **Tunnellers' Memorial**; here too is a stone which eloquently outlines the horrific story of this historic place.

Paths lead through the shell-pocked ground to the bunker on the crest between the line of small craters and the large one on the right. Remnants of other strong points are scattered over the hillside. Vestiges of dugouts and trenches can be seen in the far bank of the railway, below the Caterpillar and to the west of **the Dump**.

Supplies to the Dump were manhandled to the line from Ypres and 'Ypres Express' was the name given to the trucks on their return journey as the gradient was just sufficient to travel at a greater speed with less effort.

Trench museums, which existed until just after the Second World War, were situated on the left-hand side of the road opposite the Queen Victoria Rifles Memorial. They no longer exist. Over the years their owners changed, as did the layout of the trenches!

Continuing straight on, in ½ km we reach the road junction in **Zwarteleen**. Turn right towards **Kleine Zillebeke**. In ½ km, take a left turn through the woods. **Shrewsbury Forest** is private woodland, and contains several bunkers reminiscent of the actions fought here in 1917. On the left rises **Mount Sorrel, Observatory Ridge** and **Hill 62**. The road, having left the trees, now crosses open ground gradually rising to the Menin Road. This road was known as **Green Jacket Ride**.

Soon after passing a small road on the left, the land rises on the left and the woods of Mount Sorrel can be seen above the open fields. In the nearest copse is one of the mine craters. On the right is **Clonmel Copse**. This road was criss-crossed with trenches and was the scene of many actions, particularly those in June 1916, when the Canadian Corps captured Mount Sorrel and Hill 62. Again in the summer of 1917 this area was the focal point of much action.

Four kms from Kleine Zillebeke and the Menin Road is reached at another famous and notorious point—**Clapham Junction**. On the south side of the Menin Road stands the **Memorial obelisk of the 18th Division** whilst across the road the **Gloucestershire Regiment** erected its **memorial**. The 1st Bn. Gloucestershire Regiment took part in the battles for Gheluvelt in 1914 and the 2nd Bn. were heavily engaged in the same region around Clapham Junction in 1915. The 18th

Below left: **A German bunker, one of several remaining in Shrewsbury Forest.** *Below:* **Clapham Junction with the 18th Division and Gloucestershire Regiment Memorials.**

48

The 2nd Bn. Worcestershire Regiment Memorial House.

Above: **Hooge Château, used by the British in 1914 and Germans in 1915, stood beyond the tree in the centre of the picture. Bellewaarde Lake is in the background.**

Centre: **The late Baron de Vinckt walks in the garden of the new Hooge Château.**
Above: **Hooge Château mine craters now form ponds in the grounds.**

Division was involved here in 1917. The copse on the left is in the position of **Stirling Castle**, so named by the Argyll and Sutherland Highlanders in 1915 when they had a depot there.

Up the Menin road to the right is **Château Herentage** and behind its wood are those of **Dumbarton Lakes**, both hotly contested sites. Opposite is **Inverness Copse** and beside this woodland one of the small houses bears the **2nd Bn. Worcester Regiment Memorial**, the plaque outlining their deeds here and at Gheluvelt.

Turn left onto the Menin Road. At the bottom of the slope is the site of the **Tank Cemetery**. Here 14 tanks sank in the mud as they were disabled or put out of action.

After a further 1½ kms we reach **Hooge**. **Hooge Château** was a British headquarters in 1914 and from it Sir John French and Sir Douglas Haig watched the 1st Division rally and capture Gheluvelt. The château of the day was a red brick building with a large conservatory. It was constantly under fire and in May 1915 was captured by the Germans. It was the scene of heavy fighting during June and July, and on July 30 the Germans used 'liquid fire' (burning petrol) for the first time. In July, the British fired a large mine before the attack was made. A crater is preserved in a stylised form in **Hooge Crater Cemetery**. This large cemetery is the burial ground or memorial of nearly 6,000 men of the Commonwealth. In the grounds of the château there are two further craters, now landscaped into part of the beautiful garden of the new château which has replaced the old home of the late Baron de Vinckt which was totally destroyed. The old house stood at the end of a straight drive some distance behind the site of the present building. The Baron preserved two trees which stood near the house and survived and the stump of another. The park includes **Bellewaerde Lake** over which the old house looked.

The section of the Menin Road from east of Hooge was very heavily fortified. The Germans built a subway beneath the old road and this remains now below the new one. Concrete shelters littered the area, some of which still remain in the château grounds. One large mine, right across the Menin Road, was blown early in 1917. Even today the road suffers occasionally from subsidence caused by these old workings. On the right (at the edge of the copse before Hooge Château grounds are passed) is the **KRRC Memorial**. The site of their actions is now part of the safari park.

In ½ km, at the end of the slope down from Hooge, take the left turn—this is **Canadalaan**

Sanctuary Wood lies behind Hooge Crater Cemetery with its symbolic crater.

The King's Royal Rifle Corps Memorial at Hooge.

Sanctuary Wood Cemetery. The grave of German aviator Hans Roser.

or **Maple Avenue**. It is a road built especially to make access to the **Canadian Memorial** on Hill 62 easy. From it can be gained a magnificent view of Hooge Crater Cemetery and the ridge. **Sanctuary Wood Cemetery** is on the right in about ¾ km. In this graveyard lies Lieutenant Gilbert Talbot, MC, in whose memory Toc H was named. Here also lies the German aviator Hans Roser who was shot down by Major Lanoe G. Hawker, VC. Outside is the private grave of a friend of Lieutenant Talbot, Lieutenant Keith Rae.

A few metres further up Maple Avenue is a café behind which is a **Musée des Tranchées**. Admission fee. The family Schier, who own the café, have preserved this small part of the wood as it was found at the end of the war and it is now the only really authentic sector of trenches remaining in the Salient. The trenches belong to the **Vince Street-Jam Row** system of front and support lines of 1916. Battlefield debris of all kinds are strewn around the copse and the trench lines. In the little indoor museum, to which visitors are shown before walking through the trenches, are on display many items found in the Salient or nearby. There are, for instance, two sea mines which I have been told were from the Nieuwpoort area, and some early German gravestones.

Sanctuary Wood was so named because in

Above left: **Gilbert Talbot's grave, Sanctuary Wood Cemetery.**
Above right: **Memorial to Lieutenant Keith Rae, a close friend of Gilbert Talbot.**
Below: **The Hill 62 Canadian Memorial commemorates the 1916 battles.**

October 1914, when this was in a relatively quiet sector, stragglers were gathered together in the wood where they came under the orders of General E. S. Bulfin of the 2nd Infantry Brigade. His instructions were that they were in sanctuary and not to be employed without his permission. By 1915, the wood began to lose its original usage and was soon in the front line or close to it. The 16th Lancers were in action in Shrewsbury Forest in February 1915, as were the Leinsters. After the advance in May 1915, the Germans were in the eastern sectors of the wood and harrassed the British and French encamped on the western edges. June 1916 was the time of a violent German attack which lasted for four days; then came the Canadian counter-attack and assault on Tor Top, Mount Sorrel and ending with the Canadians regaining all the lost ground. The trees were shot to pieces and the ground was often a quagmire. Bunkers and strong points were built (of which a few remain in the private sector of the wood behind the children's playground), and a few shallow subways, or rather covered trenches, were dug to replace those of 1914. Two short lengths of these can be seen in the museum but are only passable during dry weather.

The summit of the slope is crowned with the **Canadian Memorial** commemorating the battles of 1916. Views of the immediate region can be enjoyed from the gardens which surround the memorial. The proximity of Ypres and Hill 60 can be well appreciated and on clear days Mont Kemmel appears very near

indeed. Return to Ypres via Hellfire Corner. A **new museum** has been opened by another member of the Schier family in the group of houses on the Menin Road at the end of Canadalaan. Most of the items come from the older museum.

Above and below: **Sanctuary Wood 1982. Shattered trees amongst the new growth at the Musée des Tranchées. The original headstone from Adolf Grabsky's grave for which the German War Graves declare there is now no trace.**

The Menin Road War Museum can be found behind a house at the end of Canadalaan at Sanctuary Wood.

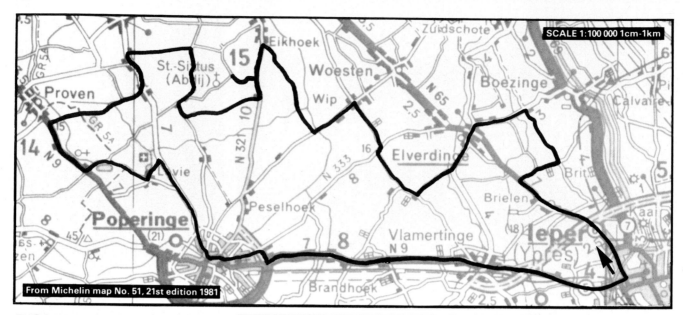

From Michelin map No. 51, 21st edition 1981

SCALE 1:100 000 1cm-1km

ROUTE IV

Leave Ypres by the Marschal Haiglaan, the N65. After 1 km cross the railway. On the right, immediately after this, is **Reigersburg Château**. This Victorian mansion was used as a base right from the early days of the war. The Royal Field Artillery were in occupation in October 1914 and there are still notices on the walls relating to their presence.

Brielen is 2½ kms further on. A small village, it was totally destroyed in the war, mainly by artillery fire as it was a forward base for the troops in action around the Yser Canal. A short way out of the village the long straight drive to **Château de Trois Tours** bears off to the left. This château was utilised as an HQ by the 1st Canadian Division in 1915 and thereafter many divisions and brigades occupied it. By some amazing chance, although the village was destroyed, this house bore a charmed life and was hardly damaged. After the war it became an hotel whose proprietors specialized in Salient tours. The Ypres League and the Anglo-Belgian Union had their headquarters here.

After 1 km **Dawsons Corner**—the name given to the camp here by the Canadian Corps in 1915. Turn right and after 1 km we reach **Solferino Cemetery** on the right. The French

The Reigersburg Château was an early billet of the BEF, and inscriptions can still be seen on the walls relating to its occupation by the Royal Horse Artillery.

An inscription at Reigersburg Château 'RFA', can still be seen at the side of the door to the stables.

had a dressing station and camp here, later taken over by the BEF. In ½ km crossroads, turn left, then after another 1¾ km crossroad, turn left again. Just before the cross on the right is a **British concrete shelter**. Half-a-kilometre further on **Bluet Farm Cemetery** is on the right. Bluet Farm was a dressing station during the 1917 battles.

In 1½ kms we reach **Elverdinge**. This large village was the centre of many camps, training areas, stores, hospitals and facilities for leisure. It was almost entirely destroyed by artillery fire being a known British base and road junction. The **château** constantly used as an HQ was also damaged and was accidentally

burnt on one occasion when a cook let some fat catch fire. Later it was rebuilt. A light railway ran from Poperinge carrying casualties and supplies. Near the church is a Belgian Krupp 95mm gun, recently reinstated after conservation.

Leave the village by the Vlamertinge road, leaving the church on the right and drive past the château grounds. An entrance to these on the right gives a good view of the house set far back. In 1 km take the right fork crossing the stream and through the meadows and beet fields which once echoed to the noise of camp life.

Another 1 km to road junction, take the right-hand road. The farm at the junction is **Hospital Farm**—the **cemetery** of this name is a little way to the left. It was a dressing station. The next ½ km goes through the site of **Dirty Bucket Camp**, so named after a farm which was near the small road on the left.

After 1 km crossroads, go straight over. **Canada Farm Cemetery** is about 1 km along on the right. There was a dressing station here between June and September 1917.

In ¾ km **Wippe crossroads**. Turn left. A **British concrete shelter** is on the right. Another is some way up on the north side of the hamlet. Then 1½ kms across the Poperongevaart and take the right-hand road in the direction of Eikhok.

After a further 3 kms, road junction, turn left. 1½ kms to **International Corner**, a junction of the British and Belgian lines. The name is to be found on the walls of a barn in the farm here. Turn right. At the next road junction—about 1 km—turn right and a short distance along take left fork and at the next crossroads turn left across this very flat area. On the right is the **Abdij St Sixtus**. This monastery, with its modern brewery producing the famous Trappist beer and its own very special mead, cultivates much of the area around here which was a very large camp. A dressing station and local headquarters were situated in the abbey buildings. (During the Second World War for a short while in 1940 it was the base of General Montgomery.) The Cistercian monks aided the care of casualties brought here in 1915. It was said that a deserter was brought here and tried after the gas attack and shot (*see page 10*).

In ½ km turn left and then in ½ km turn right for **Proven**, 2 kms further on. This was a large village which was damaged by bombing and long-range artillery fire. It was the centre of many British activities and camps. There was an aerodrome here and a large supply depot which had light railway connections with Dunkerque and Poperinge.

In the centre of the village turn left on to the N9 and in 2 kms turn left for **La Lovie**. Here, in a beautiful park, is the large **château** which from May 1915 was a British HQ of importance. As it was the centre of the training and stores region, the house was well placed. VI Corps were here until February 1916, followed by XIV and VII Corps. Then in February 1916 the Fifth Army arrived and had their HQ in the house until November 1917. In July 1917 King George V used the house as

Above: **Elverdinge Château used as a headquarters building.** *Right:* **The 95mm Krupp gun now on display.**

Although over 60 years old, this famous painted sign still remains to be seen.

one of his bases during his visit to the front that month. During 1918 various divisions and corps used its facilities among them the 41st, 49th and 34th Divisions. August 30 saw II Corps in possession until the end of the operations to clear the Salient commenced when they moved up. The château was hardly damaged. Today, the house and its surrounding buildings are used as a school and training centre for spastics. In the vicinity is the site of **Lovie aerodrome**, used by the scout squadrons in 1918. Return from the park to the right and the back road into Poperinge. In 2 kms Poperinge, and thence 12 kms to Ypres.

Above: **The fairy-tale Château de Trois Tours—haven to many divisions.** *Right:* **A bunker crumbles in the grounds.**

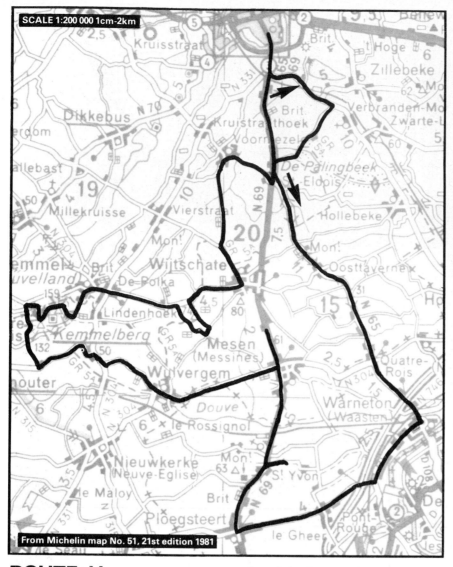

SCALE 1:200 000 1cm-2km

From Michelin map No. 51, 21st edition 1981

ROUTE V

Depart from Ypres by Rijselstraat and the Lille Gate (Rijselpoort), the N69, perhaps the most frequented route of the war. Due to the exposed position of the Menin Gate exit, most departures for the front were this way.

After ½ km **Shrapnel Corner**, a most unhealthy spot as it was constantly shelled by the German artillery and then by long-range guns in 1918. Before the railway crossing turn to the left.

Then 1 km to **Transport Farm** and **Railway Dugouts Cemetery** on the right. In the embankment behind the cemetery there are still vestiges of the shelters and dugouts. On the left is the drive leading to **Zillebeke Lake** and restaurant. A promenade encircles this artificial lake so well known to the BEF as a prairie of mud and blasted trees. It is the older of the two great ponds (the other is Dikkebus) formed in medieval times to provide for Ypres. In 1295 there was already a fish pond in existence. From 1914 onwards, there were positions all along the banks and many an artillery unit was bogged down in the mud. It was often a target for the German guns and one English gunner officer found a unique method to keep his men from being hit: take them out into the lake in an old punt he had found and sit there damply but in moderate safety. Only a few remnants of the shelters which were in the vicinity of the lake now remain on the north banks.

The eastern end of the lake is almost in Zillebeke village and the woods and fields in that area were the scenes of many terrible battles. In October 1914 the Irish Guards fought a lengthy action in holding Zillebeke Wood. Then, in 1915, the Cavalry Corps were in action and in July the 18th Division held the sector whilst the artillery were always there. In April 1918 the British withdrew from Zillebeke, returning in September. **Hellblast Corner** is at the easternmost end of the lake.

Retrace the way to the road and turn left, turning left at the next junction, noting the **British Demarcation Stone** on the corner.

After 2 kms we then reach **Zillebeke** village. Totally destroyed, it has been rebuilt on the old foundations and the church almost to the same design. Some of the earliest British burials are in the churchyard. Return to the junction, turn left and take the first right-hand road for Verbrandenmolen and Spoilbank.

In about 2½ kms **Chester Farm Cemetery** and **Spoilbank Cemetery** are on the right. A little further on is the western entrance to **Palingbeek park**. On the right here is the section of the old canal known as **Kingsway** to the BEF. Along it are two ruined locks and dugouts. Our road bends slightly round following the 1917 front line.

Another ½ km and we join the N69, turning left for the **St Eloi** (St Eloois) crossroads. Many actions were fought in this

Shrapnel Corner road junction was a regular target for German artillery.

Zillebeke Lake was the scene of bitter fighting. This is Hellblast Corner at the eastern end.

BUS HOUSE CEMETERY

TO YPRES

TO MESSINES

GERMAN DUGOUT

BRITISH DUGOUT

MINE BLOWN 7.6.17

MINE BLOWN 27.3.16

MINE BLOWN 27.3.16

MINE BLOWN 27.3.16

WARNETON

TO HOLLEBEKE

The St Eloi craters still straddle the old German lines of 1916-17. More than thirty British and German mines were fired in the area, six of the British, totalling 73,000 lbs, being fired together. The largest single mine of 95,600 lbs was blown here on June 7, 1917.

neighbourhood but it is chiefly remembered for the protracted mine warfare which began when the Germans fired their first mine in March 1915. This was part of their counter-attack to earlier British attacks for this position. In the ensuing twelve months, the British fired 13 mines and 29 camouflets and the Germans 20 mines and 2 camouflets. Six of the British mines were fired on March 27, 1916 and consisted of a total of 73,000lbs of charges but, due to the artillery barrages, it was impossible for our troops to consolidate the position and it was retained by the Germans. During the mine explosions heralding the Messines Ridge attack, the largest single charge was 95,600lbs of ammonal blown at St Eloi and this time the position was captured by the 41st Division.

Two of the largest of these craters, now circular ponds, lie on the left side of the Warneton road and are privately owned, being used as fish ponds and swimming pools. The one nearest the road is surrounded by reeds and the other by tall trees and hedges. In the apex of the Messines and Warneton roads is the third crater, but it is not easily visible from the road. On the higher ground behind it is an excellent example of a **British shelter** with a **German concrete dugout** in front of it. The British concrete retains the elephant iron (large corrugated iron) lining to its roof. It can be seen easily from the Messines road.

Above: **A German bunker near the large crater fired on June 7, 1917, and,** *below* **a British concrete shelter, still retaining the iron lining, built nearby.**

The Damstrasse—the drive to the Bayershof German HQ on the horizon.

The Oosttaverne crossroads—scene of two 19th Division actions.

Take the N65, the Warneton road. The country now undulates along gentle ridges and the road passes through pleasant meadows. A short distance, about 1 km along on the left, the ridge of the **Dammstrasse** can be discerned. In the field before it is another good British dugout. The Dammstrasse is the old drive to the White Château occupied by the Germans and known to them as the **Bayershof**.

In 2 kms **Oosttaverne crossroads**. Memorial cross of the **19th 'Butterfly' Division** on the left. This marks the site of the division's attack during the Messines battles of July 7, 1917 and later their great fight during the Battle of the Lys in April 1918. The road continues through the rolling country but after a couple of kilometres it begins to descend into the Lys Valley.

After 4 kms cross the new Lys ring-road before entering **Warneton**. The large red brick church, the cathedral of the Lys, dominates the landscape. The opening thrusts of the First Battle of Ypres were made here when the 1st and 2nd Cavalry Divisions were driven back towards Messines, attempting to gain the Lys on October 20, 1914. Warneton remained in German hands until September 1918 and was one of their most important forward bases. The Belgian frontier station is on the north end of the bridge. Turn right in the centre of the town for Ploegsteert and, in about 3 kms at Basseville, take the right fork and cross the railway, and the ring-road.

In 4 kms we then reach **Le Gheer**, a hamlet on the eastern edge of Ploegsteert Wood. A kilometre up the road on the right at the crossroad of Le Pelegrin, one of the mines laid in 1917 exploded in July 1955 when a willow tree was hit by lightning during a severe thunderstorm. Fortunately there were no casualties. Le Gheer was the scene of much activity in 1914 when the 4th Division carried out a brilliant counter-attack before withdrawing. Here is the northern limit of the 1914 'Christmas Truce' area.

Plugstreet Wood, once again a pleasant forest, was, for the most part of the war, a relatively quiet area which every now and then burst into violence. In October 1914 the British Cavalry Division captured it but later it was partially retaken by the Germans who were not finally dislodged until mid-1917. Although the lines had been fortified, on April 10/11, 1918, in the big advance, the Germans captured it completely. The British recaptured it during their advance in September.

For four years it provided comparative shelter to some one million men in its labyrinth of glades and connecting trenches. One of the main arteries was **Hunters Avenue** which is reached about 1 km from Le Gheer. At the opening is the Verderer's house and, before venturing into the wood which is private property, it is advisable to enquire here for permission. At certain times of the year, particularly in spring, it is forbidden to wander in the wood. Likewise in the autumn, when the guns are out, it would be highly dangerous to venture into the woods without the gamekeepers' knowledge.

Almost at the edge of the wood, hidden in the undergrowth, is the first of a line of concrete machine gun posts and shelters which can be seen through the trees along Hunters Avenue. There are eight of them and they provide excellent cover for the birds. Some hundred metres along the glade is a muddy footpath on the left which leads to one of the best known of British dugouts—**Blighty Hole** or Hall. A first-aid post shelter, it retains the bench for stretchers but is nearly always fairly damp underfoot.

At the second crossway, a left turn leads towards two of the British cemeteries—**Rifle House** and **Plugstreet Wood**. They are two of the most beautiful in the Salient (strictly speaking, it is beyond the southern limits of it). The former takes its name from the small fortified building whose remains can be seen close by. The tall trees here are among those which survived the holocaust.

Returning to the road, continue westward towards the village of Ploegsteert. Passing along the limits of the wood on the right, farm buildings will be seen away in the distance on the left. One of these is **Lawrence Farm** which was painted by Winston Churchill when with the 6th Royal Scots Fusiliers billeted in the area. **Lancashire Farm Cemetery** is also on the left. Here was **East Lancashire Cottage**, one of the positions of the 29th Division, when they cleared Ploegsteert of the Germans on September 4, 1918.

Two kms further on is **Ploegsteert**—a small town which was badly damaged in the war, being so close to the front line for so long. Turn right at the crossroads. The long straight road leads northwards and on it is **Strand Cemetery**, named after one of the glades of the wood which stretched across the road near here. Between two houses near the cemetery are three British bunkers in good repair as they are in use by the householders.

The site of the mine laid in 1917 near Le Pelegrin, some years after it exploded in 1955!

Left: Hunters Avenue as it was in 1917 (IWM). Above: Sixty years of growth have transformed the scene entirely—this is Hunters Avenue today.

Ploegstreet Wood, which was quickly dubbed 'Plugstreet Wood' by the Tommies, still displays the relics of both sides.

Above left: A British bunker, and above right, a German machine gun post mouldering in Plugstreet Wood today.

'Blighty Hole'—a British first aid post in Plugstreet Wood—still retains the bench for the stretchers.

Deep in the wood is Rifle House Cemetery which took its name from a small building, the ruins of which still stand nearby.

After 1½ kms, **Hyde Park Corner** is reached. On the left stands the **Ploegsteert Memorial to the Missing** and **Berks Corner Cemetery Extension**. On the right is the original cemetery. The memorial, unique in the Salient, is a circular temple with pillars guarded by two lions, one snarling in defiance whilst the other gazes serenely into the distance. The memorial was designed by H. Charlton Bradshaw, and the sculptor was Sir Gilbert Ledward. The missing from the battles of Armentières, Aubers Ridge 1914, Loos, Fromelles 1915, Estaires 1916, Hazebrouck, Scherpenberg, and Outtersteene Ridge 1918, in all 11,447 men, are listed on the panels within the colonnade. Seventy feet in diameter and 38½ feet high, it was unveiled on June 7, 1931 by the Duke of Brabant. Over 380 men lie in the cemetery beneath the flowering cherries.

The N69, begins to climb up towards **Château de la Hutte** and the highpoint, **Hill 63**, on which was a vital 'O-Pip' defended by the 25th Divison in April 1918. The château, now only a few crumbling ruins which lessen as the years pass, is in the fields on the left. It will be noted that the road surface here is extremely bad. That is due to the continual subsidence of the many tunnels which run through the hillside, often causing the road to be closed or subject to repairs.

On the crest of the hill the right turn at the crossroads leads to **St Yvon** and the alternative entrance to the cemeteries in Ploegsteert Wood. This is down a somewhat muddy lane just beyond **Prowse Point Cemetery**.

This cemetery is the only one in the area to be named after an individual, and marks the site of a gallant stand by the Hampshire Regiment and the Somerset Light Infantry in the actions for St Yvon in October 1914 at which Major, later Brigadier-General, C. B. Prowse, DSO, was the hero. Later, in the Wieltje sector near St Jean, his brigade was in violent action again and the farm was called **Prowse Farm**. It was in the field behind the **50th Northumbrian Division Memorial**, but today only a portion of the cellars remain and a large shell hole full of water.

In November 1914, the northern edge of the wood was in the sector of the 2nd Bn. Dublin Fusiliers and the 1st Bn. Warwickshire Regiment, many of whose casualties lie in the cemetery. The small pool beside the Cross of Sacrifice is part of the old line and at its side can be seen the roof of a concrete shelter.

Down the lane are **Mud Corner** and **Toronto Farm Cemeteries**, the latter, despite its name, containing entirely Australian graves, and the former mostly New Zealanders.

British Lions guard the Ploegsteert Memorial to the Missing and Berks Corner Cemetery Extension at Hyde Park Corner.

A comparison between the original and current CWGC signposts.

Peaceful reflections at Prowse Point Cemetery, named after Brigadier-General C. B. Prowse. Ploegsteert Wood is in the background.

The Messines Ridge from Kruistraat road with a British bunker in the foreground.

Return to the N69 and continue northward, with the panorama of the **Messines Ridge** ahead. The road descends into the valley of the River Douve before climbing up the ridge.

Messines (Mesen) was taken by the Wurttemburgers from the exhausted Cavalry Corps on November 1, 1914, the latter having held them at bay for over forty-eight hours after weeks of continuous fighting. The London Scottish made a gallant but fruitless charge in their support only a matter of hours after arriving in the Salient, being the first TA infantry unit to go into action. Their memorial marks the site on the northern slope before the town. From its ruins the Germans dominated the British lines until June 1917.

As early as August 1915, the first plans for the mining of the Messines-Wytschaete Ridge were made, and for eighteen months work was under way in the tunnelling and laying of charges in a number of sites on an arc from Hill 60 to east of Ploegsteert Wood. During this time the enemy blew a number of mines and camouflets, thereby interrupting the work of the British companies, but all the difficulties were overcome and finally all was ready for the big 'blow'. This was to precede the artillery barrage by a fraction and then the main attack by General Plumer's II Corps was to follow. The Inspector of Mines watched the explosion from a dugout at Kemmel and he described the scene in his diary as the nineteen mines, containing nearly 1,000,000lbs of high explosive, erupted on June 7, 1917:

'3.10 a.m. A violent earth tremor, then a gorgeous sheet of flame from Spanbroekmolen, and at the same moment every gun opened fire. At short intervals of seconds the mines continued to explode; period which elapsed between first and last mine, about 30 seconds. I found it difficult to concentrate on looking for the mines, there was so much going on, and the scene, which baffles description, developed so quickly that my attention was distracted. . . . The earth shake was remarkable, and was felt as far as Cassel.'

The New Zealand Division captured Messines and the 16th and 36th Irish Divisions captured Wytschaete. By June 10 the German salient west of Messines and Wytschaete had been straightened south from the east of Hill 60.

In 1918 Messines changed hands several times before it was finally captured on September 29 by the 30th, 31st and 34th Divisions clearing the entire ridge.

Messines Church can be seen from far and wide and from it there is an expansive panorama to the south. The only church in the area with a crypt, this was all that was left of the building and in it today can be seen vestiges of the battle. The church was also the subject of a number of water-colour drawings by a German infantryman, one Adolf Hitler.

As our road runs into the village there is a sharp left-hand turning, along which is the **New Zealand Memorial Park**. In the park a

Messines church, showing the windows of the crypt. The crypt provided a billet at one time for Corporal Adolf Hitler.

The New Zealand Memorial on Messines Ridge, captured on September 29, 1918 by the 30th, 31st and 34th Divisions.

One of a pair of German bunkers in the New Zealand Memorial Park.

white monument (similar in design to that at s'Graventafel) rises between the evergreen trees and shrubs. At the edge of the park, overlooking the Douve valley and the hills of Flanders, are **two German pillboxes**—part of the Messines line of defence. It is normally possible to enter one of them, but often the other is full of water.

The **Hôtel de Ville of Messines** is in a red brick house overlooking the wide square with its English-looking bandstand on the right of the main road to Ypres. In the Hôtel de Ville is a small but excellent **war museum** which commemorates the actions of the New Zealanders in particular, but also those of the Australians and the London Scottish. It was

The London Scottish Memorial, Wytschaete Road, Messines.

Four Huns Dugout on 'Whitesheet' Road.

the work of the then-Mayor, the late Dr. Lambelin, OBE, the Town Clerk and the local schoolmaster, M. Constandt. It is usually open during office hours in the summer. A short distance to the north on the Ypres road, on the right-hand side, is a **Memorial to the London Scottish** and a little further on **Four Huns Dugout** bunker on the left.

Take the Wulvergem road to the left on leaving Messines and, just before the road drops down into the valley, the **Messines Ridge British Cemetery** and the **New Zealand Memorial to the Missing** is on the left. The New Zealand memorial is a Cross of Sacrifice and around the base the panels bear the names of all those with no known grave from every regiment and corps of the New Zealand Expeditionary Force. In the cemetery is a pavilion similar to the New Zealand memorial at Polygon Wood.

After 4 kms, **Wulvergem** is reached after sweeping down the valley and over the **Kraaienberg** and then down again. The village was close to the front line in 1914 and was on the receiving end of a gas attack in 1916. In 1918 it was overwhelmed in the German spring advance but recaptured in September.

The Dranoutre road rises out of the Douve valley and along the undulating slopes of the **Monts des Flandres**, crossing the road direct to Kemmel (2 kms from Wulvergem). After another 2 kms, turn right on to a smaller road to begin the climb up to the western slope of **Mount Kemmel**.

In 1 km crossroad, continue straight ahead when in 1 km the road forks. Take the right fork and then, almost immediately at the crossroad, take the right-hand turn to climb steeply up to the summit of Kemmel, passing the **French Ossuary** on the right just prior to the final steep fifty metres. The mass grave set amid the trees, with the Gallic cock crowing above, is the last resting place of 5,294 unknown French soldiers.

At the summit of Mount Kemmel is the **French Memorial**. This site, 159 metres high, was chosen for the monument to the Frenchmen who died in Belgium, particularly on the Mount in 1918.

The column is 18 metres high and was originally capped with a stone representation of a poilu's helmet crowned with laurel. In the front of the column is a Winged Victory. The memorial was unveiled in September 1932 by General Petin. During a thunderstorm a few years ago, the pillar was hit by lightning and damaged. When it was re-erected the helmet was not replaced. The memorial stands in a clearing on the thickly wooded summit. As we drive on we pass the entrance to the **Belvedere Hôtel**, the Hostellerie Mont Kemmel, from where there is a magnificent view across to Neuve Eglise and the Douve valley.

Emerging from the trees into the open, the **Café Belvedere** is found on the right. This café has been rebuilt on the site of the original one which was destroyed in the battles of 1918. On

The New Zealand Memorial to the Missing and the Messines Ridge British Cemetery.

The French Ossuary on the slopes of Mount Kemmel.

The French Memorial unveiled by General Petin on the crest of the Mount.

April 25 the French division then holding the line was dislodged by a strong German force using air support. From the **look-out tower**, one can see the same view as was had by Sir John French and other senior officers of the British army during their long occupation. The hill remained in German hands, a constant and dire threat to Allied communications, until the end of August and the advance of the American 27th Division; on August 31 the British 34th Division finally drove the Germans from it. On the walls of the café are some rather interesting old prints and photographs of before and after the battles.

The road descends steeply for another 500 metres when it comes to a junction where we turn left. The descent is less steep but goes on for a kilometre into the village of **Kemmel**, passing the entrance to **Warande Château** (now an hotel). On the village green will be seen another **bandstand**. Here the military bands of the British Army, including the Brigade of Guards, played to the troops during lulls in the fighting in this area.

The **Kemmel information office** is on the right just before the road junction where we turn right and continue straight over the next crossroads (a dangerous one).

In 2 kms pass through **Vroilanhoek**. Take the second road on the right to reach the largest of the 1917 mine craters. **Spanbroekmolen**, now the **Pool of Peace** the property of Toc H. In 1930, Lord Wakefield purchased this, the **Lone Tree Crater**, at the suggestion of Tubby Clayton who thought that one of the huge craters should be preserved. The pool has a rim some 4 metres deep; it is 27 metres in depth, with a diameter of 129 metres. The charge used was 91,000lbs of ammonal which had been laid through a tunnel 513 metres long. On the northern side of the lip is the remains of one of the German pillboxes and from here one can get a good idea of its importance with a wide field of fire and view.

Away to the right, in the direction of the road, can be seen groups of tall trees. As the crossroads of **Kruistraat** is reached, it will be realised that these trees surround three more mine craters. Turn left here and then left again along a narrow road which will pass the lane up to **Spanbroekmolen Cemetery** and, just out of view as the road regains the main

Above: **Belvedere Café, Mount Kemmel, is on the site of the original building destroyed in 1918. It provided a perfect observation post for Sir John French.**

Above: **Kemmel village green was the location of several British army band concerts.**

Above: **Spanbroekmolen, the Pool of Peace. This was the Lone Tree Crater of June 1917.** *Below:* **The edge of one of the Maedelstede Farm craters.**

Kruistraat's two craters provide excellent fishing today.

Peckham Crater, Wytschaete Ridge—from here King George V viewed the battlefront in July 1917 (IWM).

As near as can be ascertained, this is the same spot today. Dr. Caenepeel stands in for King George.

road for Wytschaete, the smaller crater of the **Peckham mine crater** is on the right. This is the one visited by King George V in July 1917.

Turn right for Wytschaete and after ½ km, on the left is the site of **Maedelstede Farm** and another large crater.

Wytschaete (Wijtschate) is entered 1 km further on with the **16th Irish Division Memorial Cross** on the left just before the cemetery. 'Whitesheet' to the Tommies is on a high ridge, even higher than that of Messines in places. In 1914 the village changed hands at least three times before the Germans captured it and began to convert it into a formidable fortress. In the II Corps attack of June 1917, the 16th and 36th Division captured the ruins. Among the casualties was Major William Redmond who was mortally wounded and taken to the divisional dressing station at Dranoutre and then to 36th Division Dressing Station nearby, where he died. His body was then taken to the hospice, which was the base of 16th Irish Division, and he was buried in the garden. Now his grave is beyond the walls of the convent, just outside the Locre military cemetery. Wytschaete was lost again in the spring advance of 1918, being recaptured on September 28.

Turn left in the centre of the village, leaving the church on the right, and in 1½ kms across the ridge at the fork in the road; take the right-hand route to pass through **Grand Bois** and then on the right is **Bois 40** or **Croonart Wood** to the Germans. There is a small **trench museum** here where two German bunkers are now reached by some recently renovated trenches. The owner claims the presence of Adolf Hitler in the complex in 1917 and that he returned in 1940 to view the wood.

Crossing the Bollartbeek at the bottom of the slope, and keeping to the right at the next fork, in about 3 kms **Voormezele** is reached. This village was just behind the British line at St Eloi and was captured after very heavy fighting in April 1918. The ruins were recaptured by the American 30th Division on August 31.

At the road junction turn right, and after 1 km **Bus House Cemetery** is passed on the right. It was named after an estaminet, originally on the same side of the road, but which was later moved to the north side. The café had got its name from an old London omnibus of the 'B' type which had broken down in no man's land after bringing troops to the front in 1914. Legend has it that it was one of those used by the London Scottish.

In 250 metres we reach **St Eloi** (St Eloois).

A small trench museum can be seen in Bois Quarante, called Croonart Wood by the Germans. It was here that Adolf Hitler was reputed to have fought, and where he returned in 1940.

The 16th Irish Division Memorial above Wytschaete village—'Whitesheet' to the Tommies.

The grave of Major W. Redmond just outside Locre Hospice Cemetery. He died in the convent nearby.

A group of British concrete shelters on the site of Langhof Château.

The ruins of Rosendael Château in the grounds of Bedford House Cemetery.

Turn left and after 1 km cross the **old canal** at the western end of **Kingsway**. A **Demarcation Stone** with a British tin hat capstone will be seen on the left.

A few metres farther up on the right is **Langhof Farm** with its fine cluster of British dugouts on the island site of the old château. These shelters are not open for inspection as they are utilised by the farmer for his cattle.

Two hundred metres further on is **Bedford House Cemetery**. It is one of the largest in the Salient and has plots of 1939-45 graves as well as 1914-18. The ruins of the old **Rosendal Château** and its moats remain as integral parts of the cemetery. The drive is, in fact, in the same place.

Ypres is another 3 kms; we enter by the Lille Gate.

The road south

From Ypres to the French frontier at Le Bizet. The direct route is via the N69 and Messines, a distance of 19 kms. Via Neuve Eglise it is 21 kms.

Depart Ypres via Lille Gate; at **Shrapnel Corner** take the right fork immediately before the level crossing. Another level crossing is found directly after turning. **Ypres military barracks** are on the left—note the artillery pieces in grounds. Cross the dry canal in whose banks are remnants of trenchworks. The road travels through pretty country, firstly quite flat but gradually, as Kemmel is approached, the landscape becomes more hilly as the Monts de Flandres are traversed.

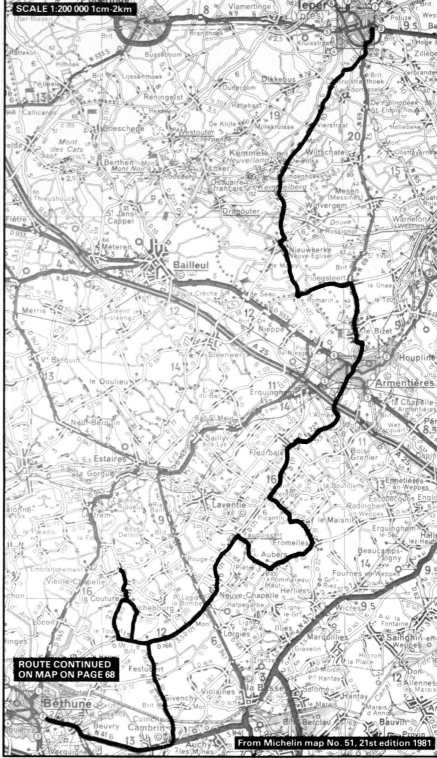

ROUTE CONTINUED ON MAP ON PAGE 68

From Michelin map No. 51, 21st edition 1981

Elzenwalle Château, an HQ in both wars.

After the crossroads of Kruistraathoek (4 kms), on the right **Elzenwalle Château**, an unusual construction of reinforced concrete with an open-ribbed dome. The lodge house is in the form of a concrete bunker, not unlike that of the Krönprinz in the Verdun area. Behind the château is **Scottish Wood** and beyond that lies **Dickebush Lake** (Dikkebus). As the road rises to Vierstraat crossroads, another well known copse comes into view, again on the right—**Ridge Wood**.

Shortly, on the left, is the **American Memorial to the 27th and 30th Divisions** who fought with the British Army in this region in 1918. The memorial was erected in 1930. There are fine views of the Wytschaete Ridge and the wooded slopes. This section of the road was known as **York Road** and was much used for bringing up supplies. Six km further

Wytschaete church crowns the ridge as seen from the American Memorial.

The Memorial to the US 27th and 30th Divisions near Wytschaete. Both fought with the British army in this area in 1918.

on the edge of Kemmel is reached; we continue straight on up to reach the next crossroad, **Lindenhoek**.

In 4 kms we reach **Neuve Eglise (Nieuwkerk)**. This village, a junction of many roads, was the scene of fierce fighting in April 1918 when it changed hands several times being defended by an exhausted 25th Division who were finally driven out on April 14. The British recaptured it on September 1.

At the T-junction turn right and, on reaching the main square overlooked by the church, turn left. The road soon begins to drop down into the Armentières-Bailleul plain with views of the Rodeberg, Mont Noir and Mont de Cats over to the right. Straight over the next crossroad. At the road junction 3 kms further on turn left for **Ploegsteert** which is 2 kms down the road. At the main crossroad in Ploegsteert turn right. The frontier station at **Le Bizet** is 2½ kms away.

Proceed into **Armentières** by the new road, D22a, sweeping behind the old road and through new residential areas. At the junction with D33, turn left into **Place Général de Gaulle** with the gothic-style town hall and **war memorial** on the left.

Armentières was, and is now again, a flourishing industrial town whose industries are centered around both brewing and linen manufacture. In 1914, the town was briefly occupied by the Germans before being recaptured by General Pulteney's III Corps on October 17. For the next three-and-a-half years, being just behind the lines, it became closely connected with the British Army for whom it was a forward base and recreation centre. Although it was intermittently bombed and shelled during these years, it was barely damaged. In the Battle of the Lys in April 1918, the German Fourth Army attacked and seized the town on the 10th after severe fighting. General Plumer's Second Army liberated the town on October 2. By then it was a heap of ruins for the Germans had mined or destroyed all the main buildings and wrecked the factories before leaving. During the British occupation the main square was called **Eleven O'clock Square**, as the hands of the Hôtel de Ville clock had stopped at this time during an early bombardment.

Leave Armentières via the rue de Lille and then the rue de Béthune, the D22, crossing the railway by the level crossing west of the station. Shortly afterwards the motorway is crossed by a bridge. Continue on the D22 bis 5 kms to **Fleurbaix**. The road passes through rather nondescript country—the scene of bitter fighting in 1916 and 1918. Continue on the D171 for 3 kms to **Petillon** crossroads passing **Rue de Bois Cemetery**. Here a diversion along the road to the left D175/22c leads in 1 km to **VC Corner Australian Memorial and Cemetery, Fromelles**. This is a very unusual graveyard as it has no headstones. The dead were brought here after the Armistice from the surrounding battle zone. On July 19, 1916 the 5th Australian Division with the 61st South Midland Division attacked the Fromelles positions. Over 400 lie buried with the names of 1,299 Australians recorded on the **Memorial to the Missing** on the panels between the shelters. This is one of the very few **British mass burial plots**.

Continue along the narrow road bearing left at the fork to reach **Fromelles** across the flat low-lying fields. Join D141 and turn right; in 2½ kms **Aubers** is passed through with its **ridge** away to the left. Go right on D41 for **Fauquissart**; the **Bois de Biez** is on the right. Thus the southern boundary of the battle area is crossed. Rejoin D171 and turn left. South of Petillon the road follows closely the 1914-1915 front line and nearby some of the incidents of the 1914 Christmas Truce took place. The area was strongly contested but there is little remaining today to indicate the destruction and devastation which the countryside suffered other than the scattered fragments of bunkers. **Mauquissart**, yet another front line village, is to the east of the road as we approach **Neuve Chapelle** in 3 kms. This was the scene of the first major operation involving the Indian Corps when on October 27, 1914 this formation was responsible for retaking the village which had been captured earlier in the German advance. Later the Allies withdrew

The graceful Indian Memorial at La Bombe crossroads, Neuve Chapelle.

and, on March 10, 1915, the Battle of Neuve Chapelle commenced with the Indian Meerut Division taking a major rôle in the attack and capture of the village by the 8th Division. Due to the inadequate preliminary bombardment, much of the barbed wire entanglements in front of the German positions remained uncut and caused heavy casualties, especially to the Middlesex Regiment and the Cameronians.

Neuve Eglise from the Kemmel road.

Armentières Grand Place. Today the Belfry clock keeps good time!

By March 14 the front had moved forward just over 2 kms before it stabilised. In the Lys battles of 1918, the Portuguese Division held the ruins of the village.

Another 1 km and we reach the crossroads of **La Bombe**, the **site of the Port Arthur Salient** of the Indian Corps in 1915. This fact is commemorated by the mention of it in the **café sign** on the right. On the opposite corner is the fine **Indian Memorial to the Missing**. Designed by Sir Herbert Baker in completely oriental style, 4,843 names are inscribed on the walls. A few yards down the D947 is the **Portuguese Military Cemetery** with its fine (if crumbling) Manueline gateway.

This road is the direct approach to **La Bassée** 6 kms away. Completely destroyed in the Allied bombardments, it had been taken by the Germans in 1914 and, heavily fortified, it formed an extremely strong bastion in their lines for over four years. It was taken by Fifth Army under Lord Birdwood on October 2, 1918. The town is once again a thriving industrial area and today it sprawls far outside its old boundaries. New roads have replaced the narrow busy ones of yore and recently a new ring-road has been instituted.

From Neuve Chapelle we remain on the D171 to **Richebourg l'Avoué**. As the **Indian**

VC Corner, Fromelles. Individuality is a cornerstone of British and Commonwealth principles in honouring war dead. Although this mass grave in the Australian Memorial Cemetery is very unusual, the names of each are inscribed in stone.

Memorial is passed a **private memorial** will be seen outside the wall. This is to the memory of 2nd Lieutenant Cyril A. W. Crichton who died on these crossroads in March 1915 and now lies buried in **Le Touret British Cemetery**, reached in 3½ kms of rather uninteresting angular road. It was just behind the front of the Indian Corps in May 1915 in the battles of Festubert and Aubers Ridge. The cemetery dates from 1914 and the **Memorial to the Missing** is for those who fell in the battles of La Bassée, Neuve Chapelle, Aubers Ridge and Festubert in 1914-15. The memorial was dedicated at the same time and day as those at Cambrai, Pozières and Vis-en-Artois in August 1930.

Just beyond the cemetery a small road to the right leads to Richebourg village outskirts and a left turn at the junction with the D170 brings one to **La Couture**. In front of the church is the unusual **Portuguese Memorial**.

In the cemetery of the next village, **Vielle Chapelle**, near the D182-D172 crossroad, is a **memorial** for which I searched for many hours. It is that of the **1st King Edward's**

Above: **La Bombe crossroads, Neuve Chapelle, where 2nd Lieutenant Cyril Crichton was originally buried.** *Right:* **The memorial records his death on March 10, 1915.**

The Portuguese Military Cemetery records that country's actions in 1917 and 1918.

The almost-forgotten cavalry memorial at Vielle Chapelle. Once standing in the village, the 1st King Edward's Horse obelisk is now to be found in the village churchyard.

Horse (The King's Overseas Dominions Regiment), a cavalry unit of the Special Reserve whose squadrons were used as divisional cavalry from early 1915 until in June 1916 they became a corps cavalry regiment. They served throughout the war in France and Flanders and were, I have always heard, a wild, hard-riding bunch. Their memorial was erected in the village after the war but with the changes in the road network and the widening that has occurred, it was moved for safety into the village cemetery . . . and almost forgotten. Return to Le Touret via the D169, noting the house on the corner at the junction. The primitive sculpture of Foch which surmounts it is just one of the examples of the work of an artist who lived here once. Bas reliefs of French and Belgian leaders are above the front door and windows, and along the garden wall a hunter seeks his prey.

Turn left and at l'Epinette take the D166 on the right for Festubert 2 kms away. Festubert figured conspicuously in the October 1914 battles, in which the Indian Corps participated with Smith Dorien's II Corps, and later in the attacks on Aubers Ridge, May

9-26, 1915. In 1918 the defence of Festubert and Givenchy in April checked the German advance in the Battle of the Lys. By then the village had been reduced to heaps of rubble (as had most of the neighbouring villages).

On the left-hand side of the D166 (after passing Festubert church), is a British blockhouse and bunker. It has two chambers and an outside shelter and is, in fact, the end of a light railway and the bunker was a ration point and officers' dugout. From January 1919 until the early seventies it was occupied by a Frenchwoman who said it made an ideal home.

Another 2 kms to Givenchy. This small village was in the thick of the battles and the scene of frequent fighting. It played a vital part in the retreat in April 1918. The crossroads just before the village was the famous Windy Corner and is commemorated by the Guards Cemetery.

Cross the La Bassée Canal and enter Cuinchy. Another front line village completely destroyed, it is reached after crossing the La Bassée canal. In January 1915, there was very heavy fighting here around the Brickstacks. There is a Guards Memorial and, here and there, craters can still be discerned in this much fought over area.

One km further on is Cambrin, a straggling industrial village. At the junction with the main road, the N41, turn right for Béthune, 8 kms away.

The Portuguese Corps Memorial to be seen at La Couture.

Le Touret Military Cemetery. The Memorial to the Missing is for all those who died at La Bassée, Neuve Chapelle, Aubers Ridge and Festubert in 1914-15.

Béthune. The ancient seat of the Counts of Flanders was fortified by Vauban in the 17th Century. The graceful Belfry, now standing in the centre of the Grand Place, was built in 1346. Most of the houses around the square have been rebuilt in the style of Flanders but those which originally clustered around three sides of the Belfry have not been replaced. As the centre of the mining villages and market gardens which abound in the locality, Béthune was a thriving town in 1914. For the next four years it was a most important British headquarters town subjected to intermittent bombardment between 1915 and 1918.

From 1914 to 1915 the Indian Corps held the town which became an important railhead and billeting area for the rear lines, besides being a corps and divisional headquarters. In the German offensive of April 1918 a particularly heavy bombardment almost destroyed the town. The great church of **St. Waast** was a mere pile of ruins but the **Belfry** bore a charmed existence as only the top was dislodged, even the well-known gargoyles surviving intact. The top has been replaced in almost identical form but the great doors on the ground floor have been replaced with glass. In 1918 the 3rd, 51st and 55th Divisions successfully held the town which only partially fell to the Germans. The town was damaged

At Festubert this British blockhouse, once a ration point and officers' shelter provided a comfortable home for a local resident from 1919 until her recent death.

The houses surrounding the Belfry in Bèthune were all destroyed.

again in 1939-45. The **town museum**, currently housed in temporary quarters near the Gendarmerie, is hoping to open a section relating to the 1914-1918 period and, in particular, the long occupation by the BEF.

Leave via N41 which joins the N43 in 3 kms. The road crosses the plain dotted with mines and slag heaps, traversing the southern sector of the **Loos battlefield** which lies between the N43 and D947 (the old main road from La Bassée) and the new N47. The D947 can be reached from Loos by the D165 just on the north of **Hill 70**. Now there is a civil airfield and an enormous hypermarket on this part of the old battlefield whilst vestiges of the mine craters and trenches can still be discerned to the west of the hill.

In 10 kms, we reach **Dud Corner Cemetery** and **Loos Memorial to the Missing** who fell in the Battle of Loos in September/October 1915, and on the Lys, Estaires and Béthune fronts in April 1918. The names are recorded of 20,589 officers and men who fell during these actions. Among those commemorated here is the son of Rudyard Kipling (on the panel of the Irish Guards).

The Battle of Loos, September 25 to October 13, 1915, was fought by the British I and IV Corps in support of Joffre's offensive in Champagne. It is remembered today as the battle in which very heavy casualties were suffered by only partially trained troops and for the first use of poison gas by the British.

From the roofs of the two pavilions of the memorial entrance, a good view of the battlefield can be gained. It is also possible on a fine day to glimpse in the distance, north of Hulloch (on the D947), the site of the **Höhenzollern Redoubt**, one of the strongly defended German positions taken by British divisions.

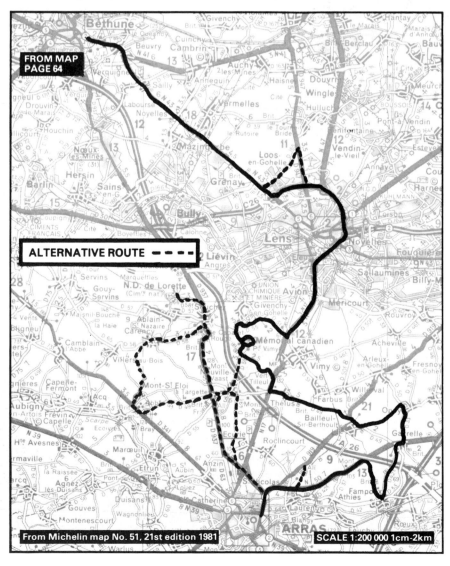

The Loos battlefield photographed from Dud Corner in 1975. British troops first used poison gas here in 1915.

The Loos Memorial to the Missing at the Dud Corner Cemetery, commemorating 20,000 British officers and men.

Continue for 4½ kms to **Lens**. This was the chief coal-mining town in France before the war almost entirely destroyed it. Now once more it is a thriving town and industrial area. Many of the mines are still working although the famous pit-head winding towers, so well known to the Tommy, are fast disappearing from the coalfield which stretches from Hulloch in the north to Avion in the south.

The Germans occupied Lens in October 1914 and, thereafter, set about fortifying it very strongly. It became the centre of a war fought from the warren of tunnels at many levels beneath the shell-torn ground. In August 1917 an Allied attack was launched from the north-west suburbs and Hill 70. The Canadian Corps forced their way through on a 2,000 yard front but the central part of the town held out. In spite of further attacks in September 1917 and January 1918, it was not until October 2 that the ruins were captured.

The Höhenzollern Redoubt today. This was a formidable German strongpoint with underground galleries, dugouts and trenches protected by thick belts of barbed wire.

The Spirit of Canada weeps for her fallen countrymen. From Vimy Ridge the view extends over the Douai plain towards Messines. The twin pillars of the Memorial stand on the summit of Hill 145.

Lens is a very busy industrial town with complicated road systems so it is probably easier to join the C26 autoroute and proceed to the south-east following the signs for Arras and so bypass the traffic-choked streets.

After 6 kms, at **Noyelles**, the Arras road becomes the N17 but for the first 3 kms it is of motorway style. Soon after the complex of the Union Chimique et Minière at Avion the road swings in a curve before the old road converges with it again below **Vimy Ridge**, thus providing a panoramic view of the twin pillars of the **Canadian Memorial** rising high above the wooded slopes of **Hill 145**.

In 7 kms, at the Vimy-Givenchy-en-Gohelle crossroad, turn right onto D51 to the latter. This straight road crosses the cornfields beneath the escarpment giving more fine vistas. The road now climbs up through **Givenchy** passing a **concrete dugout**—a German tunnel entrance to the subways tunnelled out by the men of both armies and by others in more ancient times. The largest of all, the **Vimy Cavern** was, in fact, mined out by Hugenots and chalk-burners many centuries ago. It was used for defensive purposes in the 18th and 19th Centuries and by refugees from various factions fighting to gain the supremacy of Arras.

The view from the esplanade of the **Canadian Memorial** is extensive—the Scarpe valley, the Lens minefields to the north and to the west Notre Dame de Lorette and Souchez. On a clear day the Messines Ridge can be discerned over the slag heaps.

In October 1916 the Royal Engineers commenced the construction of the tunnels which were sufficient to house large concentrations of troops on the Allied slopes of the ridge. Later, Australian and Canadian tunnelling

The shell-pocked Memorial Park photographed in March 1976—a battlefield preserved and owned in perpetuity by Canada.

Canadian trenches lead to Grange Tunnel subway.

The old German front line, surrounded by mine craters.

companies completed the work which finally amounted to more than twenty-two miles of subways on four distinct levels. The top level is some twenty to twenty-five feet underground, the next 75 feet and the other two at various levels beneath that. On the lowest floor is a narrow-gauge railway still, it is believed, carrying the small trucks used for moving ammunition. Fairly steep gradients bring the line up to higher levels in a few places. The Germans on their side were equally busy.

Mining operations had begun in 1915 by the French, being continued by the Germans and later the British. There are still relics of their work and many craters are to be seen in the 240-acre park owned by Canada. This was a gift from the French Government and is under the management of the Canadian Battlefield Memorials Commission (for whom the CWGC undertake the maintenance and gardening work).

Twelve infantry subways, each averaging half-a-mile with several more than a mile in length, were constructed by the 172nd, 176th, 182nd and 185th Tunnelling Companies, Royal Engineers, under the command of Lieutenant-Colonel G. C. Williams, Controller of Mines, First Army. In the period October 1916 to March 1917, over six miles of tunnels were dug, 6ft 6ins high and 3ft wide, lit throughout by electric light. Small lighting plants were installed in each subway and operated by the Australian Electrical and Mechanical Mining and Boring Company. Canadian tunnelling companies continued operations in the spring of 1917.

In the labyrinth were constructed assembly chambers, brigade and battalion headquarters, dressing stations, accommodation for men, trench mortar and bomb stores, signal offices, etc. Water supplies were laid on, signal cables connected up throughout and narrow-gauge railways laid. Numerous entrances and exits were provided, some for the railways (which linked up with the exterior tramways) for bringing up supplies and for evacuating wounded. Ventilation shafts provided excellent air-conditioning, the only difficulty being the risk of gas attacks when this good air flow increased the danger.

The tunnel system proved most useful and almost bomb-proof. Here and there large shells did penetrate to the first level, and one remains in situ today. Only the entrances required continuous attention and a repair gang was kept in each main subway for this purpose by the tunnelling companies.

Long before the great memorial was unveiled by King Edward VIII on July 26, 1936, work began on the preservation of the battlefield under the eye of Colonel A. F. Duguid, DSO, RCA. The front line trenches were preserved with concrete sandbags and duck-boards which today look very artificial because of their very neatness. However the sectors do follow the right lines and do provide the visitor with an inkling of the horrors which they held. At the rear of the German part of the line is a pillbox and entrance. A large German trench mortar, found within the confines of the park, has been set up and other weapons are scattered around. On the Canadian side a short length of supporting trench has been left in its natural state. The closeness between the two front lines is clearly indicated across the mine craters.

From the concrete trenches it is only a short distance to the entrance of the tunnel which is open for public inspection during the summer months. The guides are usually Canadian students. This tunnel is **Grange Tunnel** and was re-opened for visitors in 1926 by Captain Unwin Simson, Royal Canadian Engineers. Originally it was nearly 800 yards in length, with many offshoots and three exits near the 'jumping off' trenches. Grange Tunnel was completed and occupied by the 7th Canadian Infantry Brigade. The visitor can see the guard rooms, the cook house, the hospital and ammunition dumps, the general's quarters with many items of equipment lying about, including the disintegrating bed said to have been used by the general himself. The lower levels are indicated but only two of the upper levels are visited during the tour. Some of the damage done by the occupying forces in the Second World War can be seen and more recent construction to reinforce the original work of the tunnellers. At present no part of the German complex is open to visitors as much of it has flooded.

As the visitor arrives from Givenchy, the **French Memorial** commemorating the Moroccan troops who fought here with distinction in 1915 is seen on the right at the roundabout. Swing round to the left, the road behind the memorial being a one-way system as it cleaves across the shell-pocked park. A large car park is provided on the right. Here on the wall flanking the toilets is a bronze map of the battlefield. Access to the memorial is via the footpaths commencing beneath the two tall flagpoles from which the Canadian and French national flags fly. Take a look at the enchanting beavers at the bases of the poles. Beyond the car park is the Superintendent's house and office.

The circuit of the hill provides more excellent views over the **Douai Plain**. There are more car parks at the lower level to which we make our way, passing the memorial and back to the roundabout having passed a German bunker on the right. Proceed southward to take the second road to the left (a detour along the narrow road to the right will take you to two of the cemeteries in the park through acres of shell-holes and wooded enclosure) to visit the trenches and Grange Tunnel. The approach road runs below part of the line of mine craters, many blown in 1915-16, and it too is set off with trees. Driving or walking through the park, the visitor will see many wired off enclosures with small notices attached to the wires. Almost all are planted with fir trees and are definitely *not* for exploration, the signs make it obvious that danger lurks amid the pines and often rusting shells and grenades come to light as the region has not

PHOTO TAKEN MARCH 1976

GERMAN FRONT LINE

CANADIAN FRONT LINE

GRANGE TUNNEL ENTRANCE

TUNNEL EXIT

Grange Tunnel. Debris in a connecting gallery with upper floors.

A rather dangerous-looking disused entrance to the tunnel.

A first aid post gallery full of battlefield debris.

The village memorial at La Targette to those Frenchmen who died in 1916.

Trenches and craters surround the 'battlefield' cemeteries of Canadian No. 2 (top), and Givenchy Road (lower left) on Vimy Ridge.

been cleared. The areas of the park which can be explored are clearly defined and indicated by other notices and well-worn paths and the beautiful close-clipped cratered areas where, frequently, a flock of sheep can been observed doing their bit to aid the Commission gardeners.

Beside the entrance to Grange Tunnel and the preserved trench system is a small building housing the Guides' office (and toilets). Here it is possible to purchase postcards and pamphlets on the Canadian memorials. *Canada on Vimy Ridge* is a reprint from the Canada Yearbook of 1936 giving a useful

description by Colonel Duguid of the 1917 operations and after, with an excellent map. The visitor should be wary of walking in the trenches as the concrete duck-boards are lethal to anyone wearing high heels.

The narrowness of no man's land on this section of the front is extremely well demonstrated as on either side of **Winnipeg Crater** stands a sign indicating the front line. The long swerve of the craters can be observed from this point in both directions. To the left they arc up towards Hill 145, to the right they swing down to **Folie Farm**. The site of the farm is marked by a cross. Visitors are asked

to remember that the whole park is a memorial; picnics are not allowed among the shell-holes and neither are games.

One way to leave the park is by the road above the trench sector; this skirts the southern limits of the park and joins the N25 1 km north of Thélus crossroads. The other road away from the park is the D55 to Neuville St Vaast. In recent years the aspect of the countryside around Vimy Memorial Park has changed considerably due to the advent of the Calais autoroute which cuts across north of Arras. This is now crossed before entering **Neuville St Vaast**. A side road to the left leads to **Lichfield Crater**, one of two cemeteries where there are no separate graves as all fell together in the explosions. The men were all killed on April 9 or 10, 1917. The other is **Zivy Crater** which is just below the bridge which crosses the A26. Access to it is from the D49 to the east, a spur off the old road being maintained for it. The names of 48 Canadian soldiers who perished here with 5 unknown comrades are engraved below the Cross of Sacrifice.

Neuville St Vaast was completely destroyed in 1915-16. In the centre of the village take the D49 to the right to reach the D937 in 1 km at **La Targette**. **A large memorial** of unusual

A neat patchwork of graves in the huge French Cemetery at Neuville St Vaast with the British Cemetery at the top left-hand corner.

Zivy Crater Cemetery—here lie those who died in the act of blowing the mine.

design and dimensions stands at the crossroads. The huge hand holding aloft a torch is seen through a gateway bearing the inscription 'Cité des Mutilés'. It commemorates the destruction of the village in the mining operations by the French on May 9, 1916. Beneath the whole region are caverns and subways and, for many years until they became unsafe, there was a famous complex which formed part of the **Maison Blanche sector** which was reached from an entrance at the crossroad. Entombed in these caverns are many fine carvings made by the Canadians and others who were billeted in them from 1916 onwards. A short distance up the road is a farm which stands above another of these caverns. Opposite the farm is the huge **German Cemetery** of Neuville St Vaast containing 36,792 graves. There are also large French and British cemeteries in the village.

Turn right on to the D937 and travel 4 kms to **Souchez**. The French fought a fierce action here in June 1915. On the left, before descending the hill, is **Caberet Rouge Cemetery** and the **Indian Memorial**.

Continue up the hill and take the left turn, the D58e, to **Notre Dame de Lorette** 3 kms further on. At the corner by the junction is a **private museum** which is open in the spring and summer and certain weekends before and after the main season. It records mainly the French operations of 1915. An old legend declares the victor in any way in Flanders and Picardy will be the conqueror of the range of hills which culminate in the crest of Notre Dame de Lorette. A chapel stood on the eastern spur of the ridge which was won by the French after heavy fighting in May 1915. Today the **French National Memorial and Cemetery** crown the ridge, the site of the old chapel being marked by a simple stone. The cemetery covers 26 acres. A lighthouse tower, 52 metres high, and a chapel are the dominant features. In the top of the tower is a searchlight which shines all night rotating 360 degrees. From the tower magnificent views of all the surrounding countryside can be had. There is a museum within the lower floors of the tower which contains some interesting items. Between the tower and the chapel is a perpetual flame. The chapel is famous for its stained glass windows, some of which were presented by the British Commonwealth. In the crypt below are the remains of tens of thousands of dead.

Return to the D937 and Souchez. The direct route to Arras is 13 kms. A detour (7 kms) to include a visit to **Mont St Eloi** can be made by taking the D58 to **Clarency** and then, after passing through this village, taking the left fork onto an unclassified road.

Mont St Eloi was the site of an Augustinian

It was only recently that the huge German cemetery at Neuville St Vaast was landscaped and transformed from its 1918 appearance. *Above:* This is how it appeared in 1958, still with the original wooden crosses and identification discs. *Below:* Note that following general German practice, graves are now marked in pairs.

The Notre Dame de Lorette French National Memorial and Cemetery. Apart from 20,000 individual graves, another 20,000 unknown lie in the Ossuary.

The still-ruined towers of the abbey at Mont St Eloi overlook the site of the old Royal Flying Corps aerodrome.

All is quiet now at Fampoux where so many from the Seaforth Highland Battalion were cut down in the battles of 1917 and 1918. Their memorial stands to record their sacrifice.

abbey in the 7th Century but the famous ruined towers are from the 17th Century. They were all but destroyed by German artillery fire in 1914 and used by Foch's army in 1915 as an observation post. It is possible, but not advised, to climb the ancient stairs to see the view. In the valley below the village was the **RFC aerodrome of St Eloi**.

Continue via the D49 to La Targette (4 kms), and thence via the D937 to Arras (8 kms). A quieter road than this highway can be taken from Neuville St Vaast. It is the D49e and goes down the slopes of the back of Vimy ridge to **Ecurie**, once a Canadian base. It enters Arras via the suburb of St Nicholas.

Leaving Vimy via the N17, going south to Thélus, turn left when you reach the crossroads onto the D49. The **Canadian Artillery Memorial** here was built and unveiled a year to the day after the capture of Vimy Ridge. General Byng performed the ceremony on April 9, 1918. The South African Heavy Artillery Battery, who also participated, are remembered on the plaque. The memorial stands directly over a dugout, the entrance for which was under the steps in front. **Thélus** village is about ½ km from here. It was of course involved in the 1917-18 operations being captured by the 1st Canadian Division on April 9, 1917. A little to the east along our road is the **British Cemetery** and nearby vestiges of trenches can be seen. In the fields beyond stands a lone cross on a stone cairn. This is the **1st Canadian Division's Memorial** which they erected at Christmas in 1917 in

memory of their several engagements between March and July 1917. Later there was further fighting over and under these wide fields as the Germans tried to force Arras in March 1918, but the sector held.

After 5 kms we reach **Bailleul Sir Berthault**—a German front line position stormed and captured by 51st Highland and 34th Divisions on April 13, 1917 after much heavy fighting. At the far side of the village take an unnumbered road to the left for **Oppy**, 3 kms.

The notorious **Oppy Wood** is on the right as the village is neared. In the years the German Army were in occupation of this village, they transformed it into one of the strongest forts on the Western Front and defied any attack to dislodge them. It was eventually captured by 8th Division with heavy losses on both sides as they evicted the enemy, trench by trench, in September 1918. Fighting in the vicinity had gone on for months and months. It was a sea of mud and destruction from bombardments, and many British battalions had endured periods in the line here—men of the Royal Fusiliers, several Home Counties regiments and the East Yorkshires to mention just a few. Often the trenches changed hands for brief periods and soon there was little of the old wood left. It is approached by various tracks but all are private. On the right is rather an unusual **memorial** with the wood as backdrop. Here the men of **Kingston upon Hull** are remembered with their comrades from the local area, including the son of the donor of

The Canadian Artillery Memorial at Thélus crossroads to the men who fell in the Vimy operations of April 1917.

At Christmastime 1917, men of the 1st Canadian Division erected this memorial to their comrades.

The Kingston upon Hull Memorial at Oppy Wood.

the land who died on the Somme in August 1918.

Continue across the 1917 battlefield on the D33 to **Gavrelle**. Here was the scene of the attack by 63rd Royal Naval Division on April 23, 1917 and their magnificent defence for many days thereafter through innumerable counter-attacks. It was held until 56th London Division, which put up a magnificent defence in March 1918, were overwhelmed on the 28th. The 51st Highland Division recaptured it on August 27 and it was occupied by 8th Division.

Turn left and almost immediately right onto D42e across the N50. The road traverses the 1917-18 battle zones and the motorway before reaching **Fampoux** in the Scarpe valley, yet another place of evil memory to both infantry and cavalry. With its neighbour **Rouex** it was the scene of extended fighting above and below ground. The deep subways were to play a similar role in 1940.

As the road drops into the village it joins another on the immediate right. It is a very tight turn but it leads up **York Road** of 1917 towards the **Seaforth Highlanders' Celtic Cross** and 4th Division's **Sunken Road Cemetery** on the crest of the ridge. The Scottish battalion was almost annihilated on these open plains in April 1917 in the operations between Rolincourt and Monchy, on which the Vimy Ridge attack depended upon for being a success. From the crest there is a fine view and ahead can be seen **Point de Jour** and its **cairn**—our next objective. To get there our road meets the N50 in the shadow of the motorway flyover and we go left towards Arras. After 1 km we arrive at the **9th Scottish Division's old HQ dugout**, now the memorial within a ring of barely discernable trenches. A protective barrier of granite boulders, each bearing the name of a unit of the division, is before the cairn. Nearby is the broken remains of a bunker. A **British Cemetery** is along the road on the left. Continue down into Arras 3 kms distant. Up to the right, on the first road, is the **German Cemetery** for the region and nearby are two **British Cemeteries** of the Roclincourt group, both on the D919.

'Remember with honour the 9th Scottish Division who on the fields of France, and Flanders 1915-1918 served well.'

ARRAS

The focal point of many wars in this region, the various occupying powers have each left their mark on this ancient city. Long before the Romans came and established a Legion here, there was a thriving Atrebates community here. By 863 it was part of Flanders, then the Normans came and sacked it. In the centuries thereafter the English, the French, the Austrians and the Spanish held sway for varying periods. In 1431 it was the era of Joan of Arc and she was imprisoned here for a while. Then, in 1541, the English and the Spaniards fought the French for the city. Between 1633 and 1707 the great Citadel was built on designs by Vauban. Marlborough was here in 1708, and Arras was also Robespierre's birthplace; his house can still be seen.

From September 18, 1914 Arras was occupied by the Germans but they were forced to retire by General Maud'huy and many fierce battles were fought with the French army holding on to the town against von Bulow. In the years which followed the 'boves', or **underground caves**, became an underground city. Above them the town was badly damaged and in ruins after the attacks of 1915. Arras suffered also from aerial bombardment, the heaviest raid being possibly that of November 10, 1916 when forty German machines raided the town. In the aerial battle which took place, six enemy machines were shot down.

Despite all, the French and British garrisons held on to the somewhat small salient which the city formed. The Battle of Arras began on April 9, 1917 with a British attack on a twelve-mile front from Givenchy-en-Gohelle in the north to Croissilles in the south. Four Canadian Divisions advanced against the Vimy Ridge with notable success and many prisoners and guns were captured in the first few days of the offensive as the Germans retreated towards Lens. Then followed a period of indecisive engagements, very costly to both sides with few gains or losses with a return to static warfare, until the German advance of March 1918. Von Bulow's army attacked toward Vimy but the British Third Army, after falling back to Feuchy and Neuville St Vaast, held the line.

North-west of Arras beside the N39, a trench runs like a phantom image across the fields—after 60 years of ploughing.

The 'Boves' of Arras. This is the corner of a large hall on the second level.

The entrance to one of the underground caves beneath the Grand Place.

British telephone wiring and terminals in a tunnel still remain.

Arras. Place d'Héros and Hôtel de Ville.

In 1940 the city was once more under seige when the British army was involved in a rearguard action. Among the last to leave were the Welsh Guards; at the end of August 1944, this regiment was one of the first to re-enter.

Today the city has been completely rebuilt. Among the notable buildings are the **Palais Saint Vaast**, a former Benedictine abbey, rebuilt in the 18th Century and again after its destruction in the war; **the cathedral**, a 17th Century edifice which was almost destroyed in the 1915 artillery bombardment, and the **Hôtel de Ville**. This beautiful building was entirely demolished by fire and bombardment but has been rebuilt in the original style of the 15th and 16th Centuries with more modern 19th Century wings. The Belfry, which was first completed in 1553 and which collapsed in October 1914, is now one of the most beautiful. There are various memorial plaques in the foyer and on the first floor and, on the exterior near the main entrance, is the modern **1939-44 Resistance Memorial**.

On the Faubourg d'Amiens in the **British Military Cemetery** and the **Arras Memorial to the Missing**, is a beautiful colonnade with the **RFC, RNAS and Royal Air Force Memorial** as a central monument. The Memorial records the 35,928 missing in the battles of Arras, Vimy Ridge, the Scarfe, and those of Arleux, Bullecourt and Hill 70 of 1917. The **Air Services Memorial** records all those missing on the Western Front. High up at the head of the panels are the names of Major Lanoe Hawker, VC, and Major E. Mannock, VC. The globe which surmounts the pillar is decorated with a flight of doves on the exact path of the sun on November 11, 1918. In the cemetery are over 2,600 graves.

By the side of the Memorial is a narrow road which leads to the moat of the Citadel and the extremely sombre **Mur des Fusilées** with its 200 plaques forming the memorial to the French patriots who were shot in this dismal place between July 1941 and July 1944. A solitary stone post stands where the execution post was sited. Remembrance services held here are extremely moving and simple.

A **museum** of the history of Arras is being created in the basement of the Hôtel de Ville and the adjacent complex of subways beneath the Place d'Héros. Much conservation work has been made to enable the public to see just what they were like. Opening times will be made known at the Hôtel de Ville.

The grimmest place in Arras—the Mur des Fusilées with its execution post and memorial plaques.

The combined Memorial to the Missing to those of the Royal Flying Corps, Royal Naval Air Service and Royal Air Force forms the centrepiece to the British Cemetery and Memorial to the Missing at Arras.

The story and legend of Captain Albert Ball, VC, DSO**, MC, is probably so well known that it is unnecessary to go into details here but it may be of interest to visit the scene of his fatal crash and final resting place whilst in this part of France. Perhaps the simplest route is to use the A1

autoroute between Arras and Lille, leaving it at the Carvin-Libercourt turn-off, and proceed westward on to the D954 to Carvin. In the centre of this busy town, turn right on D925 for a short distance and then left on the D163 reaching Annoeullin in 4 kms. Turn right soon after the road becomes D41b to join the D41 on the edge of Carnin, crossing the flat farmland on which the Germans had a small airfield. Turn left on D41c driving for ½ km. There is a solitary house on the left-hand side of the road and immediately after it a grass track is seen in the field. It is not suitable for cars and it is only a short walk to the place where the grey stone marker stands some 30 metres in front of a small copse. This appears to be a composite of the original erected by his father made from two of the original stones which indicated the place where the aircraft fell—the third has disappeared. Today it is watched over by those who have inherited the traditions he and his fellows built so many years ago in No. 60 Squadron—still alive and well in the modern RAF.

Although Annoeullin and the other towns and villages hereabouts have grown, the immediate area around here can have changed little over the years. Maybe the lanes have deteriorated into paths and tracks but there has been hardly any development between these small fields and copse and the German Cemetery. When the German airmen carried his body from the broken plane to lay him to rest, they traversed tracks which still cross the dull land to arrive at the cemetery entrance from the opposite end of the road used by cars. From the crash-site follow the D41c into Allennes lès Marais (1 km), and turn left for Annoeullin. After 1 km at the

crossroad (traffic lights), turn left and in 400 metres left again at the T-junction and follow the signs for the German Cemetery and the Communal Cemetery, bearing left off D41 onto a cul-de-sac. This is the road which 200 metres beyond the cemeteries peters out into the field track.

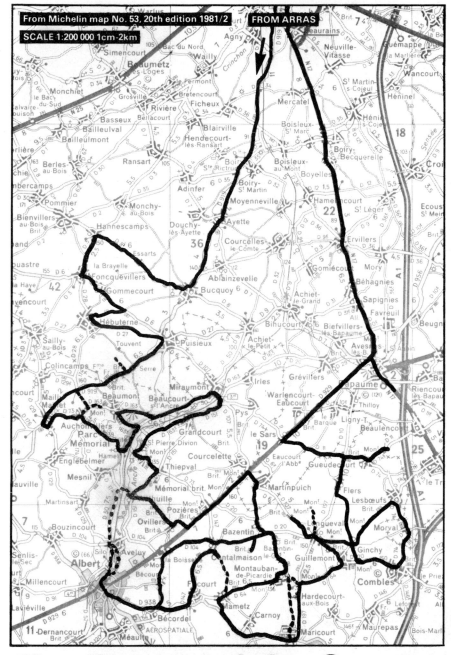

From Michelin map No. 53, 20th edition 1981/2
SCALE 1:200 000 1cm-2km

FROM ARRAS

wood and reached the outskirts of the village which did not completely come within our line until February 27, 1917. Not far from the village is the triangular-shaped **Bois de Riez** which was a landmark used by the RFC on patrol.

Taking the small road on the right, in less than a kilometre we reach **Hébuterne**, a British fortress village immediately behind the front line from which the 56th (London) Division attacked Gommecourt on July 1, 1916.

Now take the D27, the left-hand road to **Puisieux** (4 kms). This is an example of the many villages in this undulating country which were completely destroyed by artillery fire. It did not fall to the Allies until the spring of 1917 and by then it was merely a ruin.

Rejoin the D919 turning right for **Serre**, 2 kms. A little way out of the village is the **Memorial to the 12th Battalion York and Lancaster Regiment** on the right hand. The road drops down through a group of British and French cemeteries marking this area of very severe fighting on July 1, 1916. Here the 31st Division fought their way across the hilly country in a vain attempt to reach their objectives. They were mown down by hidden and well-placed machine gun nests or impaled on the barbed wire entanglements, supposedly cut up by the tremendous artillery bombardment preceeding the attack. Beside the farm on the right at the bottom of the hill a track leads up to a scattered group of small cemeteries, **Serre Road No. 3, Queens, Railway Hollow** and **Luke Copse**. This last was one of several hotly contested positions of which four were named after the Evangelists. **Sheffield Memorial Park** is a small enclosure on the reverse slope up which the British had to fight. Here a length of the front line trench and shell-cratered rear line is preserved around the shelter of the **Sheffield Memorial**. Away to the back of the crest of the hill **La Signy Farm** can just be seen. In between a clump of trees marks the site of **Basin Wood**, the casualty clearing station.

Back on the D919 **Serre Road No. 1 Cemetery** is just beyond the farm with the French one beside it and, further along on the left, the largest of the group—**Serre Road No. 2 Cemetery** with over 3,300 graves. On the roadside a **private memorial** is set on a grassy mound—the original wooden cross of the same design is preserved in the crypt of Winchester Cathedral.

In 1½ kms the crossroads at the top of the hill was once the site of the **sucrerie**, an important position in the British lines. Turn right for the direct route for Auchonvillers, but it is worth continuing on 2½ kms to **Mailly-Maillet**

The Battles of the Somme

The graceful entrance to the Indian and Chinese cemetery at Ayette, 16 kilometres south of Arras. Ayette was the scene of fierce battles in 1918.

Leave Arras by the D919. It is 12 kms to **Boiry** and another 4 kms to **Ayette**, scene of fierce fighting by 31st and 32nd Divisions in March and April 1918. It has a rather unusual **Indian and Chinese Cemetery**. We then reach **Bucquoy** 4 kms. This village was behind the German lines, providing a base and billeting area until it came within the range of British artillery. The village was captured in March 1917 and for a year was well known to the BEF. In the German spring advance, it was desperately defended by the 62nd Division after the first battle on March 26 by British Whippet light tanks.

Turn right in centre of village on to the D8 for **Hannescamps** (6 kms)—always behind the lines but heavily bombarded. Then left turn on the D3 2½ kms to **Foncquevillers**, in the lines from 1915-16 and badly damaged by artillery.

We then take the D6 road past **Gommecourt Wood**, 4 km to **Gommecourt** which was the Third Army front of July 1, 1916. The 46th North Midland Division attacked the

Above and below: Gommecourt Wood with vestiges of the trench lines which straddled the shattered treescape in 1916. After the desperate fighting of that July, Gommecourt fell almost peaceably during the German retreat in February 1917.

The church at Mailly-Maillet with its medieval doorway still intact. Its preservation during two particularly fierce bombardments in 1916 and 1918 owes much to its face being protected . . . and no doubt to the fact that the door faced west and the German shells came in from the east.

From the shelter of the **Sheffield Memorial** the view is down across the undulating ground of the former battlefield to Railway Hollow Cemetery.

Serre, scene of the 12th Bn. York and Lancaster Regiment's attack on July 1, 1916.

Sheffield Park with a sad memorial to Private A. E. Bull of the 12th Yorks and Lancs. Killed on this spot on July 1, 1916 his remains were not discovered until April 13, 1928, when they were buried in Serre No. 2 Cemetery.

Serre No. 1 British Cemetery—serried ranks of graves from the fighting in July 1916.

observing the fine views of the **Thiepval Ridge** to the east across the Ancre valley, to visit the village church to see the unexpected sight of a medieval west doorway preserved through the forethought of the curé who had it protected during the war. This village, as with all the others just behind the British lines, was a very busy place before July 1 and also, like its neighbours, had many underground tunnels in the quarries below it from which the material for building the houses was taken. These subways provided vital cover for the troops and, although no longer open to view, still retain carvings and graffiti on their walls.

Take the D73 for **Auchonvillers** 1 km beyond which is the **Newfoundland Memorial Park** entrance. Just before it a lane is signposted for **Hawthorn Ridge No. 1 Cemetery** near the clump of trees marking the site of the crater.

The D163 from Auchonvillers to Beaumont Hamel village passes through the valley behind the ridge—1 km on the left a lane runs up on to **Redan Ridge** and back to Serre. At one side is the **Memorial of the Argyll and Sutherland Highlanders** tucked under the slope and in the fields; on the other the small **Beaumont Cemetery**. Up the steep field on the right of the road, a pathway has been made up to the rim of **Hawthorn Ridge crater**, indicated by a multi-language signpost at the roadside. Although the crater is now filled with trees and bushes, the farmers having over the years tried to fill it in, a swathe has been cut down its precipitous side to show the depth. The crater was 150 yards in length, 100 yards wide and 80ft deep, 40,000lbs of ammonal being used to make it. The eruption was caught on film as it was prematurely exploded and is one of the best known and frequently screened examples of the 1914-18 cameraman's art.

Newfoundland Memorial Park covers more than 80 acres of which some 40 are in the sector of the Royal Newfoundland Regiment of 29th Division on July 1. The regiment was annihilated in the initial attacks following the explosion of the mine: being ten minutes too soon it was therefore occupied by the enemy.

At the entrance to the park is the **29th Division Memorial** and all around are the grass-covered trenches of the battlefield. All have been preserved as they were left in 1918 and, due to the fact that later battles did not alter them very much, it is possible to study and appreciate the actions fought here. Even on a fine, sunny summer's day, the park seems to have a definitely foreboding atmosphere and, after a thunderstorm, I have smelt the awful stench of battle in the still, deep, trenches. Nowhere else in my travels on the Western Front has the horror of war come nearer to me than here on one very hot evening following a clear day. It was late July and, as I wandered across the shell-torn slopes towards the

The battlefield of the Somme—at peace. The attack on July 1, 1916 began at this spot at 7.20 a.m. when the 252nd Company of the Royal Engineers blew up the German trenches held by the 119th Infanterieregiment. The explosion formed what came to be known as Hawthorn Ridge Crater. *Above:* The view from the lip of the crater down towards Beaumont Cemetery. *Below:* Looking from Beaumont village across Redan Ridge. The crater, now tree-filled, is in the centre.

German lines, the sound of thunder was heard in the distance, getting gradually nearer as might an artillery barrage. The light grew dim and black clouds gathered overhead. Lightning streaked across the sky—a veritable reincarnation of what a barrage must have been like.

As the rain drops began to fall, I dived into one of the trenches for cover and tripped and stumbled along until I found better shelter close to the great **Caribou monument** which stands guard over the park from a raised mound above a dugout. All the light I had was a tiny torch and this gave little help in avoiding the occasional shell-case or the jagged pieces of iron which litter the trenches. After the hot day, the usual smell of rain-soaked grass began to permeate my nostrils

The 29th Division's simple monument at Beaumont Hamel—all around are the grass-covered trenches of the battlefield.

Beaumont Hamel Newfoundland Memorial Park is one of the best preserved of the trench memorials on the Western Front to be seen today. St. John's Road and the Caribou Memorial above a dugout at Beaumont Hamel.

. . . but with a difference . . . I realised that this was the smell of battle. It was a never-to-be-forgotten experience, and one which I have found on return visits when the conditions have been similar.

Before the visitor to the park reaches the Caribou, along the gravel path between the trenches a memorial plaque bearing a verse by John Oxenham bids the beholder to tread softly over the hallowed ground. At the base of the Caribou is the **Memorial to the Newfoundland Missing** on land and sea and the names of over 800 men from this small country are listed on the bronze panels. Around the foot of the plinth of stone on which the monument stands is an orientation table. From this level a good view can be had of all the park and beyond to Beaumont and Thiepval. Across the expanse of the park the various lines are indicated by signboards, the British and German front lines being clearly marked amid the rough shell holes.

The modern house of the Superintendent can be seen across towards Thiepval and, over the small ridge where the skeleton of the **Danger Tree** rises in front of the German trenches, is the ridge where the **kilted Scotsman of the 51st Highland Division** gazes out across the countryside. Tall fir trees, planted many years ago when this area became the Newfoundland National Memorial, grow around the statue. The sweep of these trees is interrupted down in the hollow by the **Y Ravine Cemetery**. Hidden over to the left is **Hawthorn Ridge Cemetery No. 2.** Between it and the 51st

Y Ravine Cemetery contains the headstones of men known or believed to be buried there, their graves being lost in later battles.

A relic of 1916—the petrified Danger Tree in no man's land. Y Ravine is in the background.

Overleaf: **A trench map in reality; Beaumont Hamel Memorial Park, seen in April 1976.**

HAWTHORN RIDGE

HAWTHORN RIDGE CEMETERY No. 2

BRITISH FRONT LINE

ST JOHN'S ROAD

ROYAL NEWFOUNDLAND REGIMENT MEMORIAL

RMAN MAIN POSITIONS

Y-RAVINE

51st HIGHLAND DIV. MEM.

NTER'S
METERY

Y-RAVINE CEMETERY

GERMAN FRONT LINE

DANGER TREE

Highland Division Memorial is the smallest of the cemeteries in the park, **Hunter's Cemetery**. A small wall encircles the Cross of Sacrifice around the base of which are the headstones of 46 men, mostly of the Black Watch of the 51st Highland Division, who died here when the area was captured by the division in the autumn of 1916. The division memorial overlooks the infamous **Y Ravine** which was a German position and from which their machine guns wreaked a devastating fire. Entrances to dugouts were cut in the sides of the ravine, but these are now peacefully covered with grass.

As the visitor crosses the battle area, it is noticeable that some of the shell holes contain much battlefield debris: rusting helmets, broken shells, barbed wire and the iron pickets on which the wire was hung. These

The Kilted Scotsman of the 51st Highland Division looks out over Y Ravine.

collections are not there for the taking and it is requested that they should be looked at and not pilfered. Even today many shells and often hand-grenades can be found emerging from the greensward. Should the visitor find a dangerous item, leave it alone and advise the Superintendent or one of the gardeners working in the park.

In 1959, the Canadian Battlefield Monuments Commission took over the park and the CWGC provide the work force to keep it in beautiful condition. To aid them a flock of sheep grazes peacefully. Before the CWGC took over, long lines of pickets and barbed wire were to be seen across the park, since removed to the shell-holes. The Newfoundland Roll of Honour is kept in the

Superintendent's house together with other interesting references to the history of the regiment and park.

Leave the park and continue eastward, dropping suddenly down into the Ancre valley at **Hamel**. We then follow a short but interesting circular detour by taking the left fork in the village and joining the D50. Then, after a few hundred metres, take the left fork on the D163e for Beaumont, leaving the railway which runs between the D50 and the Ancre. In **Beaumont** take the right-hand road, the D163, for **Beaucourt**. There are several **monuments** to British units which took part in the Battle of the Somme including the **63rd Royal Naval Division** and very fine views out over the battlefield.

The tiny Hunter's Cemetery of Highland graves with the 51st Division Memorial in the background.

The 63rd Naval Division Memorial at Beaumont.

Even after nearly sixty years of ploughing, the trenches of the Schwaben Redoubt are still visible from the air.

Insets: The 36th Division Memorial *(top left)* and the Mill Road Cemetery *(bottom right)*, both visible in the aerial photograph.

PHOTO TAKEN MARCH 1976

Thiepval Memorial to over 73,000 men who have no known graves. Built on the site of the old château, it rises above land still bearing scars from 1916.

In Beaucourt rejoin the D50 and turn left for **Miraumont** where the Germans had a supply base and a reserve ammunition store near the **old watermill**, close to the railway line. This was blown up by the British artillery on August 5, 1916, destroying much of the village.

Take the D107 and cross the railway and then take the D151 to the right for **Grandcourt**, which was part of the German entrenchment on the River Ancre. Go straight through the village, taking the D163e to **St Pierre Divion**, travelling along the region where the Germans were securely dug in. At the junction with the D73 will be seen the **ruins of the mill**. Turn left and climb up the steep slopes to Thiepval. At the top of the hill the **Memorial to the 36th Ulster Division** is reached.

Set in a small park on the left of the road, on a site venerated as being the place where the 36th Division won glory on July 1, 1916 in their gallant attempt to reach Thiepval and take the Schwaben Redoubt, is a tall grey memorial. It is a copy of the memorial to Helen, the greatly loved mother of the Marquis of Dufferin, in the family park at Clanboye, County Down, where the division had its training grounds before coming to France. Within the tower are a chapel, visitors' room and an apartment normally occupied by a CWGC official. At present access to the tower can be gained as indicated on a notice by the door.

In the grounds is a flag-pole from which the flag first flew on Armistice Day 1921 when it was hoisted by the Duchess of Abercorn at the unveiling of the memorial. In the spring and autumn, after the ploughing has been done, the fields behind the memorial are crisscrossed with chalk slicks which follow the course of the German trenches leading to the **Schwaben Redoubt** which lies in the fields under **Mill Road Cemetery**, and Thiepval hamlet. Here in 1966 and 1976 great gatherings of the 36th Division survivors met to celebrate the 50th and 60th anniversaries of their heroic deed in which some 5,500 men were killed, wounded or missing.

A little higher up the road is the cemetery where many of them are buried, **Connaught**

Road Cemetery, with part of **Thiepval Wood** as a backdrop. Others lie in Mill Road Cemetery, away in the fields on the left. Here, due to the continual subsidence caused by the movement underground as the many subways and caverns of the Schwaben Redoubt crumble, the headstones in the path of one of the tunnels are laid flat. The cemetery marks one of the main entrances to the underground fortress. It was one of several in the area, the others being Stuff, Zollern and Liepzig. It was from these underground strongholds that the German forces emerged to cause such devastation among the attacking forces.

Continue one km to **Thiepval**. This hamlet, once a flourishing village, was totally destroyed by the end of 1916. It was a German fortress, both above and below ground, and was a vital position to be taken by the British. Terrible losses were suffered on both sides in the attacks which were made on that dreadful first day of the Somme, and it did not fall until September 28, 1916 when the 51st Highland Division captured the ridge. At the crossroads is a small, rather unprepossessing house, once a café which for many many years was owned by one, Isobel. She had been there in 1916 and twice had to be evacuated by the Germans because she obstinately refused to leave voluntarily. Until her death in the early seventies, she still dispensed the beer and coffee and was a great source of stories.

The great **Memorial to the Missing** is along the road behind the church on the right. This colossal arched memorial was designed by Sir Edwin Lutyens and is built of brick with stone facing. The immense central archway is flanked by smaller arches resting on 16 main pillars. On the panels of stone are recorded the names of 73,412 men who died in 1916-17 and have no known graves. Behind the memorial is a **cemetery** where equal numbers of British and French unknown soldiers lie buried

An inscription at the entrance to the memorial, which stands on the site of the grounds of **Thiepval Château** and on part of the **Leipzig Redoubt**, records that the monu-

ment is dedicated to both the British and French. The memorial was unveiled by the Prince of Wales on July 31, 1932 and can be seen from every direction for considerable distances. Beneath is the labyrinth of trenches which formed the vital arteries of this impregnable fortress. **Moquet Farm**, over the valley towards Courcelette, was the forward advance HQ of the defending German army. The majority of the casualties recorded here were lost in the attempts to capture this fortress. The siege dragged on for nearly two months but the most disasterous day was July 1 when the British lost nearly 60,000 men. In September, the 11th and 18th Divisions, following in the footsteps of the 36th, 8th and 25th Divisions, finally took the village. The ridge was retaken by the Germans in their 1918 offensive when it was only lightly defended but on August 24 it was recaptured with ease by V Corps.

Across a wide green lawn from the great edifice is the **18th Division Memorial**. This is passed as the D151 is joined for **Authuille**, 1½ kms away. The road descends to this village which clings to the east bank of the Ancre. Across the river and its bankside marshes is the railway and the road to Albert via **Aveluy Wood**. This wood is still cut by the remains of the trenches of the British lines; 36th Division's HQ was here, and **Lancashire Dump** was on the site of **Aveluy Wood Cemetery**. This road is the D50 and it rolls up and down the valley to Albert some 3 kms away.

However before we enter this historic place, take the D104 from Aveluy to visit Ovillers and La Boisselle via Pozières. Shortly after crossing the D151 there is a rise in the road and, on the right, a small road leads to **Ovillers**, passing its large **cemetery** and overlooking the valley called **Mash Valley** by the BEF. Along the ridge of this valley up which the D929 rises there were many mine craters in years gone by. They were part of the almost continuous series blown in the mine warfare of 1915-16. Ovillers was stormed on July 1, 1916, but did not fall until the 16th.

Passing through the village take the right-

Aveluy Wood Cemetery, where men sleep amid crumbling trenches, was laid out on the site of the Lancashire Dump.

The Memorial to the Fifth Army Missing at Pozières, where 14,690 names are recorded of men who died on the Somme.

hand road to join the D929. Turn left up the slope to **Pozières**. This village, astride the main Albert-Bapaume road, was the focus of much heavy fighting and, by August 1916, had ceased to exist. It was taken on August 23 by the 1st Australian Division and the 48th British Division of General Gough's Fifth Army. Beside the long straight road before the village is reached, the **Pozières Military Cemetery** and the **Memorial to the Missing of the Fifth Army in 1918** are passed. This memorial records the names of 14,690 men of the Fifth Army who died in the battles of the Somme up to April 5, 1918, and all other casualties up to August 7 with no known graves.

Continue up the gradient, which increases until the crest is reached, beside the **Tank Corps Memorial** opposite the site of **Pozières Mill**. The obelisk of the Tank Memorial is set off by four fine scale models of tanks of the 1916-18 period, one of which bears bullet marks from the Second War. It was from this area that the first tanks went into action towards Flers in September 1916. Pozières Mill is now simply a grassy mound, identified by a memorial slab giving the details of the stand by the Australians in July and August 1916 in their attempts to capture this feature, Hill 160. The mill was fortified by a German bunker of which there is little left today. By looking around, it is possible to appreciate what a fine 'O-Pip' this was. Over to the westward, the Thiepval Memorial can be seen. The sites of other prominent actions can also be discerned, even the **sugar refinery** on the ridge. The **Australian and other memorials** are on the south of Pozières.

Another 1½ km further north and the **Canadian Memorial of Courcelette** is reached which commemorates their great actions in November 1916 when they took, among other positions, the longest trench built by the

The Tank Corps Memorial, Pozières, the start point for the first tank battle on September 15, 1916.

Memorial gate to Pozières Mill, once the scene of bitter fighting by the Australian Division, now merely a grass mound.

Germans on the Western Front, which ran across this ridge—**Regina Trench.**

Turn right on to the D6 for Martinpuich (1 km). Martinpuich was battered to pulp long before it actually fell to the British 15th Division on September 15, 1916 after the attack on Flers. Some of the tanks first used that day were in action here. After it was recaptured by the Germans in March 1918, they remained here until V Corps troops retook the position in August.

We now take the small unclassified road to the right for **Bazentin-le-Grand**, another village with a similar history. Turn right onto the D104 to **Contalmaison**, going through the village to **La Boisselle**. Above the village is the **Memorial to the 34th Division** and, on the

green before the church, is the **19th Division Memorial.**

Taking the small road on the left and the immediate left fork in a few metres arrive at **Lochnager Crater.** The purchase of it in 1979 by Richard Dunning of London has made its preservation more secure and the erosion of the site by encroaching agriculture halted. The crater, the largest on the Western Front, was one of a group blown on July 1, 1916, the explosion being felt for hundreds of miles. This mine alone comprised 60,000lbs of explosives—all carefully dragged underground along saps emanating from the direction of the **Tara-Usna line** near the main road to Albert—and the crater today is some 300ft across and 90ft deep. From the rim there

Nearby is the 1st Australian Division Memorial.

The Canadian Memorial at Courcelette. Here in November 1916 the Canadians captured the longest trench constructed by the Germans on the Western Front.

In April 1976, when the photo *above* was taken, what was left of the battlefield surrounding Lochnager Crater at La Boisselle was gradually being reclaimed. Although this, the largest crater on the Western front created on July 1, 1916 by the explosion of 60,000 lbs of guncotton, still remained amid the ruins of the old German front line, other smaller craters near the village were being filled in. The latest to go now has a house built over it. In 1979 Richard Dunning decided that this gradual encroachment of a unique piece of First World War history, and the Somme battles in particular, must be reversed and he purchased Lochnager Crater personally that it might be saved as a permanent memorial. The picture *right* of the area in 1982 shows how the surrounding fields crept closer in those six short years. A new inscribed stone memorial was erected in 1980.

are extensive views over Chapes Spur—**Sausage Valley**—so called by the British for the German observation balloon which hung over it. In the slopes of the shallow valley can be discerned the positions of some of the machine gun posts which poured forth their deadly fire to cause such devastation among the troops advancing from Tara and Usna—Becort Wood and Albert —the ridge towards Fricourt and upwards to Pozières and back to Ovillers. Nearer to hand are the small craters of the **Glory Hole** blown in 1915, easily visible behind the houses of La Boisselle and along the road which connects with D929 beside the **Tyneside Scottish and Tyneside Irish Memorial** close to their positions when these battalions fought to win this sector in that infamous July. All around there is still evidence in the shell holes of the many months of fighting in this valley. **Y Sap**, another of the large mines, lay on the western side of D929. It was filled in some years ago and built over and today it is merely discernable by a white circular patch in the field immediately behind the bungalows.

Albert is 3 kms down the D929 or, taking the Bécourt-Bécordel road below Lochnager Crater, more of the battle area is traversed. Little now marks the landscape except the

The 19th Division Memorial on the village green at La Boisselle.

The 34th Division Memorial above La Boisselle.

Behind the Norfolk Cemetery artillery lines have left their mark.

chalk slicks in newly-ploughed ground or the occasional artillery position in the embankments. Such a position is very clearly seen behind **Norfolk Cemetery**. The two hamlets were in the British rear lines and were bases from which units moved into action. After Bécordel turn right on to D938 to reach Albert in 3 kms.

Albert, once called Ancre, is an industrial town which was very much in the front line in the various battles of the Somme and the Ancre. At the end of September 1914 it was almost occupied by the advancing German Second Army but the French Tenth Army stood in its way and, with the support of the British cavalry, pushed them back. For the next two years Albert was only a few kilometres from the front line and was frequently bombarded. On January 15, 1915, the **golden virgin** on the tower of the Basilica was toppled from her plinth when a shell hit the dome on which she stood. The statue did not fall but hung, precariously, head down out over the tower. The sight of the statue hanging almost at right angles was one of the most talked of incidents of Albert and led to the legend that when the 'Leaning Virgin' fell, the war would be over. In due course the base of the statue was secured, first by French and later British engineers.

Being close to the front, Albert was always filled with the military, at first mostly by French forces but, in March 1916, the British took over. Until October 1916 the town was well within the range of the German guns and was very badly damaged. On March 26, 1918 the German offensive swept through Albert after bitter fighting, and the town remained in German hands until the British advance in August when, on the 22nd, it was recaptured. As the Basilica tower was being utilised by the Germans as an observation post, orders were issued for its destruction. At 3.30 p.m. on April 16, the 35th British Divisional Artillery shelled the tower extremely accurately and, with the third shot, the tower fell with of course the Virgin—so much for the legend!

None of the buildings in Albert are old, all having been rebuilt, although the Basilica and the imposing Hôtel de Ville were rebuilt in the 1920s very much in their old style. On the front wall of the **Hôtel de Ville** is a memorial plaque to the **Machine Gun Corps**.

To resume the tour of the battlefields, leave Albert via the N338 for **Fricourt** (5 kms). At the beginning of the village, the **Fricourt British Cemetery** and the **7th Battalion, Green Howards Memorial** is on the left. This was another of the villages turned into fortresses by the Germans during their long occupation. Mine warfare was fought for many months around the village which was, in time, utterly ruined. On the left of the D147, on the crest of the rising ground, the cratered ground of the

Tambour Mine is visible. Above it is **Fricourt New Military Cemetery** out in the fields. Fricourt fell to the 17th Division on July 2, 1916 and this cemetery was one of their burial grounds. On the north-east side of the village is **Fricourt Wood**, again captured by 17th Division.

Above left: **The Leaning Virgin on the tower of the Basilica was dislodged in a bombardment in January 1915. Although secured by French and British engineers, she was finally toppled on April 16, 1918.** *Above right:* **Once again the Golden Virgin gleams over modern Albert.**

The Machine Gun Corps Memorial decorates the facade of Albert's Hôtel de Ville.

Beside the Bray road on the outskirts of Fricourt lies the British Cemetery and the 7th Bn. Green Howards Memorial.

Left: **The 12th Bn. Manchester Regiment Memorial stands hidden in Contalmaison Communal Cemetery.** *Above:* **Crumbling on the edge of Bazentin-le-Petit is the Royal Engineers' 82nd Field Company Memorial.**

Three kilometres up the D147 is **Contalmaison**, captured by the 17th and 38th Divisions on July 9, 1916, after being attacked by the 7th, 17th and 23rd Divisions since the 3rd.

To the south of the village is **Mametz Wood** which is reached by taking the first right-hand road as the village is entered. This road leads to **Mametz** itself, about 1½ kms away.

An East Surrey VC, Corporal Dwyer, at rest in Flat Iron Copse Cemetery.

On the north-east end of the village, the D104 leads to **Bazentin-le-Grand** and **Bazentin-le-Petit**, and the woods such as **Flat Iron Copse** with its **cemetery** which were scenes of fierce fighting. The battles for the **Bazentin ridge** went on for several days before the villages and woods were firmly in British hands on July 14.

An unclassified road from Bazentin-le-Petit leads to Montauban de Picardie and the D64 thence to Mametz. Mametz Wood, which is some way north of the village was, as were all the other woods in the German lines, a labyrinth of trenches and dugouts which had to be fought for every inch of the way as the British forces pushed slowly but steadily northwards during that dreadful summer. In the vicinity are several British cemeteries including **Danzig Alley**, which includes a **Welsh Memorial to the Royal Welsh Fusiliers**.

From Mametz return to the D938 and turn left. A small unclassified road climbs up to the right passing **Mansel Copse**. Hidden within

the little wood is **Devonshire Cemetery** where the men of the 8th and 9th Devons were buried by their padre and all 163 still lie as he interred them. Among their number is Lieutenant Harry Webber, at 67 the oldest man killed in action in the Somme, and Hudson the poet. The tiny **Gordon Cemetery** was created by 2nd Bn. Gordon Highlanders in one of the British support trenches which ran along here. Like the Devons, the Gordons were part of 7th Division whose memorial in Mametz has disappeared.

The next two roads to the left lead to Carnoy but continue on to **Maricourt** where

The Royal Welsh Fusiliers' Memorial in Danzig Alley Cemetery.

the British and French lines merged in 1916. Turn left either via the unclassified road to **Montauban** or the D197 which joins the D64 to the east of that village near the site of the **brickworks** captured by the Liverpool Regiment. The works were completely destroyed having provided the Germans with a magnificent OP. Only a crumbling post-war replacement chimney remains. These roads were the main routes for the men coming up from Albert to the front line.

The 18th Division marked their attacks in Trones Wood with this memorial.

The 20th Light Division's Memorial above Guillemont.

This is the tiny cemetery at Mametz created by the 2nd Bn. Gordon Highlanders. Trenches still remain below the hedges in the middle distance.

Turning on to the D64 we pass **Bernafay Wood**, captured on July 1, and soon we come to **Trones Wood**—Bois des Troncs—which was captured by the **18th Division** whose **memorial obelisk** is at the side of the road at the edge of the wood. Today the woods are healthy young forests and bear little resemblance to the muddy shattered areas the troops knew.

Guillemont is 2 kms, but just prior to reaching the village we pass on the left **Guillemont Road Cemetery** where Lieutenant Raymond Asquith, the son of the then-Prime Minister, is buried; he was killed at Ginchy in September 1916. From here there is a panoramic view over towards Delville Wood and Longueval across the railway and the derelict sucrerie on the site of **Waterlot Farm**. Guillemont fell to the 20th Division and a brigade of the 16th on August 23, 1916 after bitter fighting which had involved many units since the end of July. Take the D20 on the left to Longueval, passing over the line of advance to Delville Wood.

On reaching **Longueval** take the first road to the right, for **Delville Wood** and the **South African National Memorial**. The cemetery on

Memorial in Guillemont to Irishmen of the 16th Division killed in the battle for the village, and at Ginchy.

Delville Wood—the South African Memorial group represents Union. Delville Wood was also called Devil's Wood by the troops. The original glades, named after streets in London, Edinburgh and Capetown, have still been retained today.

the south side of the road is **Delville Wood Cemetery** which contains the graves of men of the divisions who contested this sector—the 9th Scottish Division and the 2nd, 14th Light and 17th Divisions. The **Bois d'Elville**, approximately half-a-mile square in an irregular shape, skirts the eastern flank of Longueval and reaches almost into Ginchy on the east. The battle for the wood, often called **Devil's Wood** by the troops, was the scene of the baptism of fire of the South African Brigade of the 9th Scottish Division from July 14-20, 1916. Commanded by General H. T. Lukin, the South African Brigade had a strength of 121 officers and 3,032 NCOs and men. On July 14 they had been in reserve at Montauban. Less one battalion (which went to assist in the clearing of Longueval), the brigade went into action on the morning of the 15th. Under heavy bombardment by the defending force, the battalions fought their desperate way into the wood and, despite heavy losses, had taken all the wood except the south-west corner by July 17. The 3rd Battalion was cut off and had to surrender—three officers and 150 men. The colonel of the 2nd Battalion gathered together 140 of all ranks from the four battalions and fought his way through to rejoin the brigade.

A real South African monument, the Cross of Consecration, the Voortrekker cross upon a cross.

The sole remaining tree to survive the 1916 battles, despite its shrapnel-filled trunk, is carefully tended by the CWGC.

In the depths of Delville Wood the pleasant glade of Buchanan Street intersects with Rotten Row.

At 6.00 a.m. on the 20th the brigade was withdrawn—29 officers and 751 other ranks were all that were left.

The graceful memorial is approached across a broad lawn between two double lines of oak trees grown from acorns brought from French Hook, Cape Colony. Hundreds of young trees were planted in the 1920s to form a frame for the memorial which was designed by Sir Herbert Baker, ARA. A triumphal archway, surmounted by a bronze group, is flanked by a curved wall of flint and stone with a pavilion at either end. In the lawn behind the memorial is a South African Voortrekkers double cross called the 'Cross of Consecration'. This replaces the usual Cross of Sacrifice.

The bronze group of two figures either side of a great horse is by Alfred Turner and represents 'Union' (of the two races of the Union of South Africa). The memorial itself was unveiled by Mrs Botha in the presence of General Herzog, Field-Marshal Haig and other dignatories on October 10, 1926. The Altar Stone of Remembrance, placed in front of the arch, was added after the Second World War to commemorate South Africa's 1939-45 war dead. This was unveiled by Mrs O. M. Swales, mother of Captain W. Swales, VC, on June 5, 1952.

Almost directly behind the memorial, amid the trees, is the **only surviving original tree**, carefully tended by the CWGC and, despite being full of shrapnel, it is remarkably healthy.

The memorial books of honour and items of interest can be viewed on application in the visitors' room in the Warden's house by the roadside. Plans are afoot to create a museum in the park to honour the Brigade.

In the rehabilitation of the wood the original glades, which were named after streets in London, Edinburgh and Capetown, have been maintained and make a walk through the wood a very pleasant experience. It is difficult to realise the terrible past until a trench is noticed in the undergrowth where rusty pieces of shell-case, water bottles and odd rounds of small arms ammunition are frequently found. All the glades have stone signposts at their junctions so it is quite easy to follow the course of the battles which raged in all for sixteen days before the 2nd Division finally cleared the wood on July 28, 1916. In 1918 heavy fighting again took place during the Allied advance when the 17th and 38th Divisions were engaged. On **Buchanan Street**, just north of the cross with **Rotten Row**, is a monument marking the site of the **South African Brigade HQ dugout**. From it several trenches can be followed away into the wood.

Before proceeding eastward to Ginchy it is of interest to go into Longueval village and along the D107 for about a kilometre to the

Close by this memorial are the trenches leading to the South African Brigade HQ dugout.

The Cameron Highlanders and Black Watch Memorial beyond which lies a water-filled mine crater in High Wood.

Bois des Fourceaux, or, as it is better known, **High Wood**. On the roadside is the **Memorial to the 47th (London) Division** which fought here and finally cleared the wood of its German defenders on September 15, 1916 after fierce fighting. One of their trenches ran along the edge of the wood about where the right-hand ditch is now. The British cavalry penetrated the wood on July 14 but the Germans were well dug in with concrete dugouts and positions, one of which can be seen from the road among the trees. Further along the road is **London Cemetery**. On the eastern flank of the wood, (reached by a muddy track at the edge of the field) is the **Memorial to the Cameron Highlanders and Black Watch** who fought here on September 3, the day when the large mine was blown. The crater, now filled with water, can be seen on the left beyond the memorial.

The wood is privately owned and should not be entered without the permission of the owner who lives in the large house near the road. The trenches and some of the strong points remain amid the trees, but the area has not been completely cleared of battle debris and it could be dangerous to trespass. From the edge of the wood overlooking Delville Wood is the area fought over by the London Battalions after taking the wood. It was a pocket of resistance which the capture of Flers had outflanked.

Away on the rise between the woods can be seen the **New Zealand Memorial** on the site of **Crest Farm**; it can be reached from the Longueval to Flers road, and behind is a small cratered area.

From Delville Wood continue eastwards to **Ginchy**—a forward position in the German defence line standing high on the plain above Combles. It was first captured by the 7th Division on July 3 but lost in a counter-attack only to be recaptured on July 9 by the 16th Irish Division. Turn right in the centre of the village to join the D20 in ½ km at the **20th Light Division Memorial** and turn left for Combles 2 kms. **Combles**, a small town built on a hill, was the last German redoubt to fall in September 1916. Just opposite was the junction between the BEF and the French lines. Protected by its surrounding hills, Combles did not suffer to the same degree as neighbouring villages. During their occupation of it, the German Army strongly fortified the town which eventually fell to a joint Anglo-French attack on September 26. In the rock beneath **Lamotte Château**, tunnels and shelters had been cut before the war which the Germans extended making a complete subterranean headquarters.

Two kms along the D74/D11e is **Morval** which was captured on September 25, 1916. It was re-entered again by the advancing Germans in March 1918 as it lay in the gap between the Third and Fifth Armies.

The 47th London Division Memorial outside the school at Martinpuich.

The New Zealand Memorial lies between High Wood and Delville Wood.

A kilometre further on is **Lesboeufs** captured by the 6th and Guards Division on September 25. In March 1918 the 63rd Division was in action here delaying the German advance. Machine gunners fired

250,000 rounds whilst covering the division, creating havoc among the oncoming German forces. Keep to the left and return to Ginchy by the road which crosses the heights. A stop at the **Guards' Memorial** provides excellent

The Guards' Cemetery is laid out on the slopes beyond Combles. This town, just opposite the junction of the British and French lines, was heavily fortified by the Germans. It was captured on September 26, 1916.

The Guards' Memorial on the Lesboeufs road—a windswept viewpoint.

The 41st Division's Infantryman gazes down Flers main street—his bayonet pointing to Pozières.

views of the area of the September conflict and the March 1918 advance.

Continue to Ginchy (3 kms) and take the right turn for Flers, crossing the wide expanse of **Caterpillar Valley**, the route of the tanks on September 15, 1916.

We reach **Flers** 3 km further on. At the end of the main street is the **41st Division Memorial**, a 'New Army' division with units from many parts of England; their badges decorate the enclosing pillars. The rifle of the bronze infantryman points in the direction the tanks came from Pozières. Flers was the target of three corps of the Fourth Army on September 15, 1916 when, in the early morning, the tanks first took to the fields.

Proceed northward to the next crossroad and turn right for **Gueudecourt** (6 km). The centre of many actions in September 1916, there was little remaining of the village when the site was captured. About ½ km on the Beaulencourt road, in the wide expanse of cornfields, is the small fir-lined enclosure of the **Newfoundland Memorial**, a Caribou

Allied trenches occupied by the regiment. The Newfoundland Caribou of Gueudecourt looks towards the German lines.

On the Butte de Warlencourt, a German cross, erected by a German infantry battalion in 1944, stands in the original mount.

similar to the one at Beaumont Hamel. This one stands above a strong point within a curve of trenches and a machine gun post which were the site of a regimental position in September 1916.

Leave Gueudecourt by the D11 for **Le Sars** crossing the **Warlencourt Ridge**. The hamlet of Le Sars is astride the D929 on the crest of one of the rises of the hills overlooking Bapaume, and marks the limit of the British advance on this sector in the 1916 Somme battles.

Turn right on to the D929. As we descend the hill, over to the right ahead in the fold of one of the slopes of the hills, is a wooded mound. In 1916 this was the chalk covered eminence known as the **Butte de Warlencourt**. At that time it was higher than it is today and it stood out above the rest of the battlefield. The Butte was an artificial mound which had played a prominent part in the war of 1871, and was honeycombed with many tunnels even before the Germans took it and fortified it so strongly that it was almost impossible to capture. Several times it was overrun by British units but the defenders from below counter-attacked and drove the attacking forces off until, on February 25, 1917, success was achieved and the Butte fell into British hands. During the following year, five of the attacking units erected memorials on the shell-torn crest including the **Durham Light Infantry**, the **South Africans** and other territorial units. None of these survive here today. In March 1918 the Germans retook the mound and they erected a cross on the summit. It was not until August 1918 that the Butte was again overrun.

The remains of some of the fortified entrances can be traced in the undergrowth beneath the trees and the **base of the German memorial** can be found on the crest. In 1944, the German infantry battalion in the region erected a replacement cross on the old base and this survives, hidden in the brush.

The D929 continues across the undulating country to Bapaume, five kilometres away. Vestiges of the old trench lines remain here and there with the occasional concrete shelter, such as the one on the Thilloy-Grevillers crossroad, and, nearer to Bapaume, the ridges and hedges show evidence of usage as artillery positions. To visit the town, turn right at the road junction after the rise in the road.

Bapaume is a quiet market town with a long history dating back to Roman times. Situated at a strategic crossroads, it was frequently the scene of conflict and in the 16th Century was a fortified town. Beneath the quiet streets, many of the cellars are in fact relics of this period.

The town was in the battle line in late August 1914 and, after the German push to the west, remained in their hands until March 17, 1917 when the Australian 2nd Division

Beneath the streets of Bapaume these bottles recall the German occupation of the Bastion de la Reyne.

Above: **51st Highland Division gunners shelter in a collapsed water tower in Bapaume in January 1918 (IWM).** *Below:* **The old tower survives near a modern replacement.**

captured it. All the old buildings had by then been destroyed; only one building remains today and that is a **barn** on the very outskirts of the town on the Péronne road. Opposite it is a **water tower** which is on the site of one which fell over in the 1917 battle and later became a moderately warm and dry billet for the troops, immortalised in a photograph of the gunners of 51st Highland Division entering it in January 1918. Parts of the old ramparts, stripped of their brick cladding, can be seen on the eastern side of the town in a park. The **town museum** is housed in the Lawrence School, just above the square, and includes relics from 1914-18. The school was the gift of a manufacturer from Sheffield. In the foyer of the Hôtel de Ville are huge reproductions of the Croix de Guerre and the Légion d'Honneur awarded to the town.

During the German occupations of the town in both wars, they made use of one of the underground bastions, which dates from 1551, and on occasions this can be viewed. The galleries of the **Bastion de la Reyne** lie beneath the houses north of Place Faidherbe and are in remarkable condition. The entrance is through one of the houses in rue de la République. The main gallery is some 8 metres below the level of the pavement and consists of two large halls connected by narrow vaulted passages.

In many of the old gun ports, there are piles of debris from the German occupations including hundreds of bottles, proclaiming it as the site of an old mess. On the walls are earlier relics, on one brick is inscribed 'the palindrome 1551' which legend has it was scratched by Charles V. On another is a representation of the arms of the Austrians, Spaniards and Burgundy, the three major contestants for the town in the 16th Century. The wiring for

telephone and electricity dates from 1916. Enquiries for further details should be made to the Société Archéologique de Bapaume.

When the Germans evacuated Bapaume in March 1917, they left many of the buildings booby-trapped or mined. The Hôtel de Ville was one of these and it blew up some days after the Australians had entered the town. The Germans re-entered the ruins of Bapaume on March 24, 1918 but were dislodged by the New Zealand Division on August 29.

Leave Bapaume for Arras by the N17. This road swings up and down through several small villages and hamlets well known to the BEF. In its day, this agricultural plain was a scene of utter devastation and sometimes, usually in the evening light, the tracks of a tortuous trench line can be discerned.

Four kms further on **Sapignies** and a little further **Behagnies** were both in the front line in March 1918 when they fell in the face of the German advance. Both were recaptured in August by the 2nd Division.

We then pass through **Ervillers** in 2 kms, a German garrison village until March 1917 and then in March 1918 the scene of heavy fighting with the 42nd Division trying to delay the advance. It was recaptured on August 23. **Gomiécourt** a short way to the south-west, was where the 3rd Division had a fierce fight in August 1918 when they took the village with many prisoners.

It is 6 kms to **Boiry-Becquerelle** (the modern road goes over the old highway by a bridge as the villages are entered) and three kms to **Mercatel**. This village was the junction of the **Hindenburg Line** with the old German line of 1914. We reach **Beaurains**, a suburb of Arras through which the front line ran in 1917 and where the CWGC now have their offices.

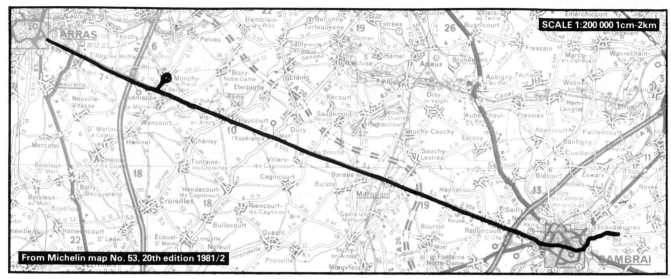

From Michelin map No. 53, 20th edition 1981/2

SCALE 1:200 000 1cm-2km

Arras to Cambrai

ROUTE I

The direct route via the D939 is 30 kms, an absolutely straight road of Roman origin.

Tilloy-lès-Mofflaines (4 kms). North of this Arras suburb is the famous **Observatory Ridge** with the **Harp position** from which the Hindenburg Line swung southwards to Croisilles and Quéant. There were many actions fought around here in 1917 during the battle for Arras but few signs are evident today. The construction of the autoroute A1 has removed the most prominent ones but, here and there, a ditch with steep sides or a long earthwork may be part of the outworks of the line.

La Chapelle de Feuchy (2 kms). Access point for the Lille-Paris motorway. This was the furthest extent of the first days' advance in the April 1917 battle and the village where the 15th Scottish Division stood in the defence of Arras in 1918. Here, too, in April 1917 the **12th Division** fought an action and their **memorial** stands on the south side of the road near the spot. This cross is one of two memorials, the other being at Malassie Farm near Epehy, south of Cambrai, a position held by the division in the capture of that town in September 1918. Both crosses are copies of a cross on York Minster.

Leave the D939 by turning to the left on the D33 for **Monchy-le-Preux** (1 km). This village, built on high ground, provided the Germans with a commanding view of the Allied lines. It was captured by the 37th British Division on April 11, 1917 during a blizzard. It was protected by wide bands of barbed wire, such as those which covered the Hindenburg Line, making an attack a very costly affair. However, Monchy, despite many counter-attacks, was retained until the March 1918 advance. Eastward from Monchy rises **Infantry Hill** which was in the 29th Division line held by the Royal Newfoundland Regiment. On a bunker in the village, in the front garden of a house, stands the Caribou of the **Newfoundland Regimental Memorial**. Monchy was recaptured on August 26, 1918 by the Canadian Corps. Return to the D939 via D34.

Vis-en-Artois (4 kms) is reached after crossing the River Cojeul. On the upward slope is the **Vis-en-Artois Cemetery and Memorial to the Missing** who fell in the 1918 advance in Picardy where 9,903 names are carved on the memorial. In the cemetery lie over 1,700 British and 573 Canadians who died in the capture of this sector on August 27, 1918.

The Memorial to the 12th Division on the HQ dugout site at La Chapelle de Feuchy.

The 37th Division's soldier trio which stands at Monchy le Preux.

Vis-en-Artois Cemetery and the Memorial to the Missing.

Dury crossroad (3½ kms) with the **Canadian Memorial** almost directly after it on the left.

Eight kms of undulating road stretch across the expansive plain before the Canal du Nord and **Marquion** are reached. To assist the 4th, 63rd and 1st Canadian Divisions to take this small town in September 1918, the Royal

Engineers built several bridges over the canal during the nights beforehand.

In 10 kms we enter **Cambrai** via the rue d'Arras and, after crossing the St. Quentin Canal, the rue des Feutriers leads into the great Place Aristide Briand, once the Place d'Armes. Cambrai, an historic town, is once more a bustling, prosperous industrial and market city.

In 1815 Wellington took the surrender of the city after the fall of Napoleon. In 1870 the Germans took it and, in August 1914, von Kluck took it again for the Germans. The Germans held the town as a large garrison base until October 8, 1918. In 1916, Prince Rupprecht of Bavaria had his headquarters here. In the autumn of 1917 the city came within the range of the Allied artillery and damage was effected on the ancient buildings. However most of the destruction was caused in 1918 when the retreating Germans mined and fired it as 3rd Canadian Division and the 57th Division converged on the city, from the north and the south respectively, to complete the operation on October 9.

The impressive **Hôtel de Ville** was severely damaged but has been rebuilt in its former design of the 19th Century. In the Belfry, above the central facade, are the oldest inhabitants of Cambrai: 'Martin' and 'Martine', the two mechanical figures of blackmoors which date from 1510 and which appear as the clock strikes the hour. In **le Mail St Martin** is the rebuilt **Belfry**, all that remains of the church of St Martin which dates from the 15th Century. Two of the city gates have survived, the **Porte de Paris** in the south and the **Porte Notre Dame** in the north-east. The **cathedral** in the rue de Paris is a Gothic church built in 1859 which was badly damaged. There is a **Municipal Museum** in the rue de l'Epée which is also a good provincial art gallery.

On the D942, the Solesmes road, about a kilometre out of town is the **Cambrai East Military Cemetery**. This cemetery was originally a German graveyard later taken over by the CWGC. As with almost all the German burial grounds, it has green lawns about which are scattered lines of graves and very Teutonic monuments with the central huge black cross within a small walled area.

Above: **One of the two original city gates to have survived in Cambrai. The Porte de Paris (on the road to Paris) survived German destruction in 1918.**

Cambrai East Military Cemetery was originally German but is now looked after by the Commonwealth War Graves Commission. Photo *above* shows the original German memorial and *below,* the British section.

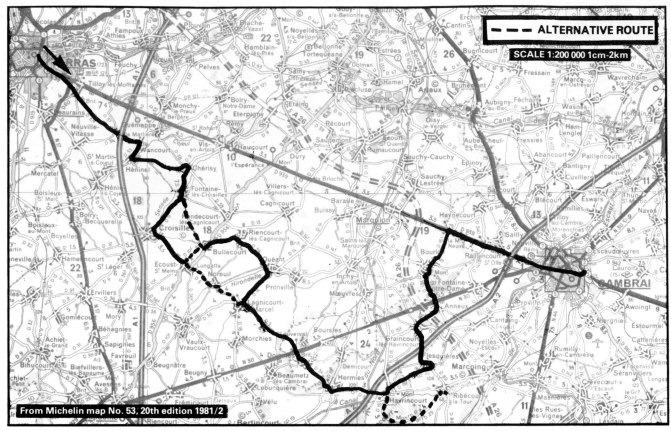

From Michelin map No. 53, 20th edition 1981/2

ALTERNATIVE ROUTE

SCALE 1:200 000 1cm-2km

Arras to Cambrai

ROUTE II

Leave Arras by the D939 and, about one kilometre after crossing the railway, take the D37e to the right through the centre of **Tilloy** and then out into the country, crossing the area of the April 1917 attacks during the Arras battles.

In 8 kms, after going under the motorway, enter **Wancourt** and, at the church, turn right on the D33 for **Héninel**, 1½ kms away. Both these villages played important roles in the attacks by General Allenby's Third Army in 1917 and General Currie's Canadians in August 1918.

Turn left for **Chérisy** (2 kms), a pleasant if narrow road across the rolling countryside which was very cut about in 1917 and 1918. At Chérisy turn right on to D9 for **Fontaine-lès-Croisilles**, (1 km). On the outskirts of the village, which lies on the east bank of the River Sensée, (and before crossing the river), on the right is a very well-preserved **German concrete dugout**.

The D5 leads to **Croisilles** and **Ecoust St Mein**, while the first small road after the church leads to **Hendecourt** and the second one to **Bullecourt**. This is all the area fought over by Australians and several British divisions during the Arras battles, and the breaching of the **Hindenburg Line**, which ran over the open country with wide belts of barbed wire entanglements. Bullecourt was the scene of many gallant deeds by the West Riding Division and has retained long associations with units which took part. Before the church is a **memorial to the British and Australians** erected in 1980, and outside the village **a plaque** recalls the Australian effort.

Either take the D5 to **Noreuil** from Ecoust or the D38 from Bullecourt to **Quéant** (thence

Memorial at Bullecourt to the British and Australian dead of April/May 1917.

German bunker near Fontaine les Croisilles.

Bas reliefs carved by C. S. Jagger on the Tank Memorial at Louverval. This remembers those who fell in the Battle of Cambrai and have no known graves.

by the D14 to Lagnicourt-Marcel) to go over the sites of the **Hindenburg Line** or the **Quéant Switch** which stretched to Drocourt in the north. This region was eventually captured by the 63rd Royal Naval Division.

From **Lagnicourt** take the D5 through **Louverval** to the crossroads on the N30 where stands the **Cambrai Memorial** to those who fell in the Battle of Cambrai and have no known graves and the **Louverval Military Cemetery**. On the walls of the memorial are some fine bas reliefs by Jagger relating to the Cambrai battles. Whichever route from Chérisy is taken, it is about 20 kms.

Turn right onto N30 for a short way and, at **Doignies**, turn left for **Hermies** on D34, 3 kms away. This is a pleasant village of which the green was once a **large mine crater** in 1917 when the I Anzac Corps were here.

Travel 3 kms further along the D5 over the motorway and **Havrincourt** is approached. The **château**, which dominates this village, was for a long time in German hands as an HQ and here, on occasion, the Kaiser stayed. Before the end of the 1917 campaign the village and château were in ruins, either through constant artillery bombardment or demolition. In 1917 British divisions could not dislodge the enemy from the village or the wood, which was fortified with concrete bunkers, when the main attack on the Hindenburg Line was begun. The village was also on the edge of the Battle of Cambrai in November to December 1917. The 62nd Division were in action here in 1917 and in 1918 the village was captured by them. The New Zealand Corps captured **Havrincourt Wood**, on the edge of which is the **62nd Division Memorial**.

As with other villages in the area, Havrincourt has retained close relationships with its liberators and, each year, the Bradford Pals Pilgrimage used to pause here to meet the Maire and other personalities to drink a 'Vin d'Honneur' before visiting the château. This large, red brick house has been destroyed three times by fire or battle this century and, after each tragedy, has been rebuilt exactly as it was. In the meadows behind the château and in the wood beyond are remains of concrete shelters and bunkers.

A pleasant detour can be made to include **Trescault** and crossing the woods, by taking the D15 to Trescault and then the D17/29 to **Ribécourt-la-Tour** rather than the direct road. Then take the D89 from Ribécourt, or the D15 from Havrincourt to Flesquières and the area of the Battle of Cambrai.

Flesquières was strongly defended by the Germans when, on November 20, 1917, the Battle of Cambrai began with the advance of 400 tanks from Havrincourt Wood to attack across the open fields on a 15 km front. From artillery emplacements in and around the village, the Germans hit hard at the Allied tanks. Although several divisions of General Byng's Third Army carried their targets, Flesquières proved to be a difficult proposition and a fierce battle ensued before the 51st Highland Division successfully captured the village.

Marcoing, 3 kms to the east, was captured by the 29th Division. The West Riding Division then went forward to take Graincourt and Anneux with many prisoners. The 6th Division took Ribécourt, whilst the 36th Division took Moeuvres in the north and 12th Division Bonvis Ridge and Lateau Wood. Meanwhile the 20th Light Division had taken, and then after a heavy counter-attack lost, Les Rues des Vignes in the south. The 51st Division went forward to capture Fontaine-Notre-Dame and, as the 40th Division were attacking Bourlon Wood, the German Second Army counter-attacked. The 40th Division took the wood following a period of severe fighting with gas attacks but, by the end of November, the British divisions had taken nearly 11,000 prisoners and 140 guns. However, by the end of the first week in December, the reinforced German army had driven back the Allies to the Flesquières Ridge.

During the Allied advance in September 1918, the area was captured by the 2nd, 3rd, 5th, 42nd and Guards Divisions with the Canadians taking Bourlon Wood. The 57th and 63rd took Anneux and Graincourt and then Marcoing before reaching Cambrai.

From Flesquières go over the motorway to **Graincourt** (2 kms), and, in the village, turn right for **Anneux** and then left on D15. Cross the N30 onto the D16 for **Bourlon**, in all about 4 kms.

Bourlon Wood is to the east of the village. The **Canadian Memorial** is on the edge of the wood on the hillside and is reached up a stepped path between ancient chestnut trees, planted in Napoleon's honour. In the undergrowth of the wood are the remains of a bunker. A path leads into the wood from the entrance to the memorial (up to the left as you face the village). There is also a **memorial to the Free French** of the Second War here.

From Bourlon take the D16 to gain the D939 in 2½ kms. Turn right and Cambrai is 8 kms further on.

Above: **Havrincourt Château served as a German HQ and was visited by the Kaiser. The 62nd West Yorkshire Division, whose memorial** *(right)* **is located on the edge of the village, captured the château ruins.**

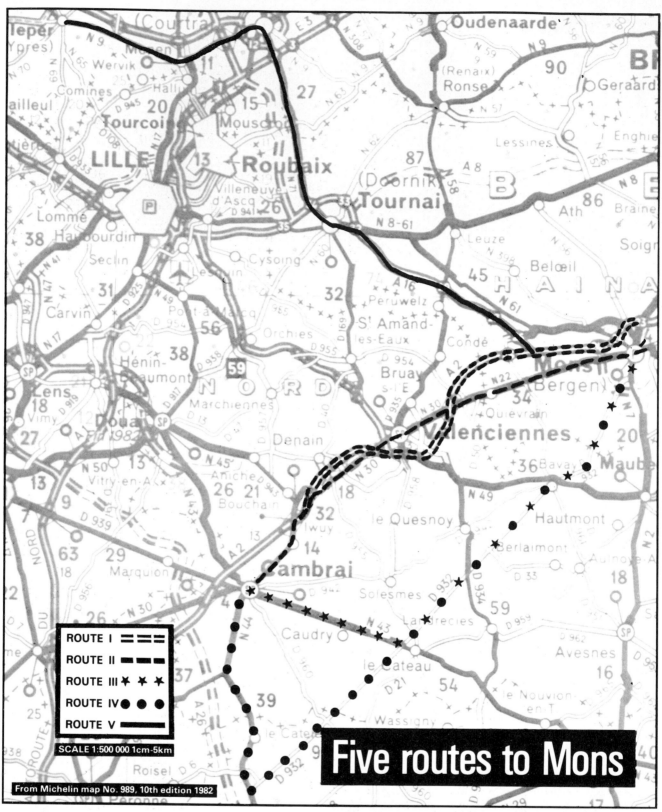

ROUTE I ▬ ▬ ▬
ROUTE II ▬ ▬ ▬
ROUTE III ✶ ✶ ✶
ROUTE IV ● ● ●
ROUTE V ▬▬▬

SCALE 1:500 000 1cm=5km

From Michelin map No. 989, 10th edition 1982

Five routes to Mons

Route I Cambrai is 65 kms from Mons on the A2 and E41 motorways.

Route II Alternatively, we can use the N30 to Valenciennes (30 kms) through some varied countryside, increasingly industrial, as the coalfields are reached between Bouchain and Douchy-les-Mines and into **Valenciennes**.

This former lace-making city was occupied by the Germans in August 1914 and suffered considerably during the next four years. Factories and other establishments were taken over for use by the invading army, converting the area into a large base. By the time the Germans were driven out of the city in November 1918, by the Canadian Corps and the 4th, 49th and 61st Divisions, much was destroyed. Damage had also been caused by long-range artillery during the Allied advance.

Twelve kms out of Valenciennes on the N30 are the frontier and customs posts at **Quiévrechain**, from where the long straight road continues 22 kms to Mons. In the latter stages it passes through the region, south of the **Condé Canal**, which figured greatly in the 1914 BEF defence of Mons. General Allenby's Cavalry Corps were defending the bridges along the canal with the 19th Brigade in support from Valenciennes. The 5th Division was in action along the canal and, after the retreat

had been ordered, the four bridges were blown. Today, however, there is nothing left to recall the brave acts of 1914.

Route III The D932 route to Mons can be joined from Cambrai either at Le Cateau or Le Catelet. Using the N43, Le Cateau is 22 kms. After leaving Cambrai there is not a bend in this old Roman road over its total length. It sweeps up and down through very open country and few towns or villages lie directly in its path. In recent years it has been greatly widened and is now a very fast road indeed, with narrow stretches only through the outlying parts of Beauvois, Caudry and Inchy.

Route IV For the more circular route via Le Catelet, leave Cambrai through the Porte de Paris on the N44, 7½ kms to **Masnières**. Here the **St Quentin Canal** is crossed not far from the **site of the bridge** which, after being mined by the Germans but not completely blown, was used by the British in their attacks in the Battle of Cambrai. However, when a tank attempted to drive across it, the much weakened structure gave way and the accident was to cause a considerable hold up to the advancing forces. On the crest of the hill going down into the town on the right is the **Newfoundland Regiment's Caribou Memorial**; the 29th Division fought here. Four kms further on is **Bonavis**, the southern end of the line for the Battle of Cambrai. Take the left-hand fork, the N44 for Le Catelet, travelling up and down across the plain (10 kms). Join the D932 7 kms south of the town.

Route V For those wanting to travel direct from Ypres (Ieper) our route follows the most picturesque and historic roads.

Take the N9 from Ypres to **Menin** (Menen), 18 kms. This industrial town (with its twin Halluin on the southern French bank of the Lys) was the major German base and supply depot for the battles of Ypres. In 1914 it was overrun before Sir John French could seize it and for the next four years the Germans retained it. On October 16, 1918, the 34th Division took the town in the great Allied advance. On the northern outskirts of the town (beside the road to Moorsele) is the **Menin German Cemetery** where 48,049 are buried.

Ten kms out of the town on the N9 is **Courtrai** (Kortrijk), also used by the German army as a large base. It fell to the 9th Division on October 17, 1918. The town was damaged during the Second World War by a number of air raids. One of its older fortifications, the **Broelen Toren,** survived. This is a bridge over the Lys with two huge towers, in one of which is a **small museum**.

A little way out of the town on the Ghent road (the N14), on the left-hand side just before **Harelbeke**, is the **Royal Newfoundland Regiment Memorial**, the Caribou marking their exploits here in 1918.

Our route is now the N71 to Tournai (Doornik), 29 kms away. A pleasant road through varying country which for the last 10 kms, follows closely the course of the Scheldt. Seven kms from Tournai at **Esquelmes**, in the little churchyard on the river bank, are a group of **British war graves** from late 1918. Away in the fields, a kilometre or so along the narrow road running parallel with the canal, is a **1939-45 cemetery**, where lie men killed in May 1940. Among the many guardsmen is the 8th Duke of Newcastle.

The ancient city of **Tournai** is entered through a long avenue of magnificent trees. The centre of the city is dominated by the enormous cathedral with its five towers. At the eastern end of the **Grand Place** is the **Belfroi**, the oldest in Belgium, and a magnificent view is gained from the gallery near the top.

Until the foundation of the modern Belgium in 1830, Tournai held allegiance to France. Many sieges have been withstood, including that by Edward III in 1340, and from 1513 to 1519 the city was in the hands of Henry VIII. He improved the old fortifications of the city and today one of these remains, the **Tour Henri VIII**. A solid two-storey building, it now houses the small but most interesting **Musée des Armes**. It includes ancient and modern weapons and equipment; at the entrance is a 'Tallboy' bomb and other smaller bombs from the Second World War.

To the German army, Tournai was a very important centre with routes connecting with their forward bases. They finally retreated in the face of the Fifth Army in the last Allied advance. The British army entered the city on November 8, 1918 to find many wrecked buildings and all the bridges destroyed.

Leave Tournai by N8 and at Warchin join

A modern bridge spans the canal at Masnières. This replaced the original one sited a few yards beyond it which collapsed under the weight of a British tank, (after German mining weakened it), causing a hold-up in the November 1917 Allied advance.

A small red brick chapel is the focal point of Menin German Cemetery where 48,049 Germans lie buried.

the autoroute A16. In 28½ kms join the E41. Leave the motorway after 11 kms at the Mons-Jemappes turn-off. Turn left onto the N22 to enter Mons (Bergen) in 2 kms.

Tour Henri VIII provides a medieval setting for the Musée des Armes at Tournai. A relic of Bluff King Hal's fortifications of the 1513-19 era.

MONS

Mons, as the run in will have shown, is a modern industrial town with a coalfield on two sides. Along the modernized Condé Canal factories stand with loading bays on the banks. In the distance, on either side, rise the hills, Mons itself being built on one.

Of the famous Battle of Mons of August 1914, or that of November 1918, no sign remains, for neither action lasted long enough to leave any lasting physical marks. There are, however, a number of memorials set at points which recall the actions of the corps to which they belong and, in spite of the German bombing of 1940 and fighting of 1944 (when the US VII Corps captured the town), the ancient municipal buildings and private houses look today very much as they did to the Old Contemptibles on August 21, 1914. In recent years, however, there have been many changes on the outskirts as motorways and their link roads have been carved through the region. Encircling the town are wide boulevards which mark the lines of the old ramparts. The large modern railway station overlooks one of these boulevards.

The **Hôtel de Ville** which dates from the 15th and 17th Centuries is on the Grand Place. The **Musées du Centenaire**, in particular the **Musée de Guerre**, through the large gate to the municipal heart of the town and the garden behind it, is one of the main reasons for visiting Mons. Housed in an old pawnshop built in 1625 is one of the finest collections of relics from the First and Second Wars in Belgium. It represents the work of two men, Georges Licope and Léon Pepin. On the ground floor is the Great War collection, and on the third floor the Second War collection. In between are fine ceramic, numismatic and archaeological displays.

The Mons Tourist Office has produced a useful guide to the ten salient points in the region. Each is clearly labelled. The earlier guide by the late Georges Licope is also still available. M. Licope was the recognised authority on all matters concerning the four battles of Mons: August 1914, November 1918, May 1940 and September 1944.

At the gateway of the Hôtel de Ville there are several **bronze** plaques one of which is that of the **5th Royal Irish Lancers**. This regiment took part in both First World War battles and an Irish Lancer was the last British soldier to be killed on Armistice Day, November 11, 1918. Another plaque is the **Canadian Memorial** commemorating the liberation by the Canadian 3rd Division.

The highest part of the old city is the site of the Citadel and the old château. Rising here today is the baroque Belfry, the only one of its type in Belgium, built in 1662. A carillon of 47 bells is housed within and a lift goes up to the top of the tower. In the 'onion' of the dome above is a panoramic explanation of the battles of Mons. The windows on each side of the dome enable the visitor who has braved the rather precarious ladders up from the top floor of the tower (*not* recommended to anyone elderly or suffering from fear of heights), a full all-round view. A similar view, almost as satisfactory and much more comfortable, can be had from the walls of the garden in which the Belfry stands. In this garden is the **monument** unveiled by Field-Marshal Earl Alexander of Tunis in October 1952 in memory of the two **Battles of Mons of 1914 and 1918**.

In 1935, at the left-hand side of the entrance into the Belfry, was buried the **Special Symbol of the Battles of Mons**, consisting of earth from the grave of every British soldier killed at Mons. Among these, of course, are Canadians including George Price, their last casualty. The place where this man lost his life

August 23, 1982—old Contemptibles at the British Expeditionary Force Memorial at Mons erected in the Citadel in 1952.

The Mons Musée de Guerre includes a comprehensive collection of weapons and uniforms.

is by the first house over the canal crossing between Havré and Ville-sur-Haine. On the wall of **No. 71 rue de Mons** a plaque was unveiled by his surviving comrades in November 1968 recording the details.

Above: **Here Private George Price became the last Canadian to lose his life in the Great War—at 10.58 a.m. on November 11, 1918.** *Below:* **A plaque was erected to his memory in 1968.**

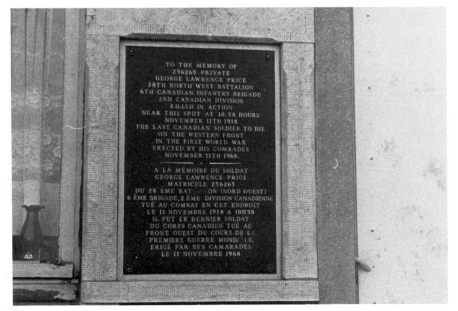

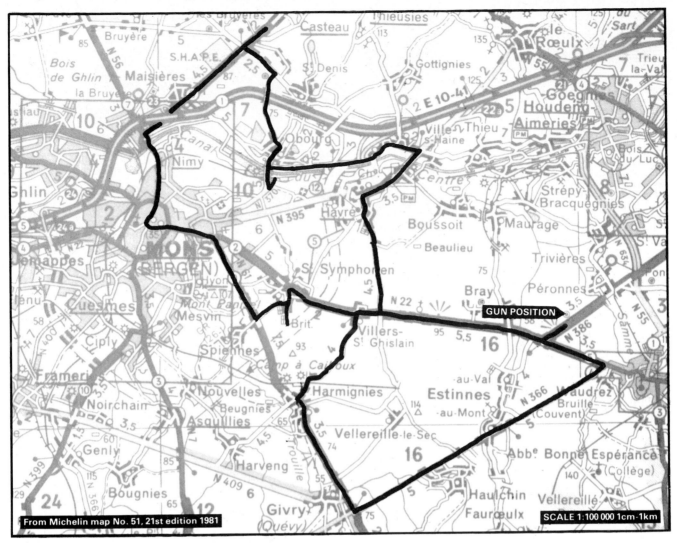

Mons Battlefield Tour

In the last ten years, the outskirts of Mons have been drastically altered with new road systems and many new buildings changing the landscape. The advent of SHAPE at Casteau is a major cause but the change of emphasis in the industrial life of the city, modern factories replacing the old smaller establishments, and the revival in the canal traffic has all played its part. The road systems are not yet complete as work on the ring-road from Ghlin and Jemappes to Frameries, Spiennes, Havré and Obourg is still in progress. New bridges, flyovers and the motorway now dominate the region.

Leaving Mons by the Chaussée de Bruxelles (N7) in 1 km reach **Nimy**, an old industrial suburb through which the main railway passes. Soon the first of the battlefield tour signboards will be seen as the road swings past the town square to the foot of the new road bridge on which it is placed. Take the small road on the right to go under the bridge and along the narrow road by the canal bank. The modern bridge spans the canal over the **site of the old swing bridge** which was so gallantly defended by 4th Bn. Royal Fusiliers. The lock-keeper's house is much the same now as then and bears scars of battle near ground level. Further along the canal is the **modern railway bridge** which replaced that defended so well by another company of 4th Bn. Royal Fusiliers. **Nimy station** is on the far side of the canal. A **plaque on the wall** supporting the bridge commemorates the actions of Lieutenant M. J. Dease and Private S. F. Godley of the machine gun section. Every man in the section was either killed or wounded as they held up the German advance permitting the battalions of their division to retire to new positions. Lieutenant Dease continued to keep the last gun firing until so badly wounded he was unable to continue. Private Godley then volunteered to man it until his wounds forbade further action; he destroyed the gun and flung it into the canal before being taken prisoner. It is said he was the inspiration for Bruce Bairnsfather's 'Old Bill'. The artist, away over in the Plugstreet Wood area, saw a photo of British prisoners from Mons entraining; in the foreground was the stocky, bushy-moustached Godley. Dease died from his wounds and both he and Godley were awarded the Victoria Cross—the first of the Great War.

A railway bridge still spans the canal where Lieutenant Dease and Private Godley of the 4th Bn. Royal Fusiliers won their VCs. On the far 'German' side stands Nimy station. This is the position of Stand 2 of the official Mons Battlefield Tour, details of which are available from the Mons Tourist Office.

It is possible to turn just beyond the bridge as the road skirts the new artificial lake and marina which provides an attractive view of Mons rising above it. Return to the N7 crossing the bridge and bear right (road signed Bruxelles and SHAPE) and go under the motorway.

Maisières where the BEF suffered its first casualties, borders the modern highway to the capital. A **plaque on the church** commemorates this event. The huge complex of Supreme Headquarters Allied Powers Europe extends over the region to the left, once wooded as is the land to the right. One impact on Mons of the presence of the organisation has been the substantial growth of residential building and another is the difficulty one has in finding hotel accommodation in the district.

At 5 kms from Mons, having passed the main gates of SHAPE and the crossroads above, lies the village of **Casteau**. Almost on the crest of the rise on the left is a **stone memorial to the first contact between the BEF and the First German Army** at 7.00 a.m. on August 22, 1914. 'C' Squadron of the 4th Royal Irish Dragoon Guards, commanded by

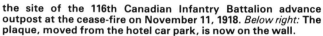

Above right: **The first shots of the First World War rang out near this monument on the Casteau road at 7.00 a.m. on August 22, 1914.** *Below:* **Almost directly opposite, a hotel now stands on** the site of the 116th Canadian Infantry Battalion advance outpost at the cease-fire on November 11, 1918. *Below right:* **The plaque, moved from the hotel car park, is now on the wall.**

Major Tom Bridges, were on patrol on the road and in the woods following reports of German cavalry between Casteau and Soignies. Captain C. Hornby, the second in command, was in the van of the first two troops when a group of German 4th Kuirassiers were sighted. Corporal E. Thomas fired the first shots of a British Expeditionary Force on the Continent for nearly 100 years and Captain Hornby, sword raised, led the first charge. Across the road on the wall of the

Hôtel Medicis is a **bronze plaque.** This memorial records that outposts of the **116th Canadian Infantry Battalion** were on this spot on November 11, 1918 when the cease-fire rang out at 11.00 a.m. 'Here beginneth and endeth the lesson . . .'

Return to the main crossroad and take the left-hand road to St Denis for 1 km and then turn right over the motorway to reach **Obourg** taking the road and bridge over the canal signed for Mons. At the south end of the

bridge a hairpin turning leads to **Obourg station**. A foot-bridge takes one over the railway line and, on the canal bank where once stood the station building, now stands a **red brick memorial**. This was fashioned in 1981 from bricks of the old station then being demolished. It was on the exterior wall of the old waiting room that the **4th Bn. Middlesex Regiment** were remembered. They had from every vantage point opened up on the oncoming Germans with fantastic rifle fire,

Obourg is a name synonymous with the first demonstration in action of the skills of the British rifleman equipped with the Rifle No. 1, Short, Magazine, Lee Enfield Mk III —the SMLE which had been adopted in January 1907. *Above:* **This was where the station stood until it was demolished in 1981. The plaque recording the events of August 23, formerly to be seen on the wall of the waiting room, has since been remounted on a memorial** *(right)* **built from bricks salvaged from the old building.**

ably displaying their skill with the Lee Enfield, typical of the regular British infantryman. All the units involved in Mons were capable of firing 16 aimed rifle shots per minute, some even more, thus giving the enemy the notion that every battalion was equipped with many machine guns instead of the pitiful few they actually had. Some of the battalion were sited on the roof of the station and the plaque recorded the events at about 8.00 a.m. on August 23. Each year a ceremony is held here on that day.

Another 4th Middlesex position was a farm at the edge of the residential area up behind the station, beyond the woods. There in an orchard the **first officer to be killed** was mortally wounded. Major Abell now lies with his men in St Symphorien British Cemetery and one of the new roads has been named Avenue 4th Middlesex.

Return over the bridge towards Obourg, turning left on to the road beneath it, and drive along to the right by the canal to **Ville-sur-Haine** 4 kms. At the junction with N395 turn right into rue de Mons passing the **house where Corporal Price was killed**. In Havré, near the ruins of the old château, turn left on the Villers St Ghislain road. In 4½ kms, at the N22 junction, turn right and then first left

Above: **The farm at Obourg occupied by the 4th Battalion. The road has been renamed 'Avenue du 4th Middlesex' in memory of their stand and the death of the first officer killed in the Great War in a nearby orchard.** *Below:* **A shell still to be seen in the ceiling of No. 2.**

for **Harmignies**. The road climbs up out of the village and in just over 1 km along on the right side will be seen **two rusty plaques**. These mark the spot of the **first crash of an RFC machine** on active patrol. The plane, from No. 5 Squadron and crewed by Lieutenants V. Waterfall and C. G. G. Bayley, came down here on August 23 in the forenoon; it was an Avro. Matters are in hand to replace the tin sheets, with their incorrect if barely legible names, with another, more fitting memorial.

Another advantage of this road is the excellent panoramic view it gives of the battle area before it drops down into Harmignies. Here the Royal Horse Artillery had their base. At the major crossroads in the village turn left onto N61 and drive 3½ kms through undulating countryside to **Givry**. Here it was that the I Corps held the line immediately before the retreat began. The commander, Sir

The spot where the first Royal Flying Corps' aeroplane fell to earth is recorded by these rusty plaques just outside Harmignies. A more fitting monument is soon to be erected.

From the field beside the slag heap, the guns of 'E' Battery fired on August 23, 1914.

General Allenby had his quarters in this red brick house belonging to the school mistress at Villers St Ghislain.

Douglas Haig, had his headquarters on the road to Bavay. Their line was Givry—Harmignies—Nouvelles, and General Allenby's cavalry were in support behind them in the Waudruz—Binche region.

Turn right onto N366 at the next crossroad; follow the very straight road and the 10 kms to **Waudrez** are soon accomplished. Turn left on to N22 and take first right on to N386 which rises over the ridge prior to dropping down into **Péronnes**. About 200 metres along on the left is a water tower opposite a factory. This is an excellent vantage point to view the countryside littered with slag heaps and belching factory chimneys. In the near foreground is one large slag heap with a cluster of houses nearby. In the fields here, 'E' Battery, RHA, fired the **first artillery round of the war** on August 22. On the right side of the road, about three metres from the pavement outside the factory boundary fence, is a small stone, almost hidden, which commemorates this event. From these positions in August 22, 1964 the same gun fired again in the presence of many of those who had participated fifty years previously. The gun can be seen today in the Imperial War Museum.

Retrace the road to the N22 and turn right for **Villers St Ghislain** (5½ kms). Here General Allenby was billeted in the **house of the school mistress**. This house, on the left, has changed little over the years.

Continue another 2 kms to **St Symphorien**. Turn left (signpost) to visit the **British War Cemetery**. The road runs through a new estate and then deteriorates somewhat as it follows a brick wall and worsens as the lane comes to a junction at the cemetery gates.

This is possibly the most beautiful of all the British cemeteries in the Western Front area. It is also very different in layout, typifying a traditional English garden. There are shady paths and glades and many varieties of trees and shrubs in addition to the flowers on the actual graves and borders. The land was originally given to the Germans for use as a cemetery by a local landowner and here they buried both their own and the British casualties of August 1914, erecting a number of **special memorials**. One of these, set in a small circular glade surrounded by the graves, is in memory of the **'Royal' Middlesex Regiment**—the German personnel could not believe that any regiment which had discipline and courage of the kind displayed by the Middlesex was not a 'Royal' regiment. This part of the cemetery is reached by taking the path to the right as you enter and is on the left, a little way up. Nearby is buried L/14196 Private J. Parr, Middlesex Regiment. It is very

probable that he was the **first man to be killed in the BEF** in the Great War. His death on August 21, in the evening when he did not return from a scout mission with his bicycle, has now been confirmed and a new headstone will soon replace that in situ (August 1982). Opposite is the headstone of the **last man to die** on November 11, 1918—Private G. E. Ellison of the 5th Royal Irish Lancers. Beyond is the **German plot** where the original headstones have been retained. In contrast to the plain white British stones, these grey granite markers differ with officers often having more flamboyant styles than those of the NCO or private soldier.

Up to the left a group of British graves can be seen. Here lies Lieutenant Dease, VC, who died on August 23, 1914. In the row behind him is the grave of Private Price of the 28th North West Bn. Canadian Infantry, who was killed at Ville-sur-Haine at 10.58 a.m. on November 11, 1918.

On the same level as the Cross of Sacrifice, which is placed at the highest part of the garden on the other side of the path, is a small rectangular lawn with a curved stone seat at the far end. In front is **another of the German memorials** to their British foes, this time to 53

Memorial erected by the German army to their gallant foe, the 'Royal' Middlesex Regiment.

The German obelisk in St Symphorien Cemetery to the dead of both armies killed on August 23/24, 1914.

St Symphorien War Cemetery contains several notable graves. One is that of Private Parr who was possibly the first casualty.

Nearby is the headstone of the last man to die before the Armistice — Private G. E. Ellison.

members of the **Royal Fusiliers**. Above this garden of rest in the spring, glorious flowering trees burst forth in clouds of creamy-white blossom.

Leaving the cemetery, the path goes through a fringe of fir trees in the centre of which is the **German memorial to the men of both armies who died on August 23/24, 1914**. From this memorial a flight of steps leads back to the entrance.

Return to the new housing estate and take the left-hand road to the west and the hamlet of **Malplaquet**. In ¾ km, turn right onto the

N61. On the left rises the **Hill of Panisel**, through the woods and fields of which run paths making very pleasant walking areas. Many fierce actions were fought in the orchards and fields on the lower slopes; this was the scene of the stand of the 3rd Infantry Division.

In 3 kms the major crossroads marks the site of **La Bascule**, a scene of heavy fighting. As one of the highest places in Mons, it was the scene of one of the first actions on August 23, involving the 2nd Bn. Royal Irish Regiment and the other units of the 7th Brigade,

The Royal Irish Regiment Memorial is tucked away on the corner of La Bascule crossroads.

3rd Division which, at great cost, delayed the advance of the enemy.

A Celtic cross on the apex of the small road which goes down the hill to Obourg and the Charleroi road is the **2nd Bn. Royal Irish Regiment Memorial**. After the action here, the battalions fell back on Mont Hyon and around Mont Erebus on the road towards Ciply to the south. The centre of Mons is one kilometre down the beautiful Avenue Reine Astrid.

Both British and German headstones are to be seen in St Symphorien Cemetery. Here lie Lieutenant Dease, the Great War's first VC, and Private G. L. Price, the last Canadian to be killed in action (rear rank on the right).

Mons to Le Cateau

The route south from Mons is basically that of the retreat but the final advance followed much the same route. Leave Mons by the N2 and in 3½ kms at **Ciply** take right fork N399. Pass straight through **Noirchain** (3½ kms), and reach **Blaregnies** 9 kms further on.

The area just passed was in the II Corps lines, the commander of which, General Sir Horace Smith-Dorrien, had his headquarters in a small château at **Sars-la-Bruyère**. The village and the château can be reached by taking the right-hand road at the crossroads in the centre of Blaregnies. In about a kilometre, near the church of Sars-le-Bruyère, go right and in a short distance the drive to the château is found on the right.

Château de la Haie, (also called Château de la Roche), a quiet white house set in delightful surroundings, was the scene of a momentous meeting on August 23, 1914, at 5.00 a.m. Present were Field-Marshal French and his corps commanders, Lieutenant-General Sir Douglas Haig, I Corps, Major-General Edmund Allenby, Cavalry Corps and of course Sir Horace Smith-Dorrien, II Corps. Also present were Major-General Sir W. R. Robertson, the Quartermaster-General, and Major-General Sir A. J. Murray, Chief-of-

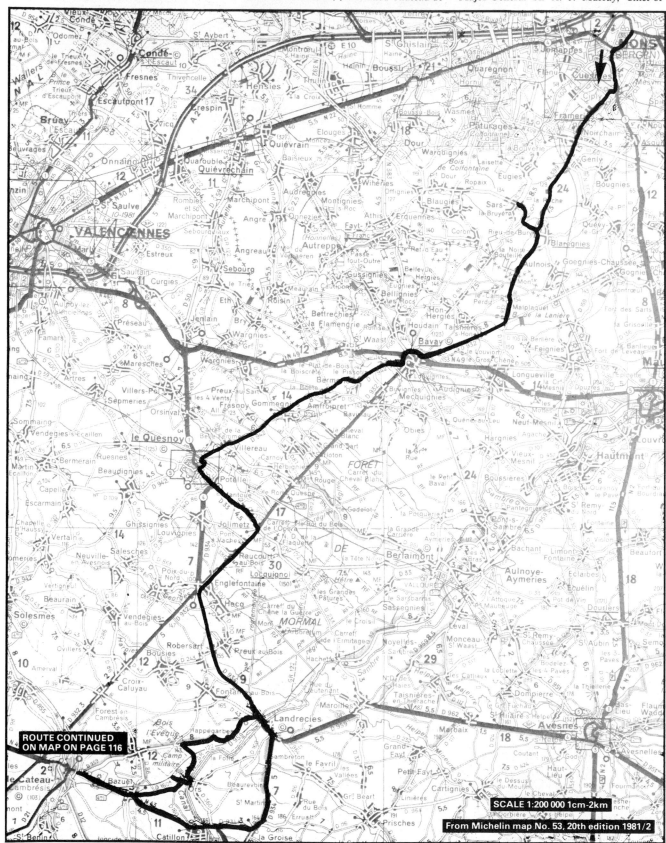

ROUTE CONTINUED ON MAP ON PAGE 116

SCALE 1:200 000 1cm-2km

From Michelin map No. 53, 20th edition 1981/2

Château de la Haie, the scene of the momentous meeting on August 23, 1914, which decided the retreat from Mons.

A plaque in the hall reminds visitors of the historic meeting between Field-Marshal French and his corps commanders.

At Landrecies, the 25th Division remember their commander, Sir Ronald Charles, who liberated the town with 600 men on November 4, 1918.

The ramparts at Le Quesnoy. Beside the site of the assault, the New Zealand Memorial depicts soldiers climbing these walls on November 4, 1918.

Staff. The conference covered all eventualities including that of retreat. A **plaque in the hall** commemorates this momentous meeting which took place in the large room to the left of the front doors. On the morning of August 24 the headquarters was moved back to Hon.

The château was owned by the Comte d'Hendécourt, who was later killed in action. His son now lives in the house which remained unoccupied for many years. In 1940 the invading Germans attempted to remove the artillery pieces flanking the front doors but left them on discovering they were mounted in concrete.

Return to Blaregnies and right onto the N399 and, within a kilometre, arrive at the frontier. Between the two stations is the **battlefield of Malplaquet** and a **monument** on the left commemorates Marlborough's victory on September 11, 1709. On November 8, 1918 there was a sharp action here as the Allies advanced. Here the N399 becomes D932.

Another 8 kms and we reach **Bavay**. This little town is situated on a hill close to which are **Riez de l'Erelle** and **Hon** where Haig and Smith-Dorrien had their respective headquarters at the beginning of the retreat. French had his advance headquarters in the **Mairie of Bavay** during the battle of Mons, General Headquarters being then at Le Cateau. By August 25, all the British corps in the vicinity were making their way south on either side of the Forest of Mormal. The Guards Division recaptured the town on November 7, 1918.

Take the D942 for **Le Quesnoy** (14 kms). Le Quesnoy is a charming old town still enclosed with its 17th Century ramparts, another of Vauban's fortresses. On August 25, 1914 the town echoed to the noises of the retreating

The 1st Division Memorial at the La Groise crossroads. Here the Division held the German advance on August 26, 1914; in November 1918 it passed back through the crossroads.

BEF and the refugees who hindered the army in their routes south. Thereafter, for four years, it was a German garrison town. On November 5, 1918, the town was attacked by men of the New Zealand Division who scaled the high walls of the outer ramparts and seized the German commander and his garrison of over 1,000 men. On the face of the walls scaled by the New Zealanders is a **memorial** to their effort which details, in bas relief, the use of mediaeval methods which proved so successful.

The D33 leads in 4½ kms to **Jolimetz** on the D932 at the western edge of the **Forest of Mormal**. The D932 was the road taken by II Corps, I Corps being on the eastern flank of the forest. The advancing German army made its way through the forest. This huge woodland, some 22,000 acres, which covers the slopes and high ground between Bavay and Landrecies, gave good cover and the wide glades provided routes for the German transport. In November 1918 the forest again lay in the path of advancing troops, this time the 3rd and 4th British Armies who drove all before them and had cleared the area by November 5.

Turn right on the D932 to **Englefontaine** (5 kms) and travel 8 kms on the D934 to the outskirts of **Landrecies**. On August 25, 1914 I Corps fought briskly here with the Guards fighting in the streets as the rest of the corps proceeded to retreat. In November 1918 the 25th Division captured the town and forced their way across the River Sambre, which is canalised here. On the bridge into the town is a **memorial to General Sir Ronald Charles**, the GOC, who, with 600 men, was killed in liberating the town on November 4.

Continue on the D934 5 kms to **La Groise**. The straight road undulates through attractive country to the crossroads of **Chapeau Rouge**. Here, on August 26, 1914, the 1st Division stood and defied the German advance and, on November 4, 1918, the crossroads were in the centre of the line held by the same division as it advanced. A rather elegant **memorial** on the left of the road recalls these facts. Just 6 kms ahead on D946 is **Etreux**, the scene of the heroic stand of 2nd Bn. Royal Munster Fusiliers. The **memorial and graveyard** mark the site with the headstones ranged in alphabetical order around the walls, the men being buried in three plots. The fields behind the cemetery and the farms close by are little changed from the dreaded day of August 27, 1914.

Return to Chapeau Rouge and turn left on D934 for **Catillon**, in 3 kms crossing the Sambre and joining the N43 for Le Cateau.

'To the Glory of God and in proud and lasting memory . . . the Royal Munster Fusiliers . . . who laid down their lives . . . in the cause of freedom and justice . . . their name liveth for evermore.' Fine words on a fine memorial at Etreux.

ALTERNATIVE ROUTE

An alternative route from Landrecies is via D959 through **Bois l'Evêque**, scene of battles in 1914 and October 1918. In 4 kms turn left for **Ors**. In the **British Communal Cemetery** by the station lie the poet Wilfred Owen, Lieutenant-Colonel J. N. Marshall, VC, MC, and 2nd Lieutenant J. Kirk, VC, all killed in 1918. At Bazuel join N43 via D160a.

Ors Communal Cemetery: 2nd Lieutenant James Kirk, VC, Lieutenant-Colonel John Marshall, VC and Lieutenant Wilfred Owen.

LE CATEAU

Le Cateau is a name engraved in the memory of all Old Contemptibles, if not as the first location of British General Headquarters as the battle honour on so many of their Colours. Here on August 26, 1914 was fought a desperate battle by the 3rd, 4th and 5th Divisions of II Corps against seven of von Kluck's Army Divisions. The Germans held the advantage, not only in infantry but also in artillery. The battle began to the west of the town, just south of the Cambrai road, and on through Caudry where the country is reminiscent of Salisbury Plain.

The site of the battle can be visited from tracks leading off the D932 or the D21. Amid a grove of trees is a **simple cenotaph** on which the actions by the 2nd Battalion of the Suffolk Regiment, the Manchester Regiment, the Argyll and Sutherland Highlanders and the Royal Artillery batteries in their support are remembered.

As you enter Le Cateau from Landrecies, look right at the crossroads with the Hostellerie du Marche on the corner. In front of the café (on the rue de la Fontaine à Gros Bouillons), is a horse trough now used very charmingly as a flower garden. This is the **Memorial of the British 66th Division** who fought here on August 10, 1918 and who liberated the town. Resistance in the station area lasted a week longer and was finally

eliminated by the South African Brigade. After that, Le Cateau was shelled heavily by the Germans until their guns were forced out of range by the Allied advance.

Many of the narrow streets which climb the hills are still cobbled including the main street. Half way up it is the **Hôtel de Ville**. The entrance is under the central tower. On the walls of the small foyer and staircase to the library and museum are pictures by one of the towns most famous sons, Matisse. Beneath them is a **British 3.7in howitzer**. This weapon was presented to the town by the 93rd Battery, Royal Field Artillery, to cement the friendship of the unit and the town for which it fought. The howitzer is of 1932 vintage. Each year, members of the battery return to the town, their headquarters being the Hôtel du Midi on the rue du Maréchal Mortier.

The **British Military Cemetery** is just north of the N43 and D932 crossroads and it gives a good panoramic view of the battlefield. The cemetery was opened originally by the Germans and there are several large memorials erected by them amid the many British and German graves. In one cluster, are a group of Russian graves. Recently the German war graves authority have made considerable renovations to their cemetery and many old crumbling memorials have been removed and the graves reset with new markers. There are now separate entrances to the British and German sections. In the British plot men lie together who died in the battle of 1914, as prisoners of war and in the 1918 actions. Among these is Lance-Corporal John W. Sayer who won the VC on March 21, 1918 and who died of wounds in April 1918.

There is another British cemetery in Le Cateau, the **Communal Cemetery** in the town cemetery. Here some 150 casualties of the battle are buried. There also is a German memorial to them and their German and French comrades.

The 66th Division's practical memorial, a horse drinking trough, is now an integral part of the town's floral decorations.

Amid a galaxy of Matisse paintings, a gun of 93rd Battery has pride of place in Le Cateau Hôtel de Ville.

Men from Germany, Russia and Great Britain lie together at Le Cateau. This is the Commonwealth War Graves section.

Le Cateau Cemetery was originally opened by the Germans and it contains several German memorials—and a mass grave.

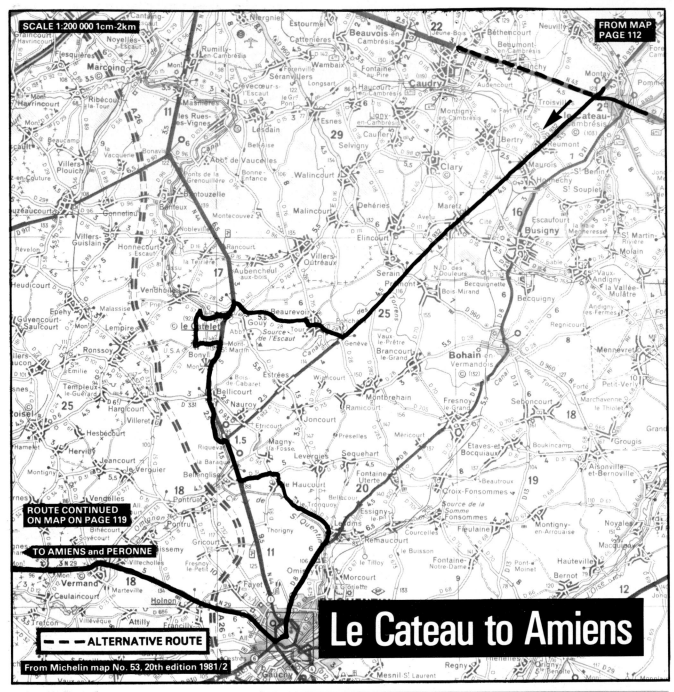

SCALE 1:200 000 1cm-2km

ROUTE CONTINUED ON MAP ON PAGE 119

TO AMIENS and PERONNE

– – – ALTERNATIVE ROUTE

From Michelin map No. 53, 20th edition 1981/2

Le Cateau to Amiens

In nearby **Caudry** is rather a unique **town war memorial**. On the plinth are commemorated four incidents in the war; the defence of the town in 1914; the trials of the occupation; the battle of 1918 and the final liberation on October 10, 1918, in which the figures carved in bas relief actually represent the personalities concerned—the officers and NCOs of the 37th Division.

Proceed from Le Cateau along the D932. This long straight highway cleaves its way across the plains of Picardy to the St Quentin canal at Riqueval, but we leave it in 18½ kms at **Poncheux** taking the D28 (on the right) for **Beaurevoir** and Le Catelet (5½ kms). This wide country was the terrain of the Australians under Sir John Monash in their advance in October 1918.

Le Catelet, is a straggling village across the N44 Cambrai-St Quentin road, and is the northern entrance of the **tunnel** of the **St Quentin Canal**. About ½ km along the D57 to **Vendhuile**, under a group of chestnut trees on the right side of the road, footpaths lead down on either side of the early 19th Century canal to the tunnel entrance. This tunnel, over 7

One kilometre south of Le Catelet lies Somme American Cemetery at Bony.

kms in length, was built in the time of Napoleon in 1802-10. During the German occupation of the area, they incorporated this tunnel and the shorter one between Le Tronquoy and Haucourt into the defences forming the Hindenburg Line.

On an average the tunnels are 16 metres below the surface and, therefore, almost impregnable. They were connected to the main works of the Hindenburg Line by shafts and were fully equipped with offices, stores, stables and hospitals. Barges were used as billets and the whole system was electrically lit.

At this northern end of the tunnel all is now peaceful and few marks recall its use as a fortress. Neither do the banks of the sleepy canal carry many reminders that they were once part of an intricate trench system. The northern end of the tunnel figured in the heavy fighting in September and October 1918, when the American 27th and 30th Division and the British 50th Division fought successfully to breach the Line.

The canal re-emerges into daylight south of **Bellicourt** village, which is 5 kms from Le Catelet. On the heights before the village and directly above the tunnel is the impressive **American Memorial**, the Bellicourt Monument of the American Battle Monuments Commission. On the west face of the monument is an interesting map of the operations of the two divisions of 90,000 men who served with the British in the battles in the region. On the terrace overlooking the battlefield is an orientation table.

About 2½ km south (via N44) of Bellicourt village at **Riqueval**, a small road (to the right) leads over the gorge at this end of the canal and eventually back to Bellicourt. Not far along this road is the actual **southern entrance** of the tunnel which is easily reached through the trees. A **memorial to the soldiers from Tennessee** who were killed in the canal battles stands near this entrance.

Right: **High above the canal tunnel, the American Memorial of Bellicourt overlooks the remnants of the old Hindenburg Line.**

Above: **The northern entrance of an unassailable fortress—the St Quentin Canal Tunnel at Le Catelet. This was an integral part of the Hindenburg Line.**

Above: **The southern entrance to the St Quentin Canal tunnel at Riqueval.** *Right:* **The Memorial to the soldiers of the American**

State of Tennessee killed in the battles for the canal stands near the entrance.

117

General Campbell, VC addresses men of the 137th British Brigade on the slopes of the St Quentin Canal from the ruined bridge at Riqueval.

Sixty years have passed. This is the author's comparison photograph taken from the same spot . . . the bridge is virtually unchanged.

Riqueval bridge is shown in one of the most impressive photographs in the Imperial War Museum when the broken arch was used by the commander of 137th Brigade of 46th Division, Brigadier-General J. V. Campbell, VC, to address his men covering the steep banks of the gorge after his brigade had captured the bridge and canal at this point.

Continue on the N44 1½ kms to **Bellenglise** also taken by 46th Division. To visit the other **tunnel** at **Le Tronquoy**, take the D31 on the left and in 1 km turn right on D71b to **Le Haucourt**. The entrance is on the right, ½ km out of the village. Five hundred metres further on is the other entrance. The D71 follows the canal to **Lesdins** where, by joining the D8 and crossing the canal, St Quentin is entered in 6 kms.

St Quentin is a large industrial town on the River Somme. The British General Headquarters was here on August 25/26, 1914 before moving to Noyon and Compiègne. Units of II Corps arrived from Le Cateau exhausted and demoralised by the continuous march. The knowledge that the advance troops of the German army were hard on their heels ceased to have any urgency for them and they fell where they stood, tired out, when the order to halt was given. Soon after, some squadrons of the 4th Hussars led by Major T. Bridges came on the scene. Bridges was horrified by the sight which met his eyes and was determined to move the men out of St Quentin. He realised that the most effective adjunct for making men march was missing—he had no band. Seeing a toy shop he went in and bought a toy whistle and a drum. With his bugler on the whistle and himself on the drum he succeeded in rousing the men and led them out of the town after the infectious music had induced others to join in with mouth organs.

The Germans held the town from the end of August 1914 until October 1, 1918. In March 1918 they had set forth from St Quentin on their Spring Offensive driving back the British Third and Fifth Armies, taking many

The impressive French Memorial at St Quentin with its interesting bas relief.

prisoners. In the Allied advance, the town was outflanked by the British and was entered by the French army of General Debeney. By then the town was in ruins, **the cathedral** had been burnt and, as the French army arrived, the Germans were completing the laying of charges in the bases of the great pillars in the church to complete its demolition. The swift intervention of the Frenchmen saved the building, but one or two pillars still show the holes that had been drilled.

Down near the station is an impressive **French memorial** depicting many different aspects of the army. The British and French lines joined opposite St Quentin and, after 1914, the British Army did not return again until 1918.

To return to the western sectors, take the N29 from St Quentin 6 kms to **Francilly-Selency**, where the Hindenburg Line is crossed. Then we reach **Vermand** (5 kms), a small town totally destroyed in the German retreat in March 1917 and again in the front line in 1918 during March and the autumn of that year. In 7 kms, at **Estrées-en-Chaussée**, turn right onto the D944 for Péronne (10 kms).

St Quentin cathedral. Bore holes drilled for demolition charges still remain.

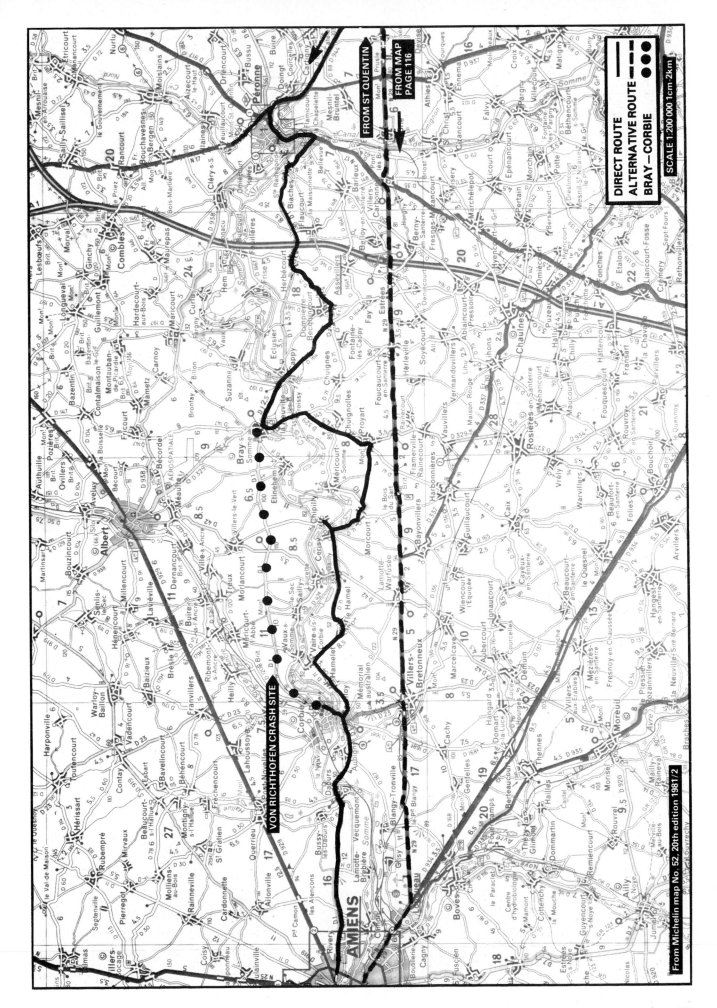

An Australian Digger stands on the 2nd Australian Division Memorial on Mont St Quentin, which replaced the original one destroyed during the Second War.

Péronne is an ancient town located at the confluence of the Rivers Somme and Cologne. It fell into German hands in 1914 and remained a most useful base, protected as it was by the artillery on Mont St Quentin, about 2 km to the north. This hill was strongly fortified with subways and deep trenches to give support and shelter for the guns. On its forward slopes many observation posts were set up commanding extensive views over a very wide area. This formidable fortress was the cause of the French Army's inability to advance in July-August 1916, although they reached Biaches, 1½ kms to the west of the city. In March 1917 the Germans evacuated Mont St Quentin when they retreated to the Hindenburg Line but, before doing so, destroyed both the fortress and the town. A year later they were back in possession of both capturing many valuable supplies. During the Allied advance, the 2nd Australian Division took the fortress on August 31, and Péronne itself was captured on September 2, 1918.

Completely ruined in these actions, the town has been rebuilt around the large square, Place du Commandant Daudre. The Renaissance town hall has been rebuilt in its old style.

Beside the Bapaume road (N17), on **Mont St Quentin** stands the **Memorial of the 2nd Australian Division**. The present monument was erected a few years ago to replace that destroyed by the Germans in the Second War. The original was a bronze figure of an Australian soldier killing an eagle, the new one is a statue of a typical 'digger'. On each side of the plinth, which was not destroyed, are bronze plaques depicting infantry and artillery in action and listing the actions in which the division fought.

From Péronne take the N17 to **La Chaplette** (1 km) and turn right on D1 for **Biaches** (4 kms) passing the **French Cemetery** and continue to **Herbécourt** after crossing the motorway (4½ km). Turn left onto the D71 for **Dompierre-Becquincourt** (2 kms) going through the village and at the crossroads in 1 km turn right on to D164. Just beyond these crossroads is a large **sucrerie** and also a **railway museum** for here is one of the **only remaining stretches of narrow-gauge track** dating from the First World War, part of which is still in regular use. From the sucrerie it runs across and then on either side of the D164 to skirt Cappy and end at **Froissy**. **Cappy**, up to March 1918 had been behind the Allied lines but after the German advance the

aerodrome became one of Richthofen's bases. It was finally captured by the Australians in August 1918. Thus it was a well-known base for all.

Crossing the Somme onto D1, **Bray** is reached in 2½ kms. This town built on the northern steep banks of the river was the junction between Third and Fifth Armies in March 1918 and was recaptured on August 24-25 in a moonlight attack by the Australians.

From Bray, the D1 is the direct road to Corbie on the north bank of the river, crossing open country with few villages. It was the route of the retreat in March 1918, but there are few signs of the battle today. From Bray the D329 goes south back across the river, and its marshes to **Proyart**, (5½ kms), notable for the stand made by the 39th Division in the March 1918 retreat, and for its enormous village **war memorial**, a miniature Arc de Triomphe complete with Poilu. The Australians took the village in August 1918.

A small unclassified road leads westward to Morcourt where it joins the D71 in 2 kms. Thence along the pretty river to Chipilly and Cerisy. On the **Chipilly** side of the river is the **Memorial to the 58th London Division**—an artilleryman with his wounded horse.

In 4 kms **Le Hamel** is reached. Near here, on the roadside, is a **Memorial to No. 57 Squadron**. From Le Hamel to Corbie the road

The 58th London Division Memorial at Chipilly—an artilleryman with his wounded horse.

is never far from the river and in 8 kms, crossing the Somme once again, we enter the quiet market town of **Corbie** with its huge church of St Pierre. This old abbey church, with its massive twin towers, was badly damaged in 1918 but the towers survived and the rest of the building was repaired in the original style.

Just outside Dompierre-Becquincourt one has the opportunity to examine a section of original narrow-gauge track which still remains from the First War.

Corbie was a very busy forward town during the Battle of the Somme.

On April 21, 1918, on the left of the D1 a few hundred metres north of Corbie, Baron Manfred von Richthofen fell to Allied guns, either those of Captain Roy Brown of No. 209 Squadron or the Australian machine gunner serving with the 53rd MG Company.

Corbie was also a headquarters of the Army Graves Registration Service and later the Imperial War Graves Commission who were responsible for the work on the cemeteries which, even during the war, in many cases quiet flower gardens where the troops went for a peaceful hour.

The D1 recrosses the Somme and follows the south bank into **Aubigny** and then recrosses the river to reach Amiens in 12 kms.

ALTERNATIVE ROUTE

If time does not permit the deviation from Estrées-en-Chaussée to include the Péronne—Somme valley, keep straight on along the N29 through **Villers-Carbonnel** (11 kms) and over the front line of 1917. This flat plain with gentle slopes was excellent tank country and, in the 1918 advance, they were used with great effect in the capture of the many positions around here. The road is now the N336 as far as Villers-Bretonneux when it reverts to N29.

The unmarked crash site of Baron Manfred von Richthofen beside the Bray-Corbie road.

The Australian National War Memorial in the British Military Cemetery at Villers-Bretonneux. The town was captured in the advance which began on August 8, 1918, led by tanks and low-flying aircraft.

Pass through **Warfusée-Abancourt** in 22 kms and 5 kms further on we reach **Villers-Bretonneux**. As the village is entered a **Demarcation Stone** will be seen. Most of this small industrial and agricultural town lies south of the road. Before April 1918 this sleepy town was well behind the British lines with an RFC aerodrome on its outskirts. Among the squadrons stationed here were Nos 11, 25 and 27.

As the Germans advanced in April 1918 it is probable that they had visions of repeating their victory of November 1870 when they defeated the Armée du Nord and went on to capture Amiens. However, the Australian Corps with the 8th, 18th and 58th Divisions stood in their way across the main road. The town fell to the Germans on April 24, and the battles that day were notable for the presence of German tanks and, for the first time, some light British Whippet tanks. The Australians and the 18th Divisions counter-attacked in the night and, during the 25th, the Australians regained the town. For the next four months a static war existed in this area with both sides digging-in and trenches were constructed in the woods south of the town.

On August 8, the Allied advance commenced with Fourth Army making a surprise attack with the Canadians and Australian III Corps together with over 400 tanks and low-flying aircraft. They advanced eastwards over the rolling downs and through the woods completely dislodging the Second German Army of General von der Marwitz. Tanks and cavalry played important roles in the advance on the Somme itself and, within a few days, Villers-Bretonneux was well behind the lines.

High on a hill, north of the village, soars the tower of the **Australian National War Memorial** and the **British Military Cemetery** lies before it. It is reached via the D23 road to Corbie. An orientation table is incorporated in the lantern at the top of the tower, which gives magnificent views of the battle area. In the spring and autumn the outlines of the old German trenches can be clearly seen as chalk slicks through the brown, tilled fields to the east. To the west, on a fine clear day, the view extends to Amiens, with the spire of the cathedral clearly in sight. To the north is Corbie, and to the south Villers-Bretonneux on its ridge. Beyond the slopes, out of sight, is the location of the old aerodrome. Further still are the woods of **Hangard** and **Demuin** —scenes of very heavy fighting.

Each year a special ceremony is held on Anzac day to recall the April and August battles, services being held at the memorial and celebrations in the town itself.

In 1975, the **Sir William Leggatt Museum** was opened in the school building which had been given to the children of Villers-Bretonneux by the Australian children whose fathers and brothers (1,200 of them) had lost their lives in the defence of the town. This museum is run by the Franco-Australian Welcome Committee. The museum, although so new, already gives a very good record of the part that the Australians and the villagers played in the battles. Access to the museum is by application to the Hôtel de Ville.

Continuing westward along the N29 the road skirts the **Bois d'Aquenne** where the Whippet tanks made their initial appearance. We then pass the **Bois d'Abbé** and, after the first level crossing, the **Bois de Blangy** is over on the left. Soon after the second level crossing **Blangy Cabaret** is passed and, on the right, the edge of **Glisy** aerodrome. Recently, a memorial to Richthofen was unveiled in the airfield precincts. Then, 17 kms from Villers-Bretonneux, Amiens is entered.

Amiens, the capital of Picardy, makes a good centre for visiting the Somme battlefields. Amiens has had a long history of contact with the English since the reign of King Edward III. There in 1550 Edward VI and Henri II of France signed a peace treaty and, in 1597, an English force assisted Henri IV to capture the city from the Spaniards. In 1802, the Treaty of Amiens brought a short respite in the Napoleonic wars.

In August 1914, Amiens was the first base for the troops arriving from the UK but, on the 30th of that month, the rapid advance of the Germans necessitated the evacuation of the city. For twelve days, until September 11, it was occupied by a German force which, after making demands for money, supplies and seizing twelve hostages, withdrew as the French army under Général d'Amade arrived and drove them back to Fricourt. The French remained in the city until it was taken over by the British in 1916. Thereafter, the town bustled with Allied soldiers. It was a centre for all manner of depots and facilities for the army, hospitals and recreation centres and, of course, for the railway to the coast and Paris. Trains from Le Havre brought in reinforcements and took away the injured. In 1918 it came within range of the German artillery until some of the large guns were captured on the Plain of Santerre, east of Chaulmes.

In the Second World War, the city was again badly damaged but today a modern city has been re-born with many new buildings. The **Picardy Museum** includes a large art gallery and collections of material relating to the history of the city. In 1966, the **Maison de la Culture** was opened in an attempt to bring together theatre, conference and exhibition halls. There are several interesting **memorials to the Allies** in the magnificent **cathedral** and also a **plaque** to Lieutenant Raymond Asquith, the son of the Prime Minister, Herbert Asquith, who lies buried at Guillemont.

A corner in the Sir William Leggatt Museum showing Australian uniforms.

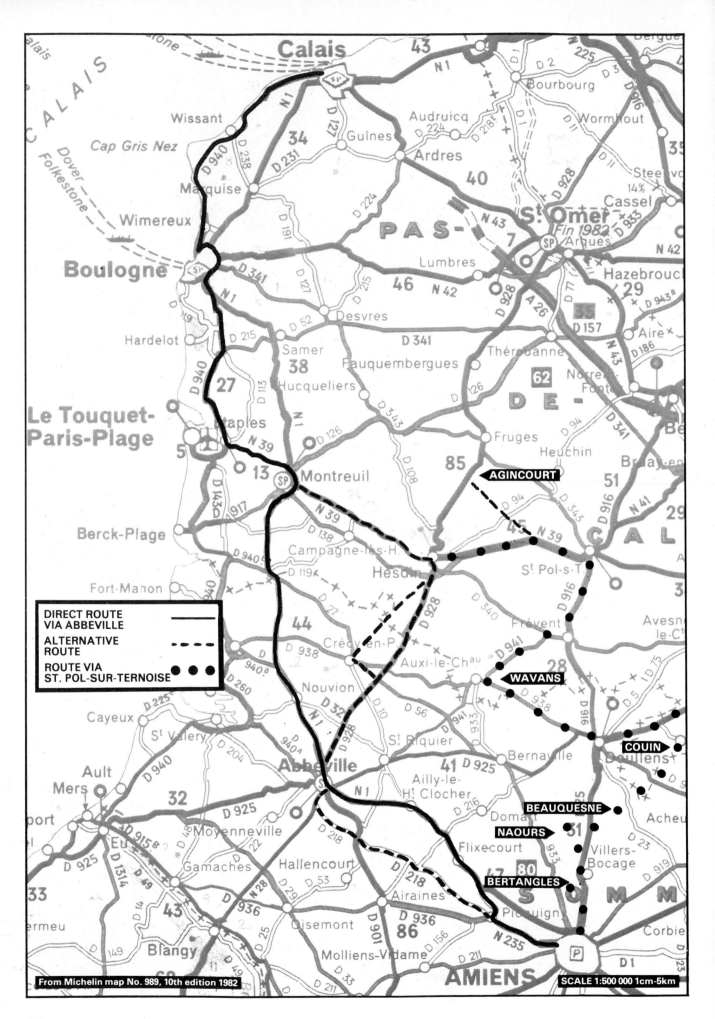

DIRECT ROUTE
VIA ABBEVILLE

ALTERNATIVE
ROUTE

ROUTE VIA
St. POL-SUR-TERNOISE

AGINCOURT

WAVANS

COUIN

BEAUQUESNE

NAOURS

BERTANGLES

From Michelin map No. 989, 10th edition 1982

SCALE 1:500 000 1cm-5km

Amiens to Calais VIA ABBEVILLE

Take the N235 to **Picquigny**, 13 kms, along the south bank of the Somme. Here the main road crosses the river joining the N1 to reach Abbeville, via **Flixecourt**, in 44 kms. The D218 keeps to the south bank of the river and is probably the more attractive route (49 kms). Both roads travel through the rear areas where training was carried out and concentrations took place before the troops were moved up to the front.

Little of the old **Abbeville**, known to all British soldiers, remains for them or their descendants to visit today, for in May 1940 the town was bombed by Stukas and the entire centre burned out. Not long afterwards, tanks entered the town and the 4th Division de Cuirassée (under the command of a certain Colonel Charles de Gaulle) were in action against German forces which had crossed the river. The defence of Abbeville continued into June with Scottish and other French forces relieving each other until it was finally taken by the Germans on the 4th.

During the First World War Abbeville, the capital of Ponthieu, was a sleepy market town with cloth-weaving as its main industry.

In 1914, groups of marauding Germans entered the town in August and September, but, by the end of that month, it was firmly in Allied hands. On October 8, Field-Marshal French set up General Headquarters here. Later it became a most important British base, a centre of communications, supply and transport. There were several hospitals and training areas in the vicinity. The main British base was outside the town and many wooden huts were erected to house the thousands of troops. In 1918 the town and surrounding area was subjected to frequent air raids. Set in very attractive country, and only 20 kms from the sea, it was a much favoured place by the BEF.

The direct route to Montreuil-sur-Mer is via the N1 and skirts the **Forest of Crécy** for a short distance some 15 kms out of Abbeville. The distance to Montreuil is 42 kms. The longer and more interesting route is via the D928 and Hesdin.

Travel north on the D928 16 kms to **Fontaine-sur-Maye**. To visit the **battlefield of Crécy** take the left road, D56, at the crossroads. In 2½ kms, an old **cross** on a modern plinth marks the **spot where John of Bohemia was killed**. The cross is said to be one of the earliest battle monuments surviving in France as it was set up shortly after the battle in 1326.

It is 2 kms to **Crécy-en-Ponthieu**, a small town amid very pleasant country. In the centre of the town is another old **monument** with an amusing English text relating to **Eleanor of Aquitaine** and her sons. Leave the town by climbing up the D111 and, on the right, a concrete transformer hut marks the **site of the windmill** from where Edward III watched his son, the Black Prince, lead his troops in the battle.

Continue 6 kms to **Dompierre** and turn right onto the D224. Then 7 kms to **Le Boisle** and left on to the D928 to Hesdin (17 kms). **Hesdin** was a 'British' town from 1916 onwards. Various branches of the Staff were quartered here and there were also hospitals. It was also the RFC headquarters. This attractive town, set amid the hills, made a pleasant leave centre.

From Hesdin, the N39 leads to Montreuil along the marshy valley of the River Canche for 23 kms. **Montreuil** is an old walled town which once was a seaport. The ramparts encircle the town on its rocky height and within them the streets are narrow, but they lead to the huge market place and the **statue of Field-Marshal Haig** on his charger, 'Miss Ypres'. The original was destroyed during the Second World War and, in the 1950s, another bronze was cast from the plaster model, now housed in the Musée des Trois Guerres at Château Diors in Indre.

From March 1916 to April 1919 Montreuil was the British GHQ. Field-Marshal Haig resided in the **Château de Beaurepaire**, some 4 kms from the town on the D138 near **St Nicholas**. A **plaque on the gateway** records his stay. The **military college buildings** housed the

Below: **Château de Beaurepaire, Haig's residence from 1916-18.** *Above:* **The old barracks nearby were used by GHQ.**

The magnificent vista at Etaples Military Cemetery where flag-bedecked cenotaphs flank the Stone of Remembrance.

In Wimereux Communal Cemetery, because of unstable ground, the gravestones lie flat around the Cross of Sacrifice.

administrative staff and it is said that over 5,000 men were attached to GHQ here. In 1918 it was within the range of German bombers and suffered several heavy raids. As a result at one time the HQ was evacuated at night.

Continue along the N39 beside the River

Dover Patrol Memorial at Cap Blanc Nez.

Canche 13 kms to Etaples. **Etaples** was one of the largest centres for reinforcements to the BEF with training depots, hospitals and facilities for 100,000 men. In the sand dunes near the railway was the infamous **'Bullring' training ground**. This is overlooked today by the beautiful **Etaples Military Cemetery** where over 11,000 men from all over the world, friend and foe, lie buried together. The cemetery is just outside 'Eat-apples' as the Tommy called it, on the D940 to **Boulogne** (27 kms).

On August 14, 1914, the first units of Sir John French's army began to disembark here and from then on Boulogne was on the main route for all troop movements from England. This famous old seaport and holiday centre became a bustling British base with hospitals, supply depots and camps being erected on the Camp de Boulogne, built in 1801 as the base for Napoleon's invasion army for England. All around the town, on the hills and coastal downs camps were built, some semi-permanent hutted camps, others just masses of bell tents.

Except as prisoners-of-war, the Germans never reached Boulogne; the nearest being in 1914 when a few squadrons of roaming German cavalry came within 40 kms. In 1917-18 the town was heavily attacked from the air and much damage was caused both to the town and the base. The Second World War saw the port and coast fortified by the Germans with many blockhouses of the Atlantic Wall, of which quite a few still remain.

In recent years there has been a great deal of new building and the town has expanded well beyond its 1918 boundaries. But, here and there, the small bungalows, which were brought from England for the use of the camp and later by homeless local population, survive.

The **Colonne de la Grande Armée**, high above the town on N1 to Calais, was erected in 1804 to commemorate the nearby Camp de Boulogne. The original statue of Napoleon in a Roman toga was in bronze and was shot off its pedestal by the Royal Navy during the Second War! The head of the first statue can be seen together with other relics in the **town museum**.

The more interesting road to Calais is the coast road, the D940, on which, in 1 km, we

'If ye break faith with us who die We shall not sleep, though poppies grow in Flanders fields.' Immortal words by Lieutenant-Colonel John McCrae. (See also page 35.)

reach **Terlincthun**. The **British Cemetery** here was one of the first to be completed with the well-known headstones and was visited by the King and Queen.

It is 5 kms to **Wimereux**. All along the coastal downs were hospitals and welfare establishments. Colonel John McCrae is buried in the **British Communal Cemetery**. His headstone, close to the Cross of Sacrifice, is one of those lying flat due to the type of ground on which the cemetery is built. This is located behind the town cemetery. For the next 36 kms, the road swings up and down just inside the coastal cliffs of **Cap Gris Nez**, through Wissant and up again over **Cap Blanc Nez**, with the **Memorial to the Dover Patrol**, and Sangatte and finally down into Calais.

ALTERNATIVE ROUTE VIA

St. Pol-sur-Ternoise

Leave Amiens by the N25 to **Poulainville** (6 kms) and in 2 kms turn left for **Bertangles**. Near this village was the RFC aerodrome. The village was also a base for other units including the artillery. It has changed very little since 1918; only the old service buildings have gone to be replaced by modern villas on the edge of the old village. It was here that the body of von Richthofen was buried on April 22, 1918 with full military honours in the **small cemetery** down a lane to the west of the village.

Take the D97 for **Villers-Bocage** (5 kms) and rejoin N25. In 3½ kms turn left onto the D60 to **Naours** (3 kms). The first turning on the right as the village is reached leads to the famous **Souterrains-réfuges de Naours**. These very extensive underground caves and connecting tunnels can house over 3,000 people and have been used for centuries. They are open to visitors and entry is via the pleasure park and the preserved windmills of Naours.

Return to the N25 in 3 kms, we reach **Vert Galant**. Take the D31, to the right, for **Beauquesne**. The **Château of Val Vion**, used by Field-Marshal Haig as a headquarters, is some 1½ kms further east. The château is on the right up a long tree-lined avenue. Here King George V stayed on his visits to the front. The present building dates only from the post-1945 era as the original house was bombed by the Germans in 1940, killing a party of Belgian refugees. The house was rebuilt almost identically.

Take next left turning at the crossroads, the D11, 3 kms to **Marieux**. Then turn right on to the D938 for 5 kms to **Louvencourt**, taking the small road to the left of the church for **Bus-lès-Artois**. This is one of the concentration areas used for the divisions before July 12, 1916.

On leaving the village by the D176, which shortly becomes the D25, we enter the Département of the Pas de Calais. The next village is **Couin**. At the bottom of the hill

Val Vion Château where King George V stayed with Sir Douglas Haig during his visits to the Front.

Above: **The funeral of the Red Baron. The firing party in Bertangles Cemetery, April 22, 1918. His body, transferred to Fricourt Cemetery after the war was reburied in Berlin in 1925. In 1975, after several years of negotiations with the East Germans, a third move came when the remains were moved to the family vault at Weisbaden.** *Below:* **The empty gravesite at Bertangles.**

before the village note the **notice on the brick barn** on the right. This direction sign for a water point was there in 1916, when the 63rd Division were gathering here, and it is thought to have been placed there by the 94th Brigade.

Continue through **Pas-en-Artois**, in 5 kms turning left onto the D6 for **Mondicourt**, another staging area, and then left on to N25 for Doullens, 8½ kms. A turning to the left just before the railway arch leads up in 1 km to the **Foch Calvary** from where there are magnificent views. **Doullens** is an industrial town of the Authie valley and the steep hills around it. In 1916 it was the BEF base and concentration area previously being Foch's HQ. On March 26 1918, the momentous meeting attended by Lord Milner, Poincaré, Clemenceau, Foch, Haig, Wilson and Pétain was held in the **Council Chamber of the Hôtel de Ville** and Foch was appointed Supreme Allied Commander. The room is open to visitors.

At **Gézaincourt**, a village beyond the Citadel, is a **British Cemetery** of which there is a model in the Imperial War Museum. It is reached from N25 and is signposted through **Bagneux**—3½ kms.

Leave the D925 for **Risquetout** (3 kms) then on to the D938 for **Wavans** (11 kms). In **Wavans Military Cemetery**, a small lonely little graveyard on the D117 on the west side of the village, is the grave of Major J. B. McCudden, VC, DSO. He was killed whilst flying from Auxi-le-Petit aerodrome not far from here.

In 4 kms at **Auxi-le-Château** turn right on to the D941, through the **Bois d'Auxi** and over the plain to **Frévent** (15 kms). Frévent is an industrial town amid hills which was used considerably by the British.

Continue via the D916 to **St Pol** (12 kms). This small bustling town was a British base for most of the war. Third Army had its headquarters here in 1916 and it remained GHQ until 1921. The Army Graves Registration Service, later the Imperial War Graves Commission HQ was here at St Pol. The choice of British Unknown Warrior was made here (in a hut near the **Cemetery of St Pol-sur-Ternoise**)

Couin. One of the few original signs to be seen . . . and the water-point is still there!

Gézaincourt Cemetery clings to the hill above Doullens.

by Colonel Wyatt in 1920 from bodies brought in from various battle areas.

A detour can be made from the N39 at **Humières**, 10 kms from St Pol, to go via **Blangy** on the D104 to **Tramecourt** to visit the **site of the battle of Agincourt** (Azincourt) 11 kms. Approaching the village, one of the two **memorials** is passed on the left. A plan of the battle is provided at this and other major positions relative to 1415, whilst others recall the Tramecourt family, a member of which was present, and his descendants who died in concentration camps in the Second World War. Their **château** is amid the avenues of huge trees. An **RFC aerodrome** was located here from 1916-18. The D71 passes through **Azincourt** and goes on to the D928 and in 12 kms to Hesdin.

The Council Chamber in Doullens Hôtel de Ville retains the original furniture in use on March 26, 1918.

After his crash near Auxi-le-Petit, Major McCudden, the famous flying VC was buried in the tiny cemetery at Wavans.

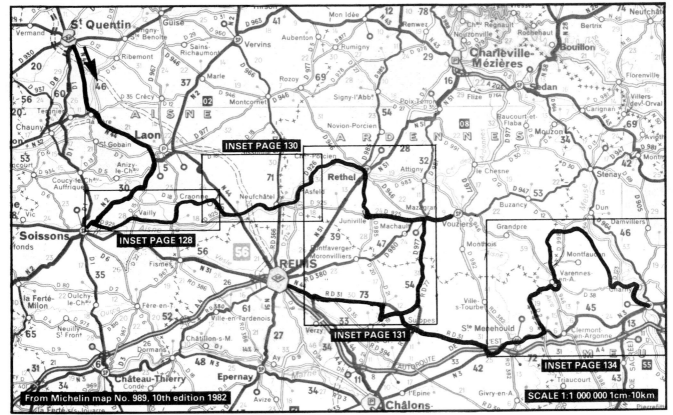

From Michelin map No. 989, 10th edition 1982
SCALE 1:1 000 000 1cm-10km

St. Quentin to Reims

This extension to the main itinerary includes the areas of British involvement in 1914 and 1918 in the regions south of St Quentin and part of the American battlegrounds in 1918.

Leave St Quentin southwards via the N44, 21 kms to **La Fère**. Continue on the N44 10 kms to **Crépy**. As the road slopes down towards a bend take the road on the left, the D26, for 1½ kms. On the left are woods and on the right, a little way from the road, will be seen a cluster of houses on the railway line. This is the **site of one of the huge German guns** which fired on Paris in 1918. The monster, which fired its first round on Paris on March 23 at 7.16 a.m., was hidden amongst the trees in the wood. Four minutes later the 210mm shell burst in north-west Paris. The distance was 74.12 miles. Today, little remains of the site of the huge railway gun with its three-part barrel, in all some 34 metres in length weighing over 300 tons. The

Below: **Traces still remain of the railway line which carried the Paris guns into these woods about 1500 metres north of Crepy.** *Right:* **The site of one of the base turning plates.**

railway siding can still be traced across the road, along a track to the main line, and into the wood where it becomes a glade through the trees which has rather unusual ridges across it—the sleepers. There are bunkers and the mounts for the base plate but nothing more.

Return to Crépy and the N44. In 5 kms the lone hill of **Laon** comes into view and the spires and towers of the old fortress town can be clearly seen 300ft above the plain.

After another 4 kms, turn right on to the N2. Drop down 9 kms to cross the Canal de l'Oise. Then 3 kms further on, on the left, are the ruins of the **Fort de Malmaison** and it is from here the **Chemin des Dames** commences. The **calvary** is a memorial to the defence of the fort in 1917.

It is another 15 kms to **Soissons**. This is one of the oldest cities in France which has been a fortress for many centuries. The Romans were defeated here by Clovis in 486. At the end of August 1914, the BEF, retreating from Mons, crossed the Aisne west of the city. The Germans held Soissons until September 12 before they retired after having blown all the bridges. On September 13 the Battle of the Aisne began. The Germans were dug in amid the

hills and quarries on the north bank and the British divisions fought their way back across the river at a number of points east and west of Soissons. The 1st Division crossed at Bourg, the 2nd at Chavonne, the 3rd at Vailly, the 4th at Venizel, the 5th at Missy and the Guards Brigade at Chavonne and at Pont Arcy. They crossed in boats and rafts, by pontoons, and by using the girders of wrecked bridges. The crossing was successful and the force moved forward only to be checked in the Chemin des Dames region. In October the BEF were relieved by the French.

Counter-attacks by the Germans were repulsed in 1915 and 1917 but in May 1918 Soissons fell. On August 2 the city was recaptured only to be ruined further by the artillery bombardment which followed.

The **Soissons Memorial to the Missing** is just below the cathedral facing the Pont d'Anglais. The memorial commemorates the missing of the British IX and XXII Corps which fought during the July and August 1918 battles alongside the French Army. There are 3,987 names engraved on the panels. The memorial is unique for the sculptural group. Three soldiers in their greatcoats stand shoulder to shoulder, two of them with their gas masks in the alert position. In front of the middle soldier is a rifle butt planted in the ground with a helmet on it. The sculptor was Eric Kennington.

Buzancy lies 13 kms to the south of Soissons

off the D1. This little town clings to the hills which were the scene of hectic fighting in the summer of 1918 and the drive there gives a good idea of the difficulties of the opposing armies. To reach the **British Cemetery** turn left off D1 and in the village turn left again up a narrow lane. The cemetery was created in July 1918 by the 15th Scottish Divison who fought here with great distinction. Their courage so impressed their French comrades that at the close of the battle they erected a **cairn** to their honour with the inscription: 'Here for all time the glorious Scottish thistle will bloom amid the roses of France'. Some years ago the rough-hewn cairn was removed to the cemetery for safety.

Leave Soissons by the D925, travelling eastwards along the pretty banks of the river on the northern side. Views of the area held by the BEF and the places at which they crossed in September 1914 can be seen all along this road. **Missy** (10 kms), **Vailly** (7 kms), **Chavonne** (4 kms), and **Pont Arcy** (4 kms), where there is still an iron bridge similar to the one blown by the Germans.

In 2½ kms we reach **Bourg-et-Comin**. Turn left onto D967 to climb up the hills to the ridge of the Chemin des Dames. Attractive

Eric Kennington's figures on the centrepiece of the Soissons Memorial to the Missing, which commemorates the missing of the British IX and XXII Corps.

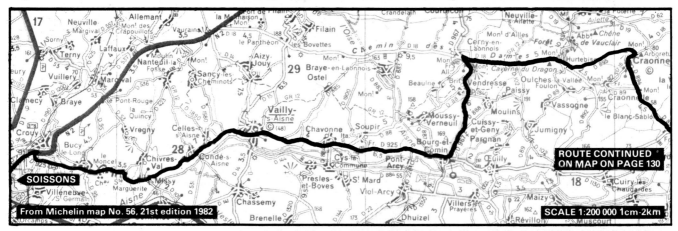

ROUTE CONTINUED ON MAP ON PAGE 130

SOISSONS

From Michelin map No. 56, 21st edition 1982

SCALE 1:200 000 1cm-2km

and beautiful as these hills and valleys are, they show the difficulties the armies must have faced.

To the south at **Braine** on the N31 Allenby's cavalry fought a delaying action in September 1914, and in 1918 it was the Americans who were in action here. In the **town cemetery** is a **small British plot** where lies Captain Harry S. Ranken, VC, RAMC, attached to the KRRC. He was mortally wounded at Hautes Avesnes in the conflict of September 19/20, 1914, suffering ghastly wounds before he would relinquish his task of tending other comrades, and he did not live to know he had won the decoration announced with the first awards. He was also Mentioned in Despatches and created a Chevalier of the Légion d'Honneur. He died here at Braine on September 25.

Vendresse is 5 km further on. On the slope above the village is a **British Cemetery**. This is the route of the I British Corps (Haig) in September 1914, and also in the sector of the 8th, 21st and 50th Divisions in May 1918.

Cerny-en-Laonnois (1½ kms) is a crossroad village on the crest of the ridge of the **Chemin des Dames**. On the left is a tall Greek pillar, the **Memorial of the 1st Bn. Loyal North Lancashire Regiment**; the 1st Brigade of the 1st Division fought here in 1914. In front of you as you reach the crossroads is the **Memorial of the Chemin des Dames**, a small elegant chapel with a modernistic column before it. Inside the chapel, in gleaming white stone and marble, are the memorials to the French units which fought here. The altar is a striking centre-piece being formed of rows of crosses in perspective. To the left of the chapel on the south side of this famous road are large **French** and **German cemeteries**.

Turn right along the Chemin des Dames,

Pont D'Arcy. A bridge still crosses the Aisne at the place where the BEF crossed in September 1914.

the D18, stretching straight and narrow along the ridge high above the surrounding country. The road owes its name to the daughters of Louis XV as it was constructed to ease their journeys between Compiègne and the Château de la Bôve situated in the upper valley of the Ailette which belonged to their great friend the Duchess of Narbonne.

The ridge is riddled with caverns and quarries which were used by both armies in the conflict. It is still possible to see the effects of the bombardments on the area in the shell-pocked chalky fields. The French gained a foothold on the ridge during Nivelle's offensive in April 1917 and the Germans fell back

to Ailette. As with Vimy Ridge, this was considered to be a very strong position and very severe casualties were suffered by both sides in repeated attacks and counter-attacks for possession of the ridge.

In 5 kms on the right **a group of guns and a 1939-45 tank** come into view with several **memorials**. They mark the entrance to one of the fortified quarries known as the **Grotte or Caverne du Dragon**. The memorials are of the **4th Zouaves**, the **164th French Infantry Division** and the **41st Batallion de Chasseurs à Pied**—the last unveiled as recently as May 1982. The complex is now a museum open daily during the season. Unfortunately the

Above: **Both in 1914 and later in 1918, the fighting swept over the wooded slopes at Vendresse as the graves in the cemetery indicate. Over the hill is the Chemin des Dames.** *Right:* **Rather unusual, the tall grey column at Cerny is a British Memorial to the 1st Bn. Loyal North Lancashire Regiment which fought here in 1914.**

Above: **Two large cemeteries dominate the Cerny-en-Laonnois crossroads, one French and one German. Over the plastic crosses of the former the grey granite of the latter can be seen.** *Right:* **A striking marble altar in the memorial chapel.**

collection has suffered more than once from thieves but security has been heightened and new display cases are now in place. Descending down a steep narrow stairway, the visitor enters a wide cavern from which passages and rooms lead off. Here the Germans set up a command post and stores depot for the troops who held the line. They had a huge arsenal and large numbers of men were housed in the various chambers. Water came from a deep well, lighting was meagre but today the guides demonstrate cleverly the modern effects with coloured lamps and, for the most dramatic effect, plunge the whole in darkness for a period. The museum has two cases devoted to the British army which took their part in the fighting here. In another cavern, a rough and ready cinema is arranged where films depicting the history of the ridge through the centuries are shown. Each time I visit the cavern I am amazed by the lack of graffiti on the walls which are all rough and devoid of other marking save the soot from a candle or two. A car park is provided.

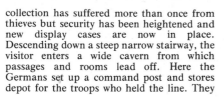

A French field-gun and a tank of 1939 vintage at the Caverne du Dragon—a memorial to French Colonial Regiments.

The interior of the Caverne Museum—once a German CP.

Battles a century apart are remembered at Hurtebise.

A matter of some hundred metres further along is one of those places which prove the adage. 'Once a good battlefield, always a battlefield.' This is **Hurtebise**. A rather striking **group in bronze** commemorates the Battle of Hurtebise Farm in 1814 and the 1914 battles, a **plaque on the crumbling wall of the farm** recalls the victory of the 4th Zouaves in 1914 and 1917 and one to the 4th Division Cuirassé in their armoured battle in 1940.

Take the D895 to **Craonne** (4½ kms), and,

Germans claimed to have taken 45,000 British and French prisoners and 400 guns. The British 8th Division, which were further east at Berry-au-Bac, lost 7,000 out of 9,000 men. There are several **French memorials** in and around Craonne relating both to Napoleon's victory over the Allies in March 1814 and to the 1914-18 battles.

From Craonne take the D894 to **Craonnelle**—about a kilometre of difficult road—and then rejoin the D89 to descend into

the valley near **Pontavart** with its important bridges over the Aisne. Turn left onto the D925.

The **Le Choléra crossroads** (with the N44) are 5 kms further on. On the east side of the junction is the **Memorial to the French Armoured Forces of 1917-18** and their commander, General Estienne. Until roadworks removed them, there were remains of a concrete bunker and a fortified farm on the west side of the road. Now all has been levelled.

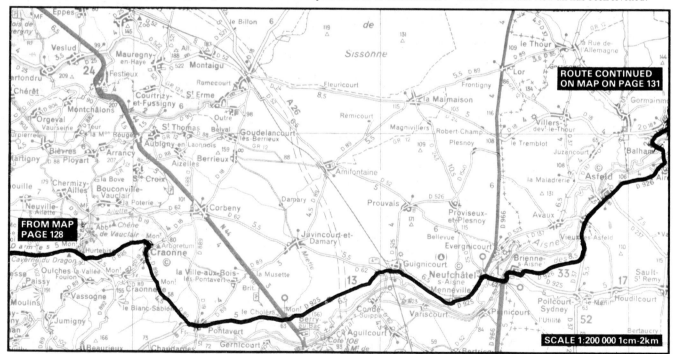

ROUTE CONTINUED ON MAP ON PAGE 131

FROM MAP PAGE 128

SCALE 1:200 000 1cm-2km

just above the village, will be seen an orientation table on the right, the **California position** used by Napoleon in 1814 and which figured again in 1914 and 1917. The table refers to the latter actions. In May 1918 the British IX Corps were in the line here enjoying a 'rest cure' after the ravages of the Somme battles earlier in the year. On May 27 the Corps was assailed by a fierce mortar and gas attack and, with many casualties, fell back across the River Aisne and the Ardres. On May 28 the Kaiser came to view the victory of his troops and is said to have looked out from the site of the orientation table at the devastation. The

The memorial at Le Choléra crossroads which commemorates the French Armoured Forces of 1917-18 and their commander, Général Estienne.

Carry straight ahead, still on the D925, for 6 kms to **Guignicourt** on the north banks of the river and parallel canal, passing **Neufchâtel-sur-Aisne** (7 kms). Turn right and take the D926 to **Rethel**, 34 kms along the pleasant Aisne valley which has a number of hotels—quite a rarity in this area. It is an ancient town which, after the fighting in 1914, was behind the German line for the rest of the war. It was badly damaged in 1940. It is a hilly

town and the **ruins of the castle** of the Counts of Rethel are on the high ridge to the north of the town.

Climb out of Rethel crossing the Aisne on the N51 and, almost straightaway, take the left fork of the D946 and then the right fork, the D985. The road passes a small airfield as it rises onto the plateau broken only by the small town of Perthes.

In 15 kms, at a road junction, turn left onto

the D925. These are the battlefields of **Champagne** fought over in July 1918 by the Americans.

At **Mazagran** (15 kms), turn right on to the D977. The long straight road, with few bends, sweeps southward across the rolling plain. Keep on it for 12 kms and, directly after entering the Département of the Marne, take the right-hand road which goes up 2 kms to the **American Sommepy Monument** on the Mont

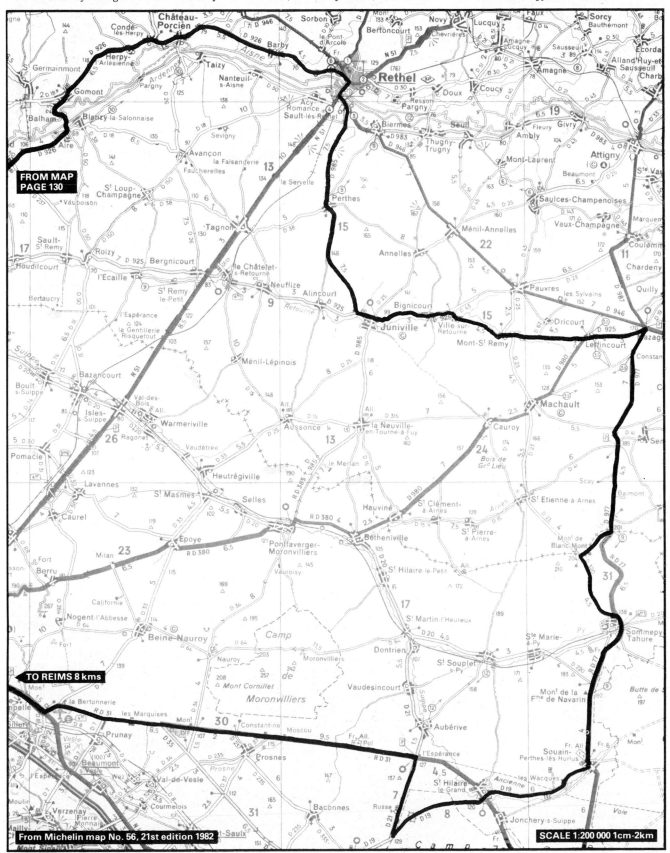

From Michelin map No. 56, 21st edition 1982

SCALE 1:200 000 1cm-2km

FROM MAP PAGE 130

TO REIMS 8 kms

Sommepy, where the American Monument now stands, was once a look-out of Kaiser Wilhelm.

Around the Sommepy Memorial, the ground has been left as it was in 1918, complete with grassy trenches and shell holes.

Blanc ridge. The tall, severe stone tower rises from the pine covered crest of a hill attacked and captured by the US 2nd Division in October 1918. All around there are vestiges of the bunkers and trenches and shell-holes in which they fought. The monument is only open on Sundays. Inside there is the usual explanation of the operations in the region which one comes to expect from the American Battle Monuments Commission. Each face of the monument bears the badge of a division with its battle honours—the 2nd. 36th, 42nd (the 'Rainbow' Division) and the 93rd. A stairway leads to the top which gives an excellent view of the battlefield.

Take the D320 for **Sommepy-Tahure** (4½ kms). On the highest point of this road, 3½ kms south, is the **Monument de la Ferme de Navarin**, one of the principal positions in the Champagne battles of 1914, 1915 and again in 1918. The pyramid is surmounted by a vigorous group of three soldiers. One is an

Below: **With unlimited views over the battlefield, the memorial at Ferme de Navarin marks one of the main positions.**

Above: The Ferme de Navarin Memorial of the Battle of Champagne rises above the tomb of Général Gouraud, GOC Fourth French Army. This area was one of the principal positions in the Champagne battles of 1914-15.

infantryman charging; the second is a machine gunner with his weapon over his shoulder as he presses forward whilst the third, with his right hand raised, urges them on. This is the work of the sculptor Maxime Real del Sarte and is a memorial to Lieutenant Quentin Roosevelt, the son of President Theodore Roosevelt, and Général Gouraud, the GOC of the French Fourth Army. The Général is buried in **the crypt**, a small chapel lit by a stained glass window bearing the likeness of him. Steep steps lead to the foot of the statues from which views of the battlefield are aided by four orientation diagrams. In the immediate vicinity, the ground has been left as it was in 1918, complete with shell-holes and trenches. Lieutenant Roosevelt was killed in 1918 in the Tardenois battles.

We continue on D77 through this huge agricultural plain, descending to **Souain-Perthes-lès-Hurlus** in 4 kms. Here there is a **German Cemetery** containing 13,783 graves. Off the road to the right is a **French Cemetery**.

Turn right on the D19 for 7 kms to **St Hilaire-le-Grand**, a small town on the northern boundaries of one of the huge military camps and training grounds associated with this part of Champagne. Take the Mourmelon road, the D19, skirting the edge of a tank training area.

In 7 kms there is a sharp fork road going off to the right, the D21. Five hundred metres along this road, on a slight incline, can be seen a group of pine trees and on the left, and most unexpectedly emerging from the trees, is the bulbous dome of a tiny **Russian Orthodox church** and beside it a **Russian Cemetery**. Here are buried Russian soldiers who fought for France in both wars with a separate enclosure for civilians. Two mass graves stand in the centre of the military graveyard.

Remain on this road for another 6½ kms and, at the **l'Espérance** crossroads, turn left onto the RD31. This highway crosses the battlefields of 1915 and 1918 as indicated by the **Franco-German Cemetery** near l'Espérance and **various French memorials** along the wayside.

In 21½ kms, the road joins the major highway to Reims, the N44, near an airfield and, on the rise in the ground as we turn right for Reims, the car park for **Fort de la Pompelle** is indicated. Access to the fort from the car park is through a narrow tunnel under the road. One emerges from it to a shattered landscape of torn chalk with the battered north-east face of the fort on the left.

As one of the forts encircling the city of Reims, it was in the line throughout the war. Bitter fighting took place in and around it and

Set amid the pine trees, the Russian Memorial church guards Russian graves from both world wars.

it changed hands several times but always the French retook it. Today it is a national musuem with a small military garrison. A varying collection of artillery pieces and equipment are displayed in front of the fort but most items are in the casemates. The internal galleries are well laid out recording the history of the fort, Reims and the Champagne district. Photographs and documents play a large part. Representative collections concerning Guynemer and other French heroes and a good selection of the uniforms and equipment of the Allies are displayed. The amazing Charles Friese collection of Imperial German Army head-dresses occupies a whole gallery. One sub-gallery has been filled with battle debris and in another series of casemates, transport is shown.

Five kms further and **Reims** is entered. Reims is a very ancient city which has played many roles in the history of France, religious and secular, military and political. It is a great industrial centre and famous for its art and learning. Here, in the massive **cathedral** so badly damaged during the bombardments but now repaired, the Kings of France were crowned.

In September 1914 the Germans occupied the city and ransacked it for a week. On September 15 the German Crown Prince made the **Grand Hôtel** his headquarters. Prince August Wilhelm was already there and, shortly, the Kaiser's brother joined them. However their stay was brief as the French Fifth Army under Général Franchet d'Esperey arrived and drove them out. For the next four years the city was in French hands but, always in artillery range, it was constantly shelled or bombed from the air. By 1917 the city was almost surrounded but in 1918 the French gradually forced the Germans back until, in October, the retreat became a rout.

For those interested in the arts there are several fine galleries; there are collections of Roman remains and of course the priceless treasures of the cathedral which were saved from devastation. The **Porte du Mars** is a fine Roman triumphal arch near the Place de la République, and not far from this at **No. 10, rue Franklin-Roosevelt** is the **war room** which is preserved as it was left on May 8, 1945 after General Eisenhower had accepted the German surrender. It is open every day.

A splendid museum is located just outside Reims in Fort de la Pompelle — still lying in ruins almost as if time has stood still since 1918.

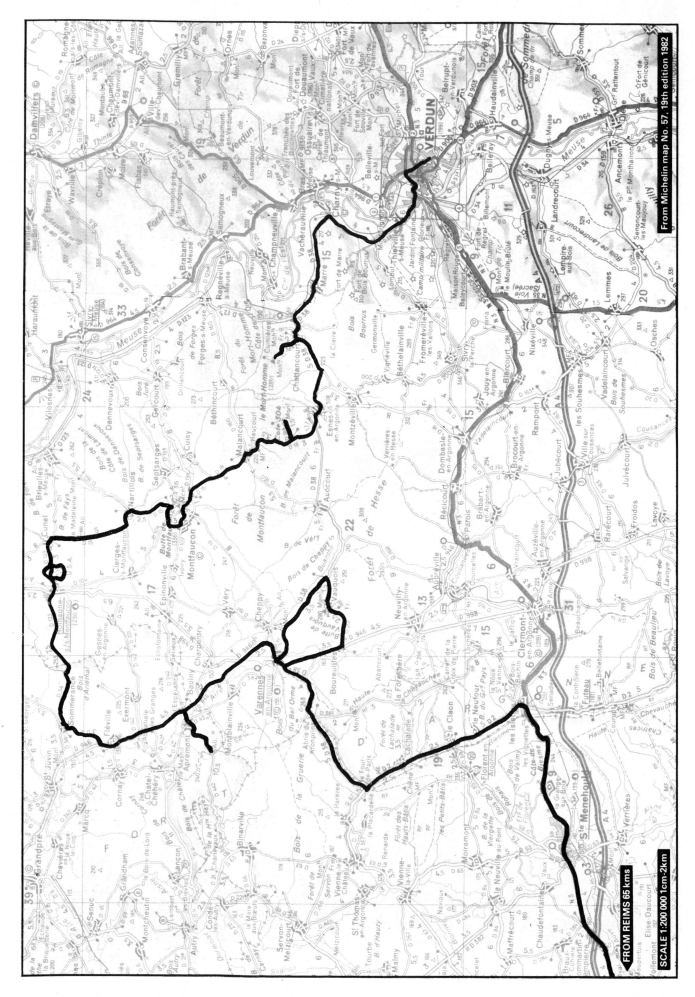

FROM REIMS 65 kms

From Michelin map No. 57. 19th edition 1982

SCALE 1:200 000 1cm-2km

Elise Daucourt

The Verdun Battlefield

One of the last places where metal Frise de Cheval entanglements can still be seen as they were in the Great War—on the mine-riven hill of Vauquois.

Beyond Reims lies the most sacred battlefield of France—Verdun—and the regions of the greatest American contribution in 1918—the Meuse, Argonne and Château Thierry fronts. This is a route for visiting those areas east and south-east of Reims. The southern and south-western region is covered in the final itinerary.

Leave Reims by the N44, branching off to the left on to the RD31 after passing Fort de la Pompelle. After 42 kms **Suippes** is reached after traversing the huge plain of almost uninterrupted grain fields among which are occasional **forts and military establishments and war cemeteries** of France, Germany and Poland.

In 23 kms at **Orbeval**, turn left onto N3 and travel 8 kms to **Ste. Menehould**. This ancient fortress town was occupied by the Germans in September 1914 and great destruction was wrought before they were driven out. Thereafter the town was a busy French HQ in the Argonne front battles over the next four years.

In another 9 kms we reach **Les Islettes**. Turn left on the D2. Then 10 kms to **Le Four de Paris**. Turn right onto D38 for 5 kms through the **Bois de la Gruerie**. A small road on the left leads into the forest; it is straight and has a good surface for approximately a

kilometre. Where it peters out into a number of mud tracks, a grubby notice will be seen on the right pointing to the **Abri du Krönprinz**. This unusual concrete shelter built into a deep trench not many yards off the road was erected for Crown Prince Wilhelm in 1915 and was used by him for quite a time. It has a front portal and large windows but is gradually disintegrating. Much of the surrounding woodland is cordoned off by barbed wire and entry into the trenches is forbidden.

Return to the D38 and continue to the left to **Varennes-en-Argonne** (4 kms). Before 1914, when the town was captured by the Germans, Varennes was only remembered in the history books as the town where Louis XVI and Marie Antoinette were arrested to be taken back to Paris and the guillotine. Now the town is dominated by the **Pennsylvania State Memorial** to her sons who died in the battles to recapture this region in September 1918. The memorial consists of a double colonnade surrounding a paved courtyard with a central monument in Grecian style. In the hillside below the monument are a number of bunkers and concrete shelters which originally led into subways.

On the right of the main street (which is the D946) is the road leading to the monument and a little further up is the modern **Musée d'Argonne** where there are ethnographical and art collections, documents relating to the arrest of Louis XVI in June 1791, and the **Museum of Mine Warfare** which contains some extremely interesting material and dioramas showing how mines were bored and blown. There are many relics of the American activities in the region and the personalities who fought here, including Harry S. Truman.

Remain on the D946 for **Boureuilles**, some 3½ kms to the south. There, turn left on D212 for **Vauquois** and the famous **Butte de Vauquois**. To visit this mine-riven hill, 290 metres high, requires a short steep walk from the car park. This was once the site of the village of Vauquois but now it is a grassy desert of barbed wire and mine craters. On the summit is a **memorial** to those who died and close by is one of two excellent orientation tables and also a machine which for a franc gives an explanation of the scene and its history in four languages. A map shows a route recommended for a comprehensive visit and each salient position is identified.

Entrance to Abri du Krönprinz, headquarters dugout of Crown Prince Wilhelm.

Bunker entrance beneath the Pennsylvania State Memorial at Varennes-en-Argonne.

Missouri's Angel of Victory surmounts its memorial near Varennes.

The imposing memorial lantern to 'Les Combattants' amid the barbed wire on the summit of the Butte de Vauquois.

The central avenue of the American Meuse-Argonne Memorial and Cemetery.

Return to the modern village at the foot of the butte and take D38 to the left to return to **Varennes**, noticing the **Memorial to the Men of the State of Missouri** on the outskirts. **Apremont** is reached in 6 km. From here a detour into the forest along D442, with the **German Cemetery** on the hillside, will in 3½ kms arrive at the **ravine** where the **Lost Battalion** disappeared for several days having become cut off from their comrades of the US 77th Division between October 2-7, 1918. A marker on the roadside up the hill indicates the valley down very steep slopes.

After 4½ kms we reach **Fléville**. Take D4 to **Sommerance** and in 3 kms the D54/D123 to **Romagne-Gesnes**, 7½ kms away, driving through more of the American battle zones to the **Meuse-Argonne Cemetery and Memorial** on the far side of the town. In this huge peaceful park 14,000 men lay buried on the gentle slopes of the valley. The administrative block looks out over the vista of gleaming white crosses, lawns and trees to the memorial chapel on the opposite crest.

Leave the park by the Cunel road. In 3 kms take the D15 to the right—**Nantillois** is 5 kms. Soon the **Butte de Mont Faucon** is in sight and is reached in 2 kms. This outstanding ridge is capped with **Hill 336** from which rises the

elegant doric column of the **American Memorial**. Shallow steps lead to the entrance and an internal and very graceful stairway up to the observation balcony below the Statue of Liberty from where the view is spectacular. The hill was the site of an ancient monastery and hamlet which the Germans heavily fortified after its capture in 1914 and used thereafter as an OP, particulary in 1916. In the ruins they built bunkers. In 1914 the

Crown Prince had his HQ on this prominence. It fell to the Americans on September 27, 1918 in their attack on the **Kreimhide Line** which ran east to Grandpré.

Leave by D15/D18 for **Malancourt**, 5 kms, and in 3 kms the D18bis on the left leads up to **Côte 304** with its **monument**. Over 19,000 men lost their lives fighting in this hilly wooded area in 1917-18. Survivors of 17th French Division erected the memorial in 1934.

Left: A German observation post in the ruins of Mont Faucon monastery. *Above:* American monument on Mont Faucon.

Apt memorial on summit of Cote 295, Mort Homme. '. . . They Shall not Pass'.

Return to D18 and continue to **Esnes-en-Argonne** (3 kms), and join the D38 to the left for **Chattancourt**, (5 kms). The infamous hill of **Mort Homme** is reached by taking the D38bis at the approach to the village. **Côte 295**, the highest in the **Forêt de Mort Homme** has a very sombre **memorial** on its summit. This was the scene of intensive tunnelling by both sides and particularly by the Germans. Their longest subway, named after the Crown Prince, was some 3,000 metres long and others were of 1,500 to 2,000 metres. These connected the three most important hills in the neighbourhood and provided support for the mine warfare in the area. From Chattancourt, take the D38 for Verdun, which is reached via **Charny-sur-Meuse** in 14 kms.

Verdun is a city with a violent history and, despite the terrible destruction of 1916 and the attacks in the Second World War, still retains the atmosphere of an ancient town. There are many monuments recalling its struggle for survival, being the hub of a circle of forts built in the surrounding hills after the war of 1870. In 1914 Général Sarrail saved the city and its military establishments from capture although it was frequently under fire. In February 1916 the Germans made fierce attacks on the fortifications and Fort Douaumont fell on the 24th. Fort Vaux held out until June when it also was overwhelmed. The next nearest fortress at Souville almost followed but, although completely ruined, the garrison held out and the city was saved. In July the German attacks eased as the Battle of the Somme began its long and murderous onslaught. In the autumn, General Mangin's massive offensive regained all the ground lost and Verdun was recaptured.

Before visiting Verdun city or the surrounding battle zone, a visit to the excellent Office du Tourisme is advised. Literature is available in several languages, including compact little guide books and leaflets outlining tours. The famous Michelin Guide, first produced in 1919, is obtainable in a reprint in English and French. The office is in the Place du Nation across the River Meuse from the handsome Porte Chaussée. From the bridge, the Avenue Général Mangin emerges and opposite the Syndicat d'Initiative is the impressive **Monument to the Fallen**—five figures represent the different corps of the French Army standing shoulder to shoulder above the columns of names. On either side are fragments of old fortifications landscaped into public gardens; a **memorial plaque for Général Mangin** is on one wall. Verdun has many fine memorials and buildings of interest but the **Victory Monument**, which towers

A tall cross rises above the seven Unknown Warriors in Verdun Cemetery; the eighth lies in Paris, beneath the Arc de Triomphe.

Symbolised in stone on the Monument to the Fallen at Verdun—the graven figures representing the five French Army corps.

over the rue Mazel and Avenue de la Victoire, dominates all. In the crypt are kept the Golden Books recording the many medals awarded to the city. The memorial, up steep steps, is flanked by two Russian guns.

An **avenue of huge statues of the Maréchals and Générals of France**, beneath the Vauban ramparts, leads to the Porte du Secours entrance to the **Citadel**. As Verdun is still a major garrison, the Citadel remains active but certain sections are open to visitors below its imposing walls and ramparts. Much of the fortress is underground—in fact there are 4 kms of tunnels which were of vital importance during the war. In one of the large chambers the selection of the French Unknown Soldier was made from eight bodies and this room is one of those open to view. The **museum** in a further chamber is confined mainly to small items and documents. There is another **museum in the Hôtel de Ville**, an Italianate Louis XIII-style building, once a small palace, where documents and decorations and flags are shown. Four old cannon flank the zero kilometre borne and a large shell or two can be seen in the Court of Honour through which access is gained to the museum.

In the cathedral crypt, the capitals of a number of the pillars represent various aspects of the Battle of Verdun, the sculptor, Le Bourgeois, depicting scenes of trench life and horrors in a simple, realistic style. There are many statues and memorials in the city but perhaps one of the most evocative is that by Rodin which is to be found in front of the Porte St Paul in the Place Vauban. It was presented to the city by the Dutch nation. There are numerous hotels in the city and nearby towns such as Etain and several camp sites provide for battlefield visitors.

Towering above the French Cemetery at Douaumont is the great ossuary.

ROUTE I

Leave Verdun by the N3 pausing perhaps to visit the **Cimitière de Faubourg Pavé**—the military cemetery where the seven unknown soldiers not chosen lie. Note also the group of captured field guns in the entrance park. In 5½ kms, turn left onto the D913. Then in 1½ kms take the right fork for **Fort Vaux**, 2½ kms up the wooded slopes. Halfway up is the **Monument des Fusilées de Tavannes** for members of the resistance massacred here in 1944. Fort Vaux was the north-eastern bastion and one of the many which surrounded Verdun. Externally it is a battered crumbling heap of stones and the advent of thousands of visitors has ruined the immediate area and gives the fort an even more desolate appearance. The iron turrets still crown the grassy cover of mounds above it. Internally the galleries, through which the guides lead parties, drip with damp and present a very sombre and chilling aspect of the life of the men who lived and died here during the bombardments. It was gallantly defended but eventually the garrison was overcome in June

The Lion Memorial at Chapelle Sainte Fine crossroads commemorates the French 30th Division and Allies.

A monument to André Maginot, once a sergeant in the 44th Territorial Regiment, near Fort de Souville.

1916 only to be recaptured again by the French in November 1916. A **memorial to the pigeon** which carried the last message from Commandant Raynal is to be found with others on the outer walls.

After visiting the fort return to the D913 and turn right arriving in 2 kms at the crossroad of **Chapelle Sainte Fine**. The road to the left, the D112, is the direct one from Verdun; it passes **several monuments** including that of André Maginot, Minister of War responsible for the famous line of forts which bear his name. He fought at Verdun as a sergeant.

The **Lion Monument** which commemorates the **French 39th Division and Allies** also marks the limit reached by the Germans. **Fort de Souville** is situated amid the trees behind the lion, a ruined heap amid the craters.

Proceed straight ahead to **Douaumont**. In a short distance, on the site of the old railway station of **Fleury**, one of the nine villages obliterated by the battles now marked only by road name boards and a chapel, stands the **Mémorial de Verdun**. This is a magnificent museum where the history of the battle is fully explained in well-designed displays of documents, photographs, specimens of battlefield equipment and relics found in the region. Captions are in three languages as are the excellent guide books. All the displays are set around a life-size representation of a sector of the battlefield beneath a huge animated map. Films are also shown continuously during opening hours.

Across the forest can be seen the tall tower of the **Ossuary of Douaumont** and, although there are many memorials and monuments in the region, this is the dominant one. The **Jewish Memorial** is on the left as the Ossuary is reached. A large car park is behind the building. The Ossuary was built between 1922 and 1932 and contains the remains of over 130,000 men, both French and German. Another 15,000 identified lay in the cemetery in front of it. The building, which is 137 metres long, was inaugurated by President Lebrun in August 1932. There is a small chapel under the tower and the long aisle is divided into 18 sections or chapels, each dedicated to a different département or city of France with other apses for the Allied nations. Services are held regularly in the chapel and the tower itself can be visited. The exterior of the building is decorated with the crests of the towns of France and others overseas which contributed to the cost of this enormous memorial. At the rear of the building the bones of the unknown can be viewed through ground-level windows. Temporary exhibitions are staged from time to time in rooms at the rear.

André Thome — the Soldat du Droit.

The Mémorial de Verdun stands on the site of Fleury railway station.

A path from the car park leads to the ruins of **Fort Thiaumont**. Resume your journey by turning left when leaving the car park and skirt the huge cemetery to take the D913b on the left for Fort Douaumont. At the roadside is the recumbent figure of **Le Soldat du Droit**, the memorial to André Thome who was killed in March 1916.

Fort Douaumont on Hill 388 was the most important of the arc of forts built in the last century. The exterior is similar to Fort Vaux with untidy paths and grassy tufts covering it. Here again the turrets remain and there is also an observation post looking out over the panoramic view. The German attack came from the region of the military camp to the north. Inside the fort, groups are conducted through the galleries and casemates, although most of the guides only speak French or German and English visitors are given typed translations.

Another interesting complex is the **Ouvrage de Froideterre** on **Côte 345**. It is reached from the Ossuary by the D913b beside the Jewish Memorial. About 1 km down through the forest is yet another. This is the **Abri Caverne des Quatre Cheminées** on the slope which falls away to the left of the road. This bunker, with others at Command Post 118 and 119 near Thiaumont, were linked. All are now under the care and control of the Association Nationale du Souvenir de la Bataille de Verdun et la Sauvegarde de ses Hauts Lieux (ANSBV) which is based at the Mémorial de Verdun at Fleury. All their sites are well

Above: **Battered Fort Douaumont surmounted by steel cupolas.** *Below:* **Several memorial plaques line the walls of Fort Vaux.**

Below: **The Ouvrage de Froideterre on Hill 345. Designed by the French army engineer Laurent in 1895, it withstood prolonged shelling during the Battle of Verdun.**

labelled with good explanatory notices, plans and orientation tables.

Just past the Four Cheminées complex, the approach road to Froideterre climbs up on the right. **Froideterre** was in action right through the Battle of Verdun and was subjected to heavy bombardments and was partially occupied by the 10th Bavarian Regiment but the garrison ejected the invaders, due in no small way to the effectiveness of the 75mm turret and its machine guns. Along the D913b and the fort road the trees are being cleared so that it is possible now to see the incredibly shell and crater-torn ground, hitherto completely hidden.

Return to the D913 and turn left before the Ossuary to visit the **Tranchée du Baïonnettes** which is on the right of the road a little way down the hill. The entrance is through a massive gateway with heavy metal doors intricately carved. Beyond, after passing a disintegrating monument, the great bulk of the concrete canopy and pillars enclosing the famous trench comes into view. This was a front line trench of the Ravine de la Dame sector in which were buried men of the 137th Régiment d'Infanterie as they struggled through the trench. They were found in 1919 when it was noticed that a line of rusting bayonets and rifles was protruding from the ground in an area where men of the regiment were known to have been and to have disappeared. Today there are few bayonets or rifles visible; in fact every time I visit the monument I see a difference. Only 17 unknown soldiers remain buried here, marked by the wooden crosses, the other 40 who were identified were reburied in Fleury Cemetery.

The D913 winds down into the Meuse valley to reach **Bras** in 6 kms and Verdun in 7½ kms south on the D964. A detour can be made northwards to visit the **Bois de Caures** made famous by the resistance of Colonel Driant and his Chasseurs à Pied. Turn right on to the D964 to **Vacherauville** (2 kms) and then take the D906 up into the woods. Here in a glade are the **regimental and individual memorials** to the gallant colonel and his men of the 56th and 59th Bataillon Chasseurs à Pied. His grave and command post are nearby. Colonel Driant, who was the Deputy for Nancy, was the author of the bill which culminated in the institution of the Croix de Guerre.

At many of the clearings in the forests, and at numerous salient positions, the ANSBV have installed boards indicating interesting walks and drives. The whole region is signposted well, and places where it is not wise to penetrate are clearly shown. The paths are labelled and the trees are marked with the relative plot number in strategic spots. All are

The successful defence of the Froideterre Casemate de Bourges was largely due to the turret-mounted 75mm canons giving covering fire to the flanks in concert with the strong point at Charny.

shown on the map 'Forêts de Verdun et du Mort Homme—Champs de Batailles de Verdun' issued in the 1/25,000 scale by the Institut Géographique National for the Office National des Forêts. The map sheet has translations in English and German. There are indeed many points of interest which are only accessible on foot and the map is invaluable for anyone studying the region in depth.

Memorial to Colonel Driant, who resisted the Germans from February to July 1916, in the Bois de Caures.

Rusty bayonets emerge beneath a concrete canopy—the infamous Tranchée du Baïonnettes at Douaumont. Only 17 unknown soldiers remain buried beneath the bayonets; the other 40 who were identified were interred in Fleury Cemetery.

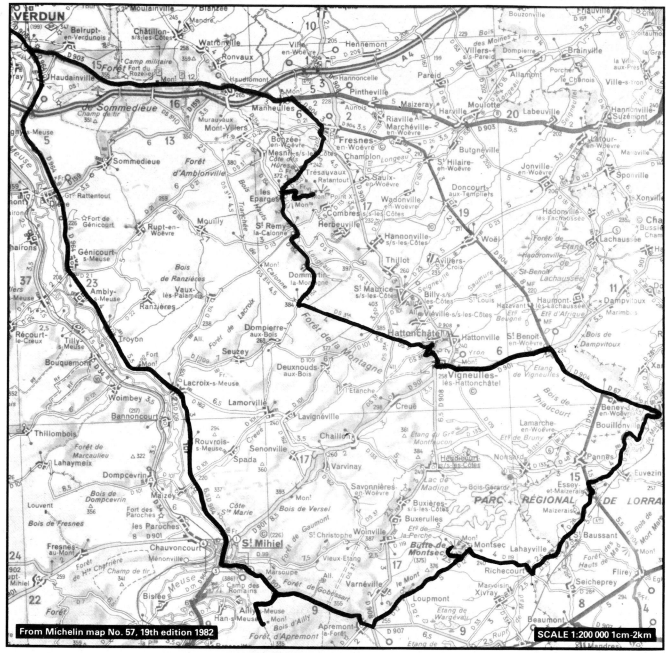
From Michelin map No. 57, 19th edition 1982

SCALE 1:200 000 1cm-2km

ROUTE II

Take the D903 out of the city and then branch off to the right on D964. This pleasant road follows the valley of the Meuse and the hills which surround it. At intervals signposts point to the various forts such as **Fort du Géniecourt** (1 km south of Dieue) and **Fort du Troyon**, 2 kms south of the village of that name.

After 23 kms we reach **St. Mihiel**. The Germans captured this pleasant town in September 1914 and the St Mihiel salient was formed. In September 1918 French Colonial troops with General Pershing's First Army made attacks on the flanks. Within three days they had reduced it, taking thousands of prisoners, many guns and much equipment, and capturing 200 square miles of enemy-held territory.

Take the D907 towards Apremont-la Forêt and the Forêt de Gobesart. in 2 kms, a small road on the right leads up to **Ailly-sur-Meuse** from which the **Bois d'Ailly** and the **Tranchée du Soif** and the **Monument of the French VIII Army Corps** is reached. Hidden in the woods behind this monument is an extremely interesting and extensive trench system with

A path leads from the obelisk of the French VIII Corps to the Tranchée du Soif.

A typical bunker entrance in the Tranchée du Soif.

The American Memorial on Mont Sec.

many bunkers and concrete shelters, some of which, no doubt, once led into subways. It is wise to keep to the path as subsidence has created gaping holes into the underground workings.

In **Apremont**, take the D12 to **Montsec** and climb up to the **American Memorial** on the crest of the **Butte** by a well-made road which ends at the wide stairway to the colonnade. The circular memorial can be seen for miles around and provides a good lookout point for the Meuse battle area. Within the pillars is a large bronze relief map of the region and between each pair of pillars are orientation points. To the north-east are seen the huge reservoirs of the Parc Régional de Lorraine.

Return to the valley and take the D119 to **Richecourt** (4 kms) and there turn left onto D33/D28 to **Essey-et-Maizerais**, (6 kms). Cross the D904 and head for **Bouillonville** and **Thiaucourt-Regniéville**, 7 kms. Turn left on the D67 and on the outskirts of the town the **St Mihiel American Cemetery** is located. The dominating monuments in this cemetery of 4,152 graves are a large eagle sundial, a chapel and a museum connected by a graceful colonnade. There is also a handsome statue of a young American officer in field uniform.

The direct road back to Verdun is the D904 via Fresnes. However it is interesting to leave this road at **St Benoît-en-Woëvre** taking the D901 to the left. In 6 kms is **Vigneulles-lès-Hattonchâtel**, an important position in the St Mihiel salient. On the rocky ridge above is **Hattonchâtel** with an **interesting old church** and a **château** rebuilt after the war by an American, Miss Skinner. These heights with their extensive views over the region were of great significance as observation posts. Take the DS31 going west of the village through the beautiful **Forêt de la Montagne** for 7 kms. At the crossroads turn right on the D154, leaving the long straight Tranchée de Calonne ahead. This road, built by Louis XVI, traverses the forest which formed an obstacle in the Eparges sector. **Dommartin**, **St Remy-la-Calonne** are passed and **Les Eparges** is reached in 7 kms. A road leads up to the **Crête des Eparges** with its **cemetery**, several monuments and huge craters to the right of the D203 to Fresnes (5½ kms). Turn left on the D904 for Verdun.

To return to Reims from Verdun take the N3 for 8 kms, when we reach the **Voie Sacrée** turning to the left. This was Verdun's lifeline in 1916 to **Bar le Duc** and 11 kms to the south it passes through **Souilly** which was Pétain's and later Pershing's headquarters. We continue straight ahead along the N3. In 36 kms we reach **Ste Menehould** and 42 kms further on **Chalons-sur-Marne**. Turn right onto the N44 to Reims which is 44 kms away.

Above: **St Mihiel American Cemetery and Memorial.** *Below:* **The French Memorial to the Missing on the summit of Crête des Eparges.**

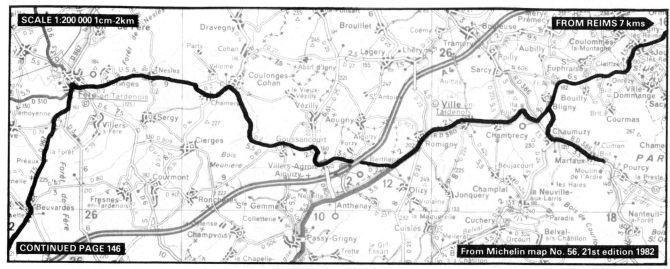

SCALE 1:200 000 1cm-2km

FROM REIMS 7 kms

CONTINUED PAGE 146

From Michelin map No. 56, 21st edition 1982

Reims to Compeigne

Leave Reims by the N380 and in 17 kms we are once more in British lines. XXII Corps were in action in this region in July 1918 and the 9th Scottish Division had a fierce struggle in the **Montagne de Bligny** sector in June.

We leave the main road, turning right down the N386 5½ kms to the village of **Marfaux**. Here is a small **British Cemetery** containing 1,129 graves and a **Memorial to the New Zealand Missing** in the battles. Among those buried here is Sergeant J. Meikle, VC, MM, of the Seaforth Highlanders, killed in action on July 20, 1918. A **German Cemetery** is close by.

The shelter at Marfaux Cemetery cloaks the New Zealand Memorial to the Missing in the attacks of 1918.

Grave of Sergeant Meikle, VC, MM, in Marfaux British Cemetery. The German Cemetery lies in the background.

One of two Italian Cemeteries in the region is at Chambrecy.

Returning to the N380 we climb up the hill towards **Chambrecy**. On the crest, an **Italian Memorial Garden** lies on the right and an **Italian Cemetery** on the left. These men, including their general, lost their lives fighting with the French armies in the defence of Reims. It is interesting to note that the graves are in order of rank although the crosses are uniform. The broken column in the Garden of Remembrance is a genuine Roman one from Italy.

The road now goes down a steep slope and, almost at the bottom, is the **British Cemetery** of Chambrecy where men of the 9th Scottish, 51st Highland and 62nd Divisions lie buried.

Theodore Roosevelt (a relative of Franklin Delano) was American president from 1901 to 1908. All his four sons fought in the Great War, Quentin being shot down just outside Chamery. This plaque still marks the spot where his aircraft crashed.

144

Two kms further on, **Ville-en-Tardenois** was one of the centres of the British defence in June 1918. In 4½ kms leave the main road taking the D2 to the right to travel across the battle area of both 1914 and 1918. It is a pleasant drive through pretty country with villages typical of the region. **Goussancourt** (3½ kms) **Coulonges-Cohan** (8 kms).

At the crossroad go left on the D14. As the road straightens out the ground rises on both sides. On the left, some ½ km further along, there is a grass track. Should the visitor be interested in the story of **Quentin Roosevelt**, the son of President Theodore Roosevelt, this is the way to reach his **crash site**. The young man was a pilot in the 95th Squadron, 1st Pursuit Group, of the American Air Service and was killed on July 14, 1918. Legend has it that not for the first time this short-sighted man was up on patrol and, instead of rejoining aircraft of his own squadron after an engagement, he tacked on to those of the enemy—who promptly shot him down. The actual site is marked by two memorials and is about ¾ km from the road, up the track and along under the hedgerow to the right. It can just be seen from the village of **Chamery** where there is also a **large fountain** in his memory. This is of cream stone with an ever-flowing water supply, and is near to the farm where the body was brought. He was later buried in Oise-Aisne American Cemetery but now lies with his brother in Normandy.

In Chamery take the right turn—just before the fountain—to return to the D2 and then turn left. In 2 kms we reach **Nesles** with its rather attractive feudal castle and then in 1½ kms the **Oise-Aisne American Cemetery**. It is the second largest of the WWI American cemeteries and lies on the right of the road

with the offices and reception room and car park on the left. On the gentle slope up to the attractive, rose-coloured memorial colonnade over 6,000 lay buried beneath the glistening marble crosses and the smooth green lawns. Below the avenues of plane trees leading to the memorial are box trees cut into shell shapes. In the chapel panels record the names of 241 men with no known graves and, in the map room, the engraved wall map explains the actions of 1918 in which the casualties occurred.

Continue 2½ kms to **Fère-en-Tardenois**.

'Only those are free to live who are not afraid to die.' The fountain memorial to Quentin Roosevelt in the village.

From September 12 to October 8, 1914, this town was the British GHQ which then moved to Abbeville. Field-Marshal French conferred with President Poincaré during the time he was here. It is a pleasant little town on the banks of the Ourcq. In the German advance of May 1918 the town was captured but was recaptured on July 28.

The Oise-Aisne American Cemetery. Here 6,012 lie buried in a 36½ acre plot to the north of the D2.

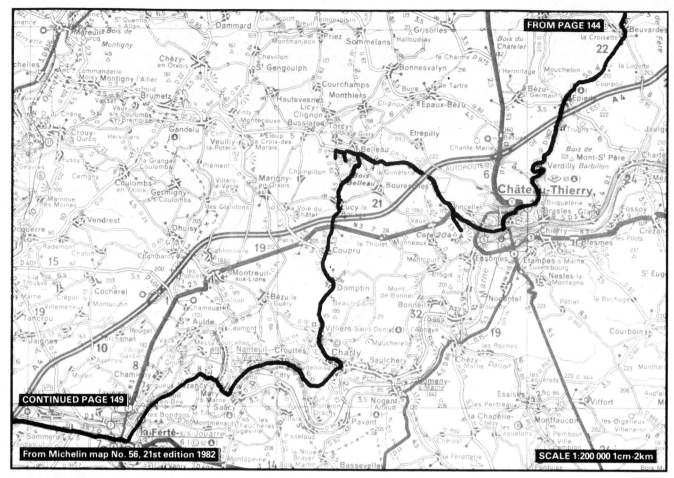

FROM PAGE 144

CONTINUED PAGE 149

From Michelin map No. 56, 21st edition 1982

SCALE 1:200 000 1cm-2km

Turn down the D967 to **Château-Thierry** (22 kms). The name comes from the castle on a hill on the northern side of the Marne which, legend says, was built by Charles Martel for the King of the Franks, Thierry IV. The site of the castle is now a public park where the ruined walls are still visible.

On September 9, 1914, a most important date in the First Battle of the Marne (when the Allies began to advance), the British I Corps (Haig) crossed the Marne here and moved forward to Fère-en-Tardenois. Château-Thierry remained far behind the line until the German advance in May 1918. As it had been with the British in 1914, Château-Thierry was to be the scene of the first American offensive. Despite many attacks the Allied line held and the town, which had fallen to the Germans on May 31, was retaken on July 21, the American Divisions pushing forward into the wooded hills north of the town. Dominating the town from the summit of Hill 204 is the huge **American Memorial**.

To reach the memorial, leave the town by the N3 and climb up a fairly steep hill. In 3 kms, on a corner, the two stone pylons marking the entrance to the memorial will be seen on the left. The drive up to the memorial is about 1½ kms. The memorial is immense and consists of a double colonnade above a paved terrace framed by an arc of fine trees. On the west face are two heroic figures representing the two countries, France and the USA. On the eastern side, a huge eagle perches above a map of the area of the American operations with an orientation table on the floor of the terrace.

Return to the main road and, with care, take the road on the far side, the D9 for **Belleau Wood**. In 7 kms we reach the village of **Belleau** and the **American Cemetery**. This is the Aisne-Marne Cemetery. The graves fan out on a curve on either side of a central lawn at the end of a tree-lined drive. Above the slopes of the cemetery, under the hill, is the chapel with its imposing tower. Here there are

2,288 graves and the names of 1,060 who have no known grave are inscribed on the walls of the chapel. There is an observation platform high in the tower giving a fine panoramic view. From the chapel paths lead up into the wood.

Opposite the gate is the **Demarcation Stone** and the **reconstructed village church**, the work being paid for by the veterans of the 26th US Division. A key of the church is held by the

cemetery Superintendent. Within are memorials and flags of the US forces and commemorative stained-glass windows. Down the village street is a **drinking trough**, filled with flowers, the gift to Belleau from the Belleau Wood Memorial Association in memory of the soldiers of Pennsylvania who lost their lives here. At the bottom of the street is the **château stables** where the Americans were housed. The road to the left takes one

The magnificent American Château-Thierry Memorial is set on Cote 204, giving fine panoramic views over the plain below. Château-Thierry was the scene of the first American offensive.

146

Above: **Captured artillery pieces in a clearing in Belleau Wood.** *Left:* **The Belleau Wood Chapel beneath the overhanging woodland.**

Memorial to the 4th US Marine Brigade.

back to the D9. Turn left to the gates of the American Cemetery passing the large **German Cemetery** where there are 8,625 graves.

Leave the American Cemetery and turn right and take the first right and the first right again thus entering the wood. The park road climbs up to the centre of the wood where a flagpole and a **Memorial to the 4th US Marine Brigade** of the 2nd US Division which took the entire wood on June 25, 1918 after having withstood many attacks since June 1. The memorial states that the wood, by order of the Commanding General of the French Sixth Army, be officially renamed Bois de la Brigade de Marine. Placed around the clearing are various artillery pieces and mortars captured by the Marines and in the wood are vestiges of the trenches and craters. Down the glade towards the cemetery is the **ruined chapel** on which is a **plaque commemorating the 2nd Division**.

Leave the wood via the road to Lucy-le-Bocage and, in 4½ kms, reach the N3. Cross this and take the D82 to **Coupru** and then the D11 for **Domptin** and **Charly** (9 kms). Turn right on the D969 to follow the course of the Marne through very pretty scenery although difficult fighting country. The river winds in large loops between steep banks with hills covered with trees.

In 8 kms we arrive at **Luzancy**. Near the

A few hundred metres away from the US Cemetery at Belleau Wood is located the German Cemetery containing 8,625 graves.

The BEF crossed the Marne in 1914 between Luzancy and La Ferté.

entrance to the village the road crosses the river close to the **site of the weir** over which the British infantry crossed as the bridge had been blown. A more modern weir is further up stream.

We then reach **La Ferté-sous-Jouarre** (7 kms), an attractive town at the junction of the Marne and the Petit Morin rivers. The BEF, which began to advance on September 6, 1914, arrived at La Ferté to find the Germans well placed on the northern banks and the bridges blown. The British artillery dealt severely with the enemy guns and the 4th Division Engineers built a floating bridge to enable the left wing of the BEF to cross. This bridge was built close to the ruined one on the main Paris road. At the southern end, today, is the **British Memorial to the Missing** who fell in the battles of Mons, Le Cateau, the Marne and the Aisne, 1914. The names of 3,888 are recorded on the panels of the memorial which stands in a small park presented by the family of Monsieur Bernard de Jussieu. Constructed of white Massangis stone, the monument is surmounted by a sarcophagus on which are laid trophies—ensigns, magazines, bayonets and a tin hat. Four columns stand at the corners of the terrace supporting urns and bearing the arms of the UK. The memorial was designed by G. H. Goldsmith and was unveiled on November 4, 1928 by General Sir William Pulteney in the presence of Maréchal Foch, Field-Marshal Milne and Général Weygand.

On the riverside, by the bridge, the **position of the floating bridge** is marked on each shore by rectangular pylons crowned with the grenade of the Engineers mounted on a circular paving.

The road bridge at La Ferté. The monument records the building of an assault bridge by the 4th Divisional Engineers close to the spot whilst under fire in September 1914.

La Ferté-sous-Jouarre British Memorial to the Missing who fell in the battles of Mons, Le Cateau, the Marne and Aisne in 1914.

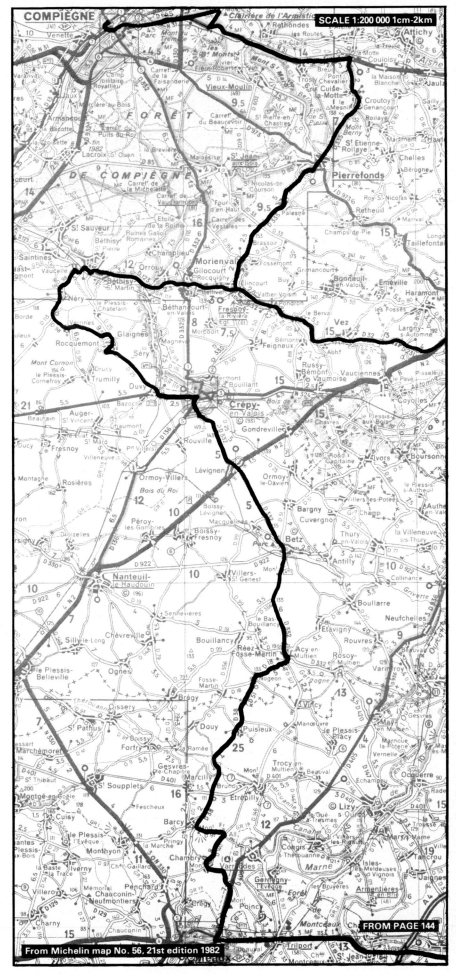

FROM PAGE 144

From Michelin map No. 56, 21st edition 1982

One wonders where the connection is in the massive American statue to French soldiery to be seen in a park outside Meaux. Possibly the most unusual of all war memorials.

From here Paris is a mere 65 kms along the N3 and it is on this road we leave La Ferté following the river to **St Jean-les-2-Jumeaux**.

In 11 kms we arrive at **Meaux**. The BEF reached this town on September 3, 1914 and, after crossing the river, blew the bridges and retired to the Fôret de Crécy some 18 kms to the south (on the N36). There they halted and on the 6th they began the return march.

From Meaux we turn north on the D405 for 1½ kms. As the road climbs out of the town there is a park to the right. Soaring above it is a huge group of sculpture which is the **American Memorial to the French Combatants of the Marne**. The figures are massive and are depicted in a fantastic pose. In 1 km turn left for Chambry on an unnumbered road and at the edge of the village, turn left on to the D140 for 1 km, then right onto D38 at the crossroads. Here is the **Monument des 4 Routes**. We now pass through the area of the French Sixth Army of Maunoury which was reinforced by 11,000 men from Paris in taxicabs.

At **Betz**, (25 kms), on the flat plateau before this town, is one of the **Memorials to the 'Army of Paris'**.

Take the D332 for **Crépy**, (10 kms), occupied briefly by the Germans as they advanced on Senlis on September 1, 1914.

Turn left onto the N324 for 2 kms and then right on the D25 to **Rocquemont**. From here take the D98 for about 4 kms and then join the D113 for **Néry**.

Memorial to the 'Army of Paris' at Betz.

Nery church stands close to the site of the artillery action in September 1914.

In this small village was fought a brief but glorious rearguard action in the mist of the morning of September 1, 1914. 'L' Battery, Royal Horse Artillery, won lasting fame and three VCs when they (and the Cavalry Brigade) were surprised by the advancing German cavalry and artillery. In the action which followed, 'L' Battery lost two guns and their crews and, in a matter of minutes, 5 officers and 49 men were killed or wounded. Five were left to man the one remaining gun: Captain E. Bradbury, BSM G. Dorrell, Sergeant D. Nelson, Driver Osborne and Gunner H. Darbyshire. Captain Bradbury, although mortally wounded, continued to direct the fire until he died, propped up against the gun which Dorrell and Nelson kept firing, supplied with shells by the other two. The 1st Bn. the Middlesex Regiment and the 1st Scottish Rifles arrived and charged the enemy, recovering the guns and capturing eight of the German field pieces. The **gun position behind the church** is now overrun by shrubs but the **farm**, in which they had sheltered, has probably changed little.

In 3 kms at **Vaucelle** turn right on the D123 for 24 kms—**Villers-Cotterêts** is reached through the attractive valley of the Automne. The delightful old town is now encircled by a ring road which relieves the traffic problems in this the birthplace of Alexander Dumas, which is also an ideal base for visiting the huge **Forêt de Retz**. It was in the forest that the 4th Guards Brigade fought a desperate rearguard action on September 1, 1914 after the Gemans had entered the town. They were pushed out and away in the Allied advance ten days later, not to return until June 1918 when they got into the forest some 8 kms distant. In July, Générals Mangin and Dogoutte gathered an Allied force in the forest and attacked on July 18, capturing 20,000 prisoners and some 400 guns as they overwhelmed a surprised enemy.

A circuit of the forest is not only very enjoyable but interesting and can be made by taking the D931 out of Villers-Cotterêts, and, almost immediately as the forest is entered, the D80 to the right. After 5 kms **Fleury** and then turn left along a typical forest road to the D2 in 2½ kms. In places the forest is really dense and in others the enormous beeches soar over a clear forest floor and it is no wonder that an army could hide here. Turn left and carry on for 2 kms and then left again onto N2 for 1 km before taking the second right exit from the carrefour to once more enter the cathedral of huge trees. In 1 km, where the beeches seem even more massive, hidden on the right is a track leading up to the **Mangin Memorial** marking the site of his OP. Here he watched his troops from the eminence of a forest fire-watchers' tower.

For a further km the road dips and rises and curves through the forest and then descends to join the D811 where there is a **private British memorial** to a fallen Guards officer. Turn right and soon the **Cross of Sacrifice of the Guards' Grave** comes in sight.

Carrefour de la Reine—memorial to a Guards officer in the Forêt de Retz.

Here 98 officers and men of the Guards Brigade are buried in a single grave below the level of the road. The ring-road is gained 2 kms further along, and a right turn and yet another right reaches the D973 for **Pierrefonds** via **Taillefontaine**.

If a visit to Villers-Cotterêts is not required, after Vaucelle turn left off the D123 at **Elincourt** and onto the D335 and Pierrefonds which is 17 kms. The **fairy-tale castle** stands out as the town is approached; it was reconstructed in the 19th Century by Viollet Le Duc and is considered the finest example of his work. Continue through the town on the D335 to turn left onto N31 in 7 kms. Then 8 kms later take a right turn signposted for **Carrefour de l'Armistice**.

Guardsmen at rest in a French forest—98 men out of the 1,114,744 British Great War dead. Casualties from the United Kingdom and Colonies totalled 888,367 (including 412,991 missing); Australia 61,860 (23,397 missing); Canada lost 64,665 (19,507 missing); Undivided India 72,407 (64,518 missing); New Zealand 18,148 (6,299 missing) and South Africa 9,297 (2,815 missing).

The famous photo taken on November 11, 1918. The signatories descend from the Armistice coach; Admiral Wemyss flanked by Général Weygand (left) and Maréchal Foch (right).

A replica of the original coach preserved as a museum piece. (The original was taken to Berlin after the 1940 Armistice and was last seen 80 kilometres south of the city in April 1945).

Here is the famous clearing where the Armistice was signed on November 11, 1918 in the Wagon Lits Company coach No. 2419D, which, with another train bearing the German plenipotentiaries, was drawn up on the two sections of railway line from Rethondes. These spurs were originally laid down for heavy artillery firing on Noyon. The two trains stopped there for the first time on November 8 when the terms were put before the Germans by Maréchal Foch and Général Weygand, with Admiral Wemyss leading the British delegation. They returned on the 11th and the Germans signed just after 5.10 a.m. The ceasefire sounded at 11.00 a.m.

After the war, the marshy area where this event had taken place was transformed and the Glade of the Armistice was laid out in the circular fashion it still retains. The opening ceremony was performed on November 11, 1932 by Millerand and Poincaré. The coach used by Foch had been returned to normal service but it was then taken to the Invalides where it became a popular exhibit. In 1927, it returned to the forest where it was housed in a special shed and the interior laid out as it had been nine years previously. A monument to the Armistice was erected in the avenue and in 1937 the statue of Foch was unveiled.

In June 1940 the coach was brought out of its shed and, amid much pomp and splendour, Hitler reversed the roles. The Germans then took the coach to Berlin where it went on display. The coach disappeared between Elsterwerda and Grossenhain in April 1945.

On November 11, 1950, the carrefour having been repaired and a new shed built (the old one had been destroyed during the Occupation when the Germans defaced the whole area), a railway carriage, similar to the original, was run into the shed and fitted out with replicas of the documents, furniture and pictures. The monument of the eagle being struck down by a sword, which had been smashed in 1940 and taken in pieces to Germany in packing cases, was found after the war and was repaired and replaced on its own site. The railway lines into the shed have now been removed just outside the doors to prevent further removal of the coach!

Armistice at Compiègne. The memorial slab marking the exact spot where the coach stood on November 11, 1918.

The Commonwealth War Graves Commission

The origins of the Commission go back to 1914 when a British Red Cross unit headed by Fabian Ware went to France in September. It was a Mobile Ambulance Unit working with the French Army. In October, Ware visited Béthune cemetery with Dr Stewart, a Red Cross medical assessor. The latter, on seeing a number of British graves with their plain wooden crosses, suggested that although they were adequately marked, there seemed to be no evidence that they had been recorded or registered and that the unit should undertake this work when and where it was able.

From that day onward, the unit searched for, located, identified and registered thousands of graves. Gradually this task superseded the medical side as the Army's medical services improved and the need for the work on graves was appreciated by the authorities. In March 1915, it became the Graves Registration Commission and was attached to the Adjutant General's department.

Major Ware, as he had then become, made one of his first tasks that of negotiating with the French government for the permanency of the cemeteries. This led to the passing, in December 1915, of a law that the French nation would acquire the necessary lands and make a free gift of them to the British Empire, in perpetuity, and the British would be responsible for their maintenance.

Early in 1916, a National Committee for the Care of Soldiers' Graves was established with the Prince of Wales as its President. With representatives from the Dominions and India, one of its aims was to deal with the question of permanent memorials to be erected after the war.

In February 1916, the Commission had become the Directorate of Graves Registration and Enquiries and was an integral part of the Army. This Directorate was the sole unit with authority to negotiate between the French military and civil authorities in all matters relating to graves. Similar arrangements were soon made with the Belgians.

In May 1916, Colonel Ware moved his headquarters to London as the horizon of the department widened beyond the Western Front with the huge task of registering, burying and recording the dead. An early result of the work of the Directorate was the introduction of a double identification tag made of compressed fibre in place of the old oblong metal plaque or glazed linen tunic label.

Long before this, Colonel Ware had realised the need for photographs of graves for relatives who frequently contacted the unit for information. He organised the systematic photography of the graveyards and, by April 1917, some 12,000 photographs had been sent to relatives. By that date 150,000 graves in France and Belgium, 2,500 in Salonika and 400 in Egypt, had been registered.

The horticultural work on the cemeteries began in 1916 when the aid and advice of the Royal Botanic Gardens was sought and plants and seeds from Kew were sent to France through funds supplied by the Red Cross. The flowers and shrubs were chosen with considerable care. The graves at the time were either individual mounds or trenches, being planted with flowering annuals with grass paths separating them. Characteristic plants from overseas were planted to provide a more local atmosphere for the graves of the men from Canada, Australia and New Zealand. Care was taken with Indian and Chinese graves only to use plants which those nations regarded as sacred and suitable for cemeteries. Nurseries were set up but in 1918, some of these as well as many cemeteries were overrun and all the work was destroyed. In time, of course, this was repaired.

The moral advantage of these almost English gardens was recognised from the beginning as oases of peace and quiet amid the hurly-burly of the battle area or the large base camps and hospitals. Men found the pleasant, colourful graveyards ideal for spending short periods to read letters from home — or to write them.

On May 21, 1917, the Imperial War Graves Commission was created by a Royal Charter with the duties of marking and maintaining the graves of all members of the Services of the Empire who died during the First World War. They were also to construct cemeteries and memorials, to keep registers and records and to publish them. The principles which guided the Commission all those years ago have been maintained to this day. To quote from a recent Commission report:

'That each of the dead should be commemorated individually by name either on the headstone on the grave, or by an inscription on a memorial; that the headstones and memorials should be permanent; that the headstones should be uniform and that there should be no distinction made on account of military or civil rank.

'The whole cost of the work is shared by the partner governments — the United Kingdom, Canada, Australia, New Zealand, South Africa, India and Pakistan — in proportion to the numbers of their graves.'

Each headstone bears the badge of the service, corps or national emblem; the name rank and number and decorations with, at the base, an inscription chosen by relatives. The headstones are 2ft 8in in height and 1ft 3in wide. The appropriate religious emblem is also included. Normally the top of the stone is gently curved but variations exist to identify foreign nationals or civilians. Headstones of soldiers awarded the Victoria Cross bear the emblem of the decoration in place of any other cross. Until recently Portland or Hopton Wood quarries provided the stone used for headstones but now Botticino limestone is being used as it requires less maintenance. The headstones stand in narrow borders planted, where conditions allow, with roses and perennials offset with lawns, shrubs and trees.

Where some doubt exists as to the exact location of a grave in a cemetery the words 'Believed to be buried in this cemetery' prefix the inscription. In places where the graves were destroyed by later battles, 'Known to be buried in this cemetery' or 'Buried near this spot' are used.

Graves of the unidentified bear the inscription chosen by Rudyard Kipling: 'Known Unto God'. He also suggested the wording inscribed on the Stone of Remembrance found in all but the smallest cemeteries, 'Their Name Liveth for Evermore' (Ecclesiasticus 44:14). The Stone of Remembrance was designed by Sir Edwin Lutyens and the beautifully-proportioned Cross of Sacrifice, found in all the cemeteries, was designed by Sir Reginald Blomfield.

Immediately after the war ended, work on the permanent cemeteries began and, within a few years, these beautiful gardens of rest appeared in the once devastated regions. The first three were completed in 1920 and included two in the battle zones: Forceville and Louvencourt.

The pilgrimages, individual and collective, had also commenced and the Commission began its close contact with the British Legion and with travel agents Thomas Cook which organised cheap trips to the battlefields. Throughout the years the Commission's offices have been offering a first-class service with help and advice to those wishing to visit the cemeteries and memorials.

In the 1920s work commenced on the erection of the memorials to the missing at certain selected sites. These ranged from the gigantic Thiepval Arch and the Menin Gate to the smaller ones such as that at Zeebrugge or the Nieuwpoort Memorial. The countries of the Empire also had their memorials and, at home, the Naval and Mercantile Marine memorials were erected at the naval ports of Portsmouth, Plymouth, Chatham and at Tower Hill, London.

The Commission also undertakes to care for, on a repayment contract, private Service memorials and certain individual graves of officers and men buried before the Commission came into being.

Almost every cemetery has a small bronze door let into a wall behind which will be found a copy of the cemetery or memorial register. There is also a book for visitors to sign before leaving the cemetery.

In March 1960, the title of the Commission was changed to The *Commonwealth* War Graves Commission and in June 1964 its terms of reference were further defined by a supplemental Charter.

A series of international agreements protect the Commission's work in foreign countries and many Governments have generously purchased land at State expense and given it for perpetual use as cemeteries by the Commission.

Copies of the Registers are published for the Commission by Her Majesty's Stationery Office. They can be seen at all the main offices abroad. The area offices in France and Belgium are:

France:
Rue Angèle Richard
Beaurains
62012 Arras Cedex
Telephone: (21) 230324
North-West Europe:
Elverdingestraat 82
B 8900 Icpcr (Ypres)
Telephone: Ypres (057) 200118
The Headquarters of the Commission are at
2 Marlow Road,
Maidenhead,
Berkshire, SL6 7DX
Telephone: Maidenhead (0628) 34221

For further, more detailed reading on the work of the Commission, I recommend *The Unending Vigil*, a history of the Commonwealth War Graves Commission, 1917-1967, by Philip Longworth, published by Constable of London in 1967.

I cannot, however, close this account without expressing my very deep gratitude for all the advice, encouragement and friendly help I have always received from the staff of the Commission over many years.

***

Addresses of the headquarters of other War Graves Commissions in Europe are as follows:

FRANCE
Secretariat d'Etat Chargé des Anciens Combattants et Victimes de Guerre
139 rue de Bercy
Paris (12c) France

GERMANY
Volksbund Deutsche Kriegsgräberfürsorge
35 Kassel,
Werner-Hilpert-Strasse 2
West Germany

ITALY
Commissariato Generale Onorauze di Caduti in Guerra
Ministero della Difesa
Piazza Luigi Sturzo 23
00144 Rome, Italy.

USA (European Office)
The American Battle Monuments Commission
68 rue 19 Janvier
92 Garches,
France

Nine villages were totally destroyed in the battles around Verdun. This is the site of Bezonvaux, ten kilometres north-east of the city, completely obliterated and never rebuilt. The plaque on the memorial depicts Bezonvaux prior to 1916.

INDEX

A

One of the many plaques in the cathedral at Amiens.

The Canadian Memorial at Dury Crossroad near Vis-en-Artois on the road between Arras and Cambrai.

Memorial at Notre Dame de Lorette to the glory of Général Maistre and the French XXI Army Corps.

London Cemetery on the eastern side of High Wood.

The US 77th Division's 'Lost Battalion' ravine near Apremont.

Damage to the American Memorial repaired at Monsec.

The impressive village war memorial at Proyart on the Somme.

These enchanting beavers guard the twin flagpoles at the Canadian Memorial on Vimy Ridge.

T

U

Buzancy near Soissons. 'Here for all time the glorious Scottish thistle will bloom amid the roses of France'.